The Responsibility Trap

*A Blueprint for Treating
the Alcoholic Family*

Claudia Bepko
with Jo Ann Krestan

THE FREE PRESS
A Division of Macmillan, Inc.
NEW YORK

Collier Macmillan Publishers
LONDON

THE FREE PRESS
A Division of Simon & Schuster
1230 Avenue of the Americas
New York, NY 10020

THE FREE PRESS and colophon are trademarks
of Simon & Schuster Inc.

Manufactured in the United States of America

10 9 8 7 6 5 4 3 2 1

Library of Congress Cataloging-In-Publication Data

Bepko, Claudia.
        The responsibility trap.

        Bibliography: p.
        Includes index,
        1. Alcoholism.   2. Family psychotherapy.   I. Krestan, Jo Ann.   II. Title.
RC565.B464   1985   616.86'185-1588
ISBN: 978-0-743-23642-3

For information regarding special discounts for bulk purchases, please contact Simon &
Schuster Special Sales at 1-800-456-6798 or business@simonandschuster.com

The Responsibility Trap

To the Memory of *Susan Bragg*
and to *Helen, Rudy, and Dorothy*

Contents

Foreword

CLAUDIA BEPKO and Jo Ann Krestan have performed a valuable service in this book by integrating a number of areas in the family treatment of alcoholism that have previously tended to be kept separate. *The Responsibility Trap* presents alcoholism as a systemic process, bridging the gaps between family therapy and alcoholism counseling and between systems theory and clinical practice. The authors present an elegant theoretical model that integrates individual experience, couple dynamics, and multigenerational family patterns and generates clear clinical interventions. They also effectively discuss the experiential meaning of alcoholism within a wider systems context.

I hope this book stimulates more mental health professionals in general, and family therapists in particular, to consider seriously the challenges and opportunities of alcoholism therapy. Like many of my colleagues, I spent a good part of my career avoiding working with alcohol problems. Then I took a job with the National Institute on Alcohol Abuse and Alcoholism because it was the only way I could fulfill my Public Health Service commitment while doing family therapy. Much to my surprise, I found that working with alcoholics and their families has been satisfying and rewarding and that it has transformed the way I approach all other problems.

It strikes me that three major challenges in working with alcoholism serve as seemingly insurmountable obstacles to most therapists. Once addressed, they provide a remarkable springboard for liberation in the therapist's professional and personal life.

The first challenge is that the desired outcomes of alcohol treatment are very specific, are easily measured, and require considerable rigor to be achieved. Much of therapy for other problems aims at more diffuse outcomes, such as increased insight, better emotional expression, and improved communication. Some of us get in the habit of learning one type of psychotherapy and offering it to all clients who enter our offices. We routinely reflect their questions back to them, get them to ventilate their feelings, or coach them on more effective communication skills. Our interventions with most clients often seem helpful and rarely are harmful.

With alcoholics and their families, the results are more clear-cut. The alcoholic is drinking, or he or she is not, and the drinking is demonstrably correlated with job performance, hospitalization, arrest record, and family violence and disruption. Many traditional mental health techniques unthinkingly applied, at best, will be irrelevant to the problem and, at worst, will reinforce the drinking problem, putting off or foreclosing effective treatment. Conversely, appropriate interventions will lead to dramatic improvement, with grateful clients and gratified therapist.

The second challenge is that alcoholics and their families are often immersed in truly dangerous situations. Issues such as the possibility of intentional or unintentional suicide or homicide arise and have to be directly addressed before sobriety can be achieved. The "pragmatic" therapist with standard approaches such as prescribing the symptom or restructuring the family is likely to be immobilized by her anxiety, or to deny it, with potentially tragic consequences. The therapist must know when to "resign" as helper and expert and starkly present the dangers in the current situation to the appropriate family members, trusting them to take responsibility for the potential catastrophe looming over them. If one can, in fact, back away from therapeutic overresponsibility, it is rewarding how few potential tragedies ever come to pass. In addition, one acquires considerable detachment about the "tragedies" in one's own life.

The third challenge, which is probably crucial for most therapists, lies in the importance of spiritual factors in the development of and recovery from alcoholism. Psychotherapy as practiced today is based on theory that is largely reductionistic and deterministic, the ultimate cause of problems being variously seen as rooted in biochemistry, in the psyche, in the family, or in cybernetic feedback loops. The emphasis by Alcoholics Anonymous on accepting one's powerlessness over drinking and asking for help from one's Higher Power does profound violence to the prevalent therapeutic world view. For some reason we can accept with relative equanimity that we are only mechanisms of one type or another or, conversely, that we are "masters of our fate," but are profoundly disquieted by the idea that there is a loving and powerful presence throughout our inner and outer worlds that transcends our comprehension.

The resistance by most therapists to the spiritual message of AA is isomorphic with the "drunk pride" of most alcoholics at hearing the same message. The alcoholic may admit that she has a "drinking problem" which she is sure she can control without declaring herself an alcoholic, and the therapist may admit that AA seems to produce positive results which can probably be explained by group hypnosis or by the substitution of an addiction to AA for the alcoholism. In both cases, there is an attempt to maintain a mind-set that offers logic, predictability, and the illusion of control and an avoidance of a way of being that offers mastery, peace, and self-acceptance.

The therapist who is not working with alcohol problems can afford to continue to go through life with his world view intact; the alcoholic cannot afford that luxury. His situation gets worse and worse until he hits bottom and turns over his drinking problem to his Higher Power. Whenever he wholeheartedly asks for help, it is always there, and a true miracle occurs that allows him to no longer have to drink and to begin to see the possibility of serenity in his life.

If I had read—much less written—the previous paragraph twelve years ago, I would have been angry, amused, or repelled. I would have regarded it as wishful thinking or wooly-headedness or arrogance. Since then, working with alcoholics and their families and exploring my own relationship with my Higher Power have taught me that there is a way out of the condition of desperation and suffering in which all human beings sometimes seem to be mired. The way out requires rigorous work on thought and feeling that eventually allows one to see as an empirical "fact" that love is real and suffering is illusion.

The Responsibility Trap is aptly titled. Along the way to being fully responsive to the transcendent reality that is within us and around us, we all get trapped in variations of over- and underresponsibility, some of the more interesting variants appearing in the families of alcoholics and among therapists. One cannot work effectively with alcohol problems for long while carrying the burden of therapeutic overresponsibility. One has to start letting in some of that mysterious Higher Power and serenity that members of AA talk about—not a bad reward for difficult work.

Bepko and Krestan do an excellent job of integrating theory and practice in describing the treatment of families with alcohol problems. This is a book worthy of its subject matter.

David Berenson
University of California
at San Francisco
School of Medicine

Preface

THIS BOOK IS the outgrowth of seven years of work in which we have made an attempt to integrate our own understanding of alcoholic dynamics within the framework of systemic family therapy. Since we share both a commitment to the principles of Alcoholics Anonymous, as well as a commitment to approaching problems from a systemic viewpoint, it has always been a source of concern for us that the fields of alcoholism treatment and family therapy seem so polarized in their respective views on the nature of alcoholism as a symptomatic process. Our hope is that this book can provide a bridge between those two viewpoints as well as some new ways of looking at alcoholism that can be clinically useful and relevant to other practitioners.

There is a great deal in this book that is not new. We have drawn heavily on the work of Murray Bowen and David Berenson in particular, and their ideas have become so ingrained a part of our thinking and our clinical practice that sometimes the boundaries between their thinking and our own have become blurred. The work of Gregory Bateson and Ernest Kurtz provided a basic intellectual and spiritual context that we adopted as essential to our work. We have aimed at an integration of the ideas of many different people in both the alcoholism field and the field of family therapy, and we have attempted to look at the contextual issues raised by alcoholism at many different levels.

As is probably typical, our work and thinking evolved because we were stuck. We were finding it entirely too difficult to facilitate movement toward sobriety in the families we worked with and we found that symptomatic behavior often shifted after sobriety to another family member. Because more often than not we saw the female members of families in the beginning of treatment, we decided to put a few of them together in a group and see what happened. These groups, described in Chapter 9, became a research laboratory from which we learned and within which we experimented with different ideas and different approaches. The group experiences were tremendously exciting and rewarding and led to some general understanding of the kind of reciprocity that occurs in alcoholic systems, which we then took back to our work with couples and families. Gradually, our focus shifted to the issues of families in postsobriety phases of treatment, and this focus deepened our understanding of the delicate processes of adjustment and rebalancing that occur once the family environment is free of alcohol.

This book is not meant to represent a "theory" of alcoholism treatment, nor are we suggesting that our approach to treatment is the only effective one. For us, the constructs that we outline have been useful in organizing our thinking, and thus informing our action. They are the result of clinical observation, not rigorous research. They represent a beginning, a point of departure. Ultimately, we would like to see our thinking evolve further in response to concrete research and the feedback of others on some of the interactional paradigms we describe.

We see what we see because of the particular personal and professional perspectives we bring to our work, and having finished this phase of our own explorations, often we experience a need to be able to stand back and look again, see differently, see more. Often, it seems as if an understanding of alcoholism is truly in its infancy and that simpler, more effective solutions must be within reach.

Writing a book is certainly a communal event and takes place with the help of a whole host of people who may not even know they're involved. Putting words on paper is only the end result of a very complex process that takes place over time with the input of many people. For the two of us, the collaborative process has truly been an enriching experience, both intellectually and clinically. If our ideas and even our identities tend to blur now and then, the fusion is a small price to pay for the intense experience of shared accomplishment.

We have many people to thank. While we couldn't list the names of each of our clients here, we should, since their struggles have really been ours, and ours theirs. It is not unusual for clients to grow more and achieve better integration than their therapists and we thank our clients, particularly the men and women in our groups, for keeping us humble.

The person most significant to our development, both personally and professionally, has been Monica McGoldrick. She has been a mentor and a generous source of encouragement and help. She has provided a forum for the development and presentation of our work, and as a woman who is a leader in her field, she has been a consistent model of the ability to share power. We thank her here, not only for her help with this project, but for her help with many other projects for which she was not adequately thanked.

Other people have been so much a part of the fabric of our lives that no work would have been possible without their belief, encouragement, and support. Pat Webb, Mary Nolan, Jeff and Marsha Ellias-Frankel, Norman Levy, and Jennifer Hanson are primary figures who nurtured us, listened interminably to our obsessive preoccupation with our "work," as well as to our chronic complaints about the demands of trying to live, work, and write all at the same time. Our other friends are to be thanked for tolerating our unavailability and what became, at times, very one-sided relationships. Finally, our families, as well as all those significant people in our pasts who helped shape our "self-experience" are thanked for their love and support.

For technical assistance, we are grateful to the staff at the library of the Center for Alcohol Studies at Rutgers University and the staff of the Monmouth County Office of the National Council on Alcoholism. Finally, Renita LaBarbera, who typed the many evolutionary phases of the manuscript, has been an invaluable collaborator on this project.

Theoretical
Constructs

1

Alcoholism: A Systemic Perspective

THIS BOOK focuses on the identification and treatment of dynamics that occur in families and in relationships affected by alcoholism. To provide a framework for looking at these problems it is important to clarify how we think about alcoholism, because, ultimately, the way we think about a problem directs what we do about it.

The clinical and etiological aspects of alcoholism are issues that have been debated and researched in great depth and at many levels from many different scientific and sociological perspectives.[1] The collective results of this research are as yet inconclusive. Every day new aspects of study, particularly in the areas of neurochemical and biomedical research, seem to suggest different evidence about the very complex and multifaceted dimensions of alcoholic behavior. At present, there exists no unitary or agreed-on definition in the scientific or medical community relative to questions of etiology or clinical progression that are generalizable to all problem drinkers in all situations. Present theories tend to point more to differences than to similarities. The effects of certain patterns of drinking, however, tend to be more predictable and identifiable than their causes, and ultimately, in clinical treatment, it is the effects of drinking behavior to which we must address ourselves. Consequently, instead of asking why a person drinks, we try to understand what changes occur for the individual and those around him when drinking occurs in certain problematic ways.

This particular approach to alcohol problems derives from our orientation as family therapists who operate within the larger framework of general systems theory.

One contribution of systems theory to the mental health field has been to remove our thinking about human behavior from the frame of causality. In systems terms it is more relevant to view complex human behavior from the perspective of interactive process than it is to attempt to identify a specific cause or "reason" for behavior that can be located within a specific individual. Even supposing, for instance, that a genetic or hereditary predisposition exists in a given individual that may render him susceptible to alcohol addiction, numerous other factors in his environment *in interaction with* that particular biological reality will ultimately affect whether or not he drinks alcoholically.

A systemic perspective on alcoholism suggests that we view alcoholism not as an individual problem but as an interactive one that affects and is affected by interaction and change at many systemic levels.[2]

While this focus on interaction is our primary context for viewing alcohol problems, we feel that it is equally important to have a basic understanding of the nature of alcoholism as it is defined medically and scientifically because it represents a specific type of symptomatic process. Alcoholism calls for family therapy approaches that may differ from those that are applied to a general range of nonaddictive, interactional, and communication problems in families. Intervention with the family system of an alcoholic may represent necessary, but not sufficient treatment, and it is important for the clinician to integrate many different levels of information and understanding about alcoholic behavior processes and events into her general repertoire of clinical technique.

It is only recently that the family therapy field has begun to acknowledge the need to develop a clinical approach to alcohol-affected families that addresses the specific dynamics set in motion by alcoholic drinking. Peter Steinglass's comment that "growing research and clinical interest in the alcoholic family has tended to outpace the development of conceptual models useful in viewing alcoholism from a family perspective" (1980:21) speaks to a gap in our understanding of alcoholic dynamics as well as a lack of specific technique that relates to those dynamics. This book represents one attempt to bridge that gap.

The purpose of this chapter is to outline the basic assumptions about alcoholism that direct our treatment and to set the stage for the specific theoretical constructs that follow in chapters 2, 3, and 4. In the interest of conciseness, we assume a basic understanding of both alcoholism and family systems on the reader's part. We will mention relevant principles only briefly as they relate to our own theoretical constructs.

What Alcoholism Is: Premises and Assumptions

Our primary assumption is that alcoholism represents a systemic, that is, circular process. The behavior of ingesting a psychoactive drug affects and is affected by change and adaptation at many different systemic levels including the genetic, physiological, psychological, interpersonal, and spiritual.

Drinking behavior occurs within a larger social or systemic context; it is shaped by cultural influence and at the same time it represents a type of feedback or commentary about the larger context in which it occurs.

Abuse of alcohol or addiction is a multidetermined phenomenon. Alcohol use may become problematic at different times for different people under different conditions for different reasons. While some patterns are more typical and generalizable, no one set of deterministic or clinical variables holds true for all people who drink.

These assumptions represent our understanding of alcoholism as a process or sequence of events that evolves over time. They do not attempt to explain what causes alcoholism nor do they view alcoholism as a secondary symptom that masks other psychodynamic problems. They suggest that alcoholism is both a cause and an effect of systemic changes that are or become dysfunctional.

Secondly, these assumptions do not speak to the issue of whether or not alcoholism is a disease. This particular question has been the subject of a great deal of controversy and polarization in the mental health field. While the model of classification and progression developed by Jellinek (1960) is generally accepted by most professionals in the alcoholism field as a standard rule of thumb for defining and classifying alcoholism as a distinct disease syndrome, other professionals tend to view alcohol addiction from a more psychological or sociological orientation.

If one accepts the premise that alcoholism is a multilevel phenomenon, it seems clear that the controversy over definition of the problem relates to specific orientations that may define one level of the problem as more dominant than another, and it relates to our capacity to use language in a way that invests certain words with political and psychological power.

If one views the alcoholic process in terms of its effect on human tissue and in terms of the very real organic damage alcohol may cause in the body, alcoholism is certainly a medical problem that has diseaselike effects. If viewed strictly on the level at which addiction represents a compulsive behavior, a more psychologically oriented person may define alcohol abuse as a behavior disorder. Approaching the issue from a holistic perspective, Alcoholics Anonymous defines alcoholism as a "disease of the mind, body, and spirit." But, whether or not one thinks about the process of alcoholism specifically as a medical disease, it still has diseaselike effects. It does damage to the healthy integration and functioning of an individual and the larger environment at all levels. In its most extreme forms, it is fatal. Certainly, the therapist needs to develop an understanding of appropriate responses to the medical complications always associated with end-stage drinking just as the physician can be of greater help to his patient in the early stages of alcoholic drinking if he understands the more psychological components of the process.

In the sense that it refers to a state of damage, dysfunction, and lack of healthy balance or equilibrium within the individual and within the larger system at many levels, we prefer to use the term disease with respect to alcoholism. It is a word that has a therapeutic psychological valence for our clients when used in a context in which ultimate responsibility for all behavior is assumed to rest with the individual. At the very least, it conveys our belief in the very serious, destructive, and potentially life-threatening effects of a failure to interrupt the process.

Alcoholism as an Interactional Process

We make the assumption that alcoholism constitutes a sequence of interactional events which occur between the drinker and the alcohol, the drinker and himself, and the drinker and others. The physiological and psychological effects of alcohol, over time, set in motion changes that shift the way the drinker interacts with himself and with others in his environment. In turn, interaction with others shapes the way the drinker drinks.

One way that alcoholism or drug abuse differs from most problems treated from a family systems perspective (e.g., schizophrenia) is that it is a behavior which introduces another substance into the informational circuitry affecting a system. The symptomatic individual interacts and exchanges information not only with others in her environment but, in effect, she interacts with the substance as well.

Alcohol is a psychoactive drug with properties that provide mood and behavior altering experiences when ingested into the body. It provides feedback to the drinker in the form of physiological effects that permit certain experiences such as warmth, relaxation, euphoria, and loosening of inhibition. The relationship with the alcohol becomes one in which, at least intermittently, the drinker is given information about himself that is more palatable or acceptable than his experience of himself in a sober state. Consequently, his feeling state is being continually modified by the added dimension of a relationship with a mood altering chemical.

This factor significantly distinguishes systems in which drug or alcohol abuse is a factor from ones in which it isn't, but more importantly, it adds a dimension of *subjective*, experiential information that is crucial to the understanding of the disease process.

In other words, when one works with most families with a symptomatic member, the communicational sequences that "surround" or constitute the problem are primarily contained within that family system and the larger contextual structures within which it operates. When the family member is alcohol-involved, however, another dimension of information and communication is introduced into the system—communication based on the distorted feedback about self that one family member receives from her interaction with a substance.

To work effectively with an alcoholic system, it is critical to understand this subjective aspect of the individual's relationship with alcohol. Both Vernon Johnson (1973) and John Wallace (1977) talk about the individual's relationship with alcohol as one that is compelling because it is confusing. Johnson indicates that the drink functions initially to cause a shift in self-experience—" the new drinker is on to a good thing. The fact that he can make himself feel better is a real discovery—in due time he knows that when he comes home and feels like this, with one drink he can feel like that" (1973:11). Over time, however, the drinker needs to drink more to achieve the same self-correction, and the more he drinks, the more subtle changes in himself and his environment begin to exact a greater price for his drinking. Increasingly, the effects of drinking become negative, but they are not consistently so, so that the drinker experiences what Wallace refers to as an "epistemological quandary" (1977:7)—he does not know how to know about himself given "the subtly changing perception, feeling, and cognition" (1977:8) and the discontinuity of the experience with the alcohol itself.

Eventually, the behavior that is motivated by an attempt to achieve a corrected experience of self shifts as the drinker experiences the need to correct the negative effects or feedback of the drinking itself. As Johnson says, "the drinker now starts from a position of feeling bad and drinks to try to get to "normal."

The struggle that Johnson and Wallace describe is one in which the individual uses alcohol to achieve an experience of herself or a "feeling" that appeals to her as more "correct" or comfortable than the one which she experiences in a sober state. This fact presumes that on some level she tells herself that the feeling or experience that she has is not consistent with how she ought to or could feel. In other words, her need or impulse to self-correct is based on certain premises about herself, about who she is and how she "should" be. These premises, of course, are based on interactional feedback received and incorporated from others in her environment. One could argue then that alcohol functions initially to reduce a kind of "cognitive dissonance" in self-experience. In the end, it creates more of that dissonance than it reduces.

Approaching the problem from another systemic level, the anthropologist Gregory Bateson (1972) views this subjective aspect of the relationship with alcohol as directly related to a false set of beliefs about self and about the world that are inherent in the thinking of Western culture. Bateson suggests that the major flaw in the thinking of the alcoholic is a kind of pride—an assertion that one can change, control what one wants to control—as he says, "a repudiation of the proposition, I cannot." Bateson suggests that the alcoholic's pride becomes the context for a struggle to achieve domination over self and others (1972:321). The subjective experience of the alcoholic in Bateson's terms might look something like this:

Joe A takes a drink.
The drink enhances or diminishes some self-perception that reduces Joe's sense of disharmony with self or others.
Joe takes another drink.
The effect is intensified. Joe comes to feel that he can regulate his emotional status by taking a drink. He gains a false sense of his own power that enables him to feel differently about himself and to operate differently with others.

Joe drinks too much to the point where his attempt to control his own emotional status leads to loss of control. Over time, Joe denies or "forgets" that loss of control and continues to relate to alcohol in such a way that he feels he can regain his "empowered" self by "losing" it to the relationship with the alcohol. He feels equal to the alcohol because he still thinks that he is in control. The more he tries to be in control, the more he loses control to the alcohol. The more he periodically and intermittently loses control and experiences negative feedback about self in terms of the fact that he is out of control, the more he drinks to prove that he is in fact in control. Over time, the singular event of taking the drink becomes a sequence of events in which a fundamental shift occurs in Joe.

In the beginning, according to Bateson's typologies of relationships,[3] Joe relates symmetrically to the alcohol. He feels "equal to it." Over time, as the consequences of drinking behavior shift his self-perceptions from positive to more negative, and as his views of self are challenged by those around him, he drinks increasingly as a way of asserting his power over the alcohol—that is, his power over himself. The relationship to the alcohol becomes a complementary one at this point in which the alcoholic seeks to assert that he is, in fact, "one-up," in face of all existing evidence that he is actually "one-down," or out of control of the relationship. In the initial phase of drinking, when the relationship to the alcohol is experienced as symmetrical, or equal, drinking is an attempt to correct self-perceptions evolved over time during sober states. Eventually, as the perceptions of self become more distorted during the course of the compulsive drinking to correct sober self-perceptions, the alcoholic begins to use the alcohol to correct the corrections—in other words, he drinks more compulsively to change the reality that he is, in fact, out of control of his drinking.

Addiction may be hypothesized to occur at the point where the alcoholic insists that she controls the action of the alcohol instead of experiencing that the action of the alcohol alters or controls her.

In the sense that the person who interacts with alcohol feels and acts one way when he is involved with alcohol, and another way when he isn't, his experience of self as well as his behavior acquires an oscillating quality. He becomes the Dr. Jekyll/Mr. Hyde so often described by those who relate to alcoholics.

Over time, the oscillations of self-experience become distortions of self-experience prompting the alcoholic to rigidly deny the "sober" aspect of self while insisting that the perceptions and experiences of the drunk state are true representations of self. In the face of mounting negative evidence to the contrary, she denies that the feedback resulting from her interaction with alcohol is now negative rather than positive. She continues to drink in a frantic attempt to achieve self-corrections. Her drinking acquires the nature of a struggle with alcohol to "force" it to provide the perceived "correct" sense of self.

As the alcoholic's feelings about himself may oscillate from extremes of self-loathing to grandiosity, depression to euphoria, so interactionally, his relationship to alcohol may shift from a symmetrical correction of self-perception to a complementary correction of the one-down status of someone in a relationship who must insist he is one-up (to others) to the alcohol.

Over time, these shifts from one state to the other become more extreme as the alcoholic's sober behavior increasingly begins to resemble drunk behavior so that the self-perceptions sober and drunk become more alike than different. Eventually, complete breakdown, represented by physical collapse or a succession of extreme consequences for drunkenness, occurs.

The primary characteristic of the interaction between the drinker and the alcohol, then, is the drinker's attempt to correct or regulate how she feels or experiences herself. She develops assumptions about how she should "be" or feel—as well as the conviction that she can or should change those feelings—from her interactions with others in the environment. In turn, the drinker's interaction with the alcohol influences the behavior of others toward her.

For instance, if in relationship to person B, person A feels tense, anxious, angry, inadequate, or any other emotion that person A experiences as unacceptable or inadequate based on his perception of how person B experiences him, then one option is in some way to alter behavior or to alter something about the self that gives rise to the discomfort. The classic example of this self-altering or corrective behavior is the person who walks into a social situation feeling tense, anxious, and uncomfortable, and immediately heads for the bar to take a drink. The drink has the effect of correcting tension and shyness, and eventually person or persons B are reacting to a much altered person A who is livelier, more charming, more outgoing and relaxed. A new level of interactional sequences is thus established based on the altering or "corrective" influence of alcohol. Two different versions of person A have attended the party that night—the tense, uncertain and fearful person A, and the corrected, relaxed, "life of the party" person A.

It seems clear that the interactional context in which person A operates both affects and is affected by the process of A's continued self-corrective drinking. The tense, withdrawn person A progresses to the outgoing, charming person A, who eventually becomes the "passed out" person on the couch. Not only person A's feelings, responses, and behaviors have been altered during the course of the evening, but the responses and reactions of those relating to A will have been altered as well. By the end of the evening the host who so glibly kept pouring the drinks and who enjoyed A's quick wit and irreverent humor may eventually become the caretaker who drives him home or otherwise assumes responsibility for his nonfunctional state. Over the course of time, should this sequence of events continue to occur, the relationship between A and the host will be irrevocably altered—the context of their interaction will shift depending on the host's desire to continue his caretaking of the drunk person A or on his perception that the drunk person A is not worth the trouble of having around.

Thus, the drinker's drinking or self-altering behavior takes place within a given interactional context and the roles or alterations that evolve on the parts of the others involved with the drinker change as the progression of the drinking process provides new behaviors to respond to. These drinking events take place discreetly at given specific points in time—that is, once a week, or once a day—but they also evolve a pattern over time as the events of each drinking sequence slowly shape the self-perception of the drinker and the attendant responses of others in the interactional system. Just as the drinker's self-perception is changed by alcohol, the self-perception of others in the system changes and adapts in response to interaction with the drinker.

As the alcoholic drinks and successive events of self-correction occur, people relating to the alcoholic develop adaptive behaviors in response to the cyclical, discrepant, discordant representations of self presented as the alcoholic shifts from sober to drunk states. Once drinking has become a central focus of concern in a given system, other members of the system are adapting to the full sequence of behavior constituted by the oscillation from sober to drunk back to sober again. Their responses and adaptations will tend to enhance or minimize the likelihood that oscillations in the drinker will become either a sustained pattern of behavior or will recede in frequency. In most cases, the more dysfunctionally adaptive the system becomes, the more the drinker will drink, and the more the drinker drinks, the more dysfunctionally adaptive the system will become.

As a result of the adaptive nature of their behavior, their roles as reactors rather than actors, others in the system begin to acquire the same types of attitudes, feelings, and behaviors that are characteristic of the alcoholic, even though they don't drink. Their self-perceptions become inextricably linked to the actions of the drinker, and their adaptive behaviors represent their own attempts to self-correct in the face of the feedback generated by the alcohol-affected person.

What becomes clear is that in the system organized around alcohol, all members of the family or larger system are essentially alcohol-affected—that is, their self-corrective behavior is always generated by patterns of feedback that originate in a relationship with alcohol.

It must be noted that drinking may occur over phases that differ in different systems and that trigger mechanisms may be different for different families and different individuals. Life cycle events, developmental pressures, work, peer relationships, traumatic events or losses, shifting power hierarchies and family structures may all provide different trigger events in different families. The trigger for drinking or self-correction may be inside or outside the family system, but the system's response will always affect the drinking and the drinking will always affect the system.

Finally, the individual's notion of "correct self" is influenced by a series of messages or communications transferred from the macro level of social values and institutions to the micro level of interpersonal interactions within the given family context. Thus, notions about correct self are defined by cultural norms, peer group norms, gender and sex role norms, and, finally, family norms that are a collective expression of all the others.

Issues in Alcoholic Systems: Implications for Treatment

If we view the act of drinking in its extreme and repetitive forms as having a self-corrective function for the drinker, the fact that he experiences a need to self-correct represents a statement to the larger system in which he operates that something is wrong. If one observes the interactions that typically characterize alcoholic families, it is possible to evolve some statements about the social context, the interpersonal interactions, and the internal dynamics that serve as the framework for the corrective functions of alcohol.

In terms of the social context, from which one derives norms regarding appropriate hierarchies related to power in the family, it can be observed that in alcoholic families, to an extreme degree, there exists a serious inability to define appropriate hierarchial roles as well as a very covert struggle for power and control. Often there are no clear boundaries around the parental subsystem in the family so that children may be "triangled" into the parental relationship to the extent that they may replace one or both of the parents in fulfilling the parental functions. Within the spouse system, there is often significant confusion regarding the rules defining the relationship. While there is an attempt to define the relationship along very traditional lines in terms of sex role socialization such that the male is assumed to be the head of the household and the independent one, while the woman is assumed to be the dependent one and the emotional caretaker in the family, in fact, the emergence of alcoholism as a symptom creates adaptive modes of functioning in which these roles may be very much reversed, but persistently unacknowledged.

In the social context, the major effects or adaptive consequences of alcoholism seem to emerge in the dimension of sex role socialization and gender role function. It appears to us that one of the self-corrective or adaptive functions of alcohol may be that it either *permits expression* or *allows suppression* of impulses, feelings, and behaviors that violate traditional sex role norms. Given the system's focus on the alcoholism as the problematic behavior, these norm violations are never directly acknowledged.

The effects of this power/dependency conflict and the adaptive shifting of behaviors around expectations regarding sex role behavior are most clearly manifested interactionally in the alcoholic system around behaviors that may be characterized as either over- or under-responsible. In its self-corrective function, alcohol permits not an assertion of self so much as an evasion of responsibility for self. Therefore, in response to the individual's relationship with alcohol, or to the individual's tendency to have engaged in avoidance of self-responsibility prior to drinking, interactional roles in the family become reciprocally balanced around extremes of behavior that are either over- or under-responsible. Drinking may create an extreme reciprocity in terms of these two roles, or the extreme role reciprocity may be maintained by the drinking. There is strong reason to believe that patterns of reciprocal over- and underresponsible behavior transmitted between family members intergenerationally may in large part set the stage for the emergence of alcoholism in succeeding generations.

Finally, the individual for whom alcohol functions as a self-correcting substance typically takes great pride in the idealized image of herself that the alcohol permits, or she may need to self-correct because some idealized image of herself that she does hold to be true is not, in fact, validated by reality-based feedback from external events or people in her relational system. The more her idealized sense of self is threatened, the more adamantly she asserts its validity and, therefore, the more she needs to drink. Since an individual's "idealized" or inaccurate belief about self has typically been generated as a protection in response to feedback or communications from his original family system that are inconsistent, negative, or self-negating, pride is a self-corrective mechanism in itself that often requires the reinforcement and further self-correction of alcohol to be sustained.

In response to the negative and self-negating feedback that the alcoholic usually transmits to others, all people in an alcoholic system tend to evolve adaptive, idealized images of themselves which are sometimes reinforced and sometimes attacked in their interaction with the alcoholic. As a result, their sense of self and behavior become pride-based, distorted, and corrective—in short, a mirror of the process that occurs for the alcoholic, but without the alcohol.

Finally, what characterizes the alcoholic system at all levels is untruth—the attempt of the self to be not self or an altered self, and the participation of all the cast of characters surrounding the alcoholic in increasingly dysfunctional patterns of behavior based on distortion and confusion about self in relationship to self and self in relationship to others.

Ernest Kurtz (1982) would say that the erroneous belief that one can fundamentally alter the nature of self is based on a false pride generated by some belief that the human being can be *god*—that is, not fearful, not limited, not inadequate, not a being who experiences discomfort, confusion, and anxiety about his own identity. On a more basic level, self-corrective behavior seems generated by the fear of being inadequate to live up to perceived human expectations and the realistic demands and stresses of life that have been generated by a culture or society whose own values and power structures are perhaps erroneous. It seems clear that in a broadly generalizable way, alcohol-involved people encounter incongruity in their experience of their prescribed sex role behavior as it relates to power, autonomy, and dependence; that they engage in extreme forms of reciprocal interpersonal behavior that permits an avoidance of responsibility for self; and that in order to maintain prideful or adaptive versions of their own sense of identity, they use alcohol to distort their experience of self in a vain attempt to force reality to adapt to their notions of the way things *should* be.

Our assumption about treatment is that it must address these three critical levels on which the alcoholic process occurs. It must address the unbalanced interpersonal interactions that result from and maintain the alcoholic's need to self-correct. It must address the alcoholic's thinking about self—what Bateson defines as pride—because this pride mediates the interaction occurring between the alcoholic, the alcohol, and the other. And, finally, it must address issues in the larger social context— the way the society thinks about itself—because ultimately, the need for the individual to self-correct occurs in response to her perception that her "true" self exists in a state of alienation from and opposition to the norms, expectations, and rules of the larger culture.

Family therapy and the techniques described in this book are best equipped to address imbalance in interaction at the interpersonal level as well as the pride issues that mediate that interaction. However, ultimately what needs to occur for the alcholic and those around him is an entire shift in the context within which he operates—a shift in the way he thinks about himself. We feel that Alcoholics Anonymous, for reasons that will be more thoroughly explained in Chapter 3, represents the most effective means we have at hand for helping the alcoholic to accomplish this shift because it directly addresses problems and patterns of thinking particular to this culture. Consequently, any treatment strategy we outline in this book is best accomplished if used in conjunction with the AA program.

The next three chapters will elaborate on the three contextual issues that serve as our framework for viewing the alcoholic system: over- and underresponsibility, pride, and sex role socialization.

CHAPTER 2

Alcoholism and the Interpersonal Context
The Dimensions of Responsibility

In working with alcoholic families, a first point of intervention is to assess the ways family members do and do not assume responsibility for self. Patterns of over- and underresponsibility in the families we work with seem to be highly significant in maintaining alcoholic behavior and in insuring the perpetuation of the symptom in succeeding generations within the family. The manner in which people in a family do and do not assume appropriate developmental responsibility for self and for tasks related to their specific family roles represents to us the "nodal point" of dysfunction in the family. To the degree that issues of sex role socialization and pride affect the regulation of self-responsible behavior, they provide the contextual determinants within which certain behaviors will or will not evolve. However, in this chapter we are concerned with behavior, with what people do and do not do, and how their behaviors become reciprocal and mutually reinforcing along dimensions of self-focus and responsibility.

Concepts of over- and underresponsibility are not new either to family systems thinking or to the field of alcoholism treatment. It has been a main tenet of Alcoholics Anonymous and Al-Anon groups that the alcoholic must assume responsibility for her own life, her feelings, and her behavior, and that the most helpful response by the non-alcoholic is to make this necessary by focusing on his own behavior rather than the alcoholic's. The concept of "enabling" grew from a recognition that an alcoholic could continue to behave irresponsibly to the degree that others in her environment behaved responsibily *for* her. The person who attends Al-Anon meetings is coached to "detach" from the alcoholic in the sense that that person should stop taking responsibility for the emotional or practical consequences of the alcoholic's drinking behavior.

Murray Bowen (1978:155) speaks about the person who "overfunctions" in a relational context. This person tends to "do more" or to emotionally pursue more than his partner. He is anxious enough to take on the primary responsibility for maintaining one or many aspects of the relationship. Bowen's belief in terms of clinical intervention is that it is always easier to get an overfunctioner to do less than it is to get an underfunctioner to do more. He would define the transactional outcomes of over- or underresponsibility as resulting from the inherent fusion or lack of differentiation in the relationship.

Finally, David Berenson (1976b:288) also uses the terms overresponsible and underresponsible in the context of alcoholism in describing aspects of the oscillation that occurs between the wet and dry states. He characterizes "wet" or drunk behavior as underresponsible and "dry" or sober behavior as overresponsible. He makes the point that in an alcohol-affected family, one does not actually have to drink to be in a "wet" or underresponsible state. He defines any "out of control" behavior as wet behavior, so that if one spouse becomes highly anxious and reactive to the other's drinking behavior, that spouse is equally "wet" or underresponsibly out of control.

Berenson appears to have been the first clinician to suggest in the literature on alcoholism that over- and underresponsible behaviors are both dysfunctional if they become fixed patterns and that one type of behavior is really only the flip side of the other. If one views the precipitant of anxious, out-of-control behavior in the nondrinking person as a tremendous experience of overconcern or overresponsibility for what the drinker does, then it is a feeling of overresponsibility that results in underresponsible or out-of-control behavior. Thus, it is clear that overresponsibility is as nonresponsible as underresponsible behavior, and that both the nondrinking person and the drinker share a mirrored process of abdicating responsibility for self.

Building on Berenson's concepts of over- and underresponsibility as they related to alcoholism, we began to attempt in our clinical work to define more precisely how these patterns function to maintain drinking behavior and the general dysfunction in the family. It is important in facilitating a discussion of our ideas to review briefly certain systems concepts that are important to an understanding of the dynamics that occur in any interpersonal relationship.

Complementary and Symmetrical Behavior

Gregory Bateson (1958) first introduced the concepts of complementarity and symmetry as a result of anthropological studies in which he attempted to evolve a theory of human interaction. His observations led him to define two specific interactional patterns which have become incorporated, as mentioned in Chapter 1, into a general theory of interaction in family or dyadic systems as represented by the proponents of the communications school of family systems thinking.[1] Fundamentally, Bateson defined the nature of an interactional process between two people as being either complementary or symmetrical. A complementary relationship or interaction is one in which more of a certain behavior on A's part results in more of a different but complementary behavior on B's part. The behaviors mutually fit. Bateson uses the example of dominance or assertiveness and submission. The more assertive A becomes, the less assertive and more submissive B becomes. A cannot continue his assertive behavior unless B continues to communicate that the relational rule is acceptable by being submissive.

Some relationships are automatically defined as complementary by virtue of biological or structural fact or function. For instance, the relationship between a mother and child is by its nature complementary, as is that between a teacher and student. In other relationships, however, complementarity occurs because one person defines himself as "one-up" in the relationship, that is, the person in control or in charge, while the other, by virtue of submitting, agrees to be in the "one-down" position.

In a symmetrical relationship, both parties define themselves as equal and they exchange the same behaviors. If A gives, B gives; if A takes, B takes. Both assume the right to define the rules of the relationship.[2]

Both complementary and symmetrical relationships may change or develop over time in a process referred to by Bateson as schismogenesis in which the sequence of either complementary or symmetrical interactional events may lead to a "runaway," an escalation without limits that leads to a breakdown of the system. For instance, in a complementary relationship between a sadist and a masochist, too much and too extreme sadism/masochism over time or during a given incident may lead to the injury or death of the masochist. In a symmetrical relationship between two nuclear powers, the continued assertion of equality may result in an arms race that will result in nuclear war.

Thus, neither form of relationship in and of itself is inherently negative or positive. Schismogenesis, or the progression toward change lead-ing ultimately to runaway, is in part a normal process usually contained by a system of checks and balances inherent within the rules of the given relationship. Progression to a runaway or breakdown of the relationship usually results when the fact of equality or the assertion of dominance is *not* overtly accepted or acknowledged by both parties, but rather when the one partner acting one down in a complementary relationship makes covert attempts to become one up, or when the person asserting equality in a symmetrical relationship tries to assert that equality by being better than the other.

For purposes of this discussion it will be helpful simply to conceptualize a complementary relationship as:

A does more: B does less.

and a symmetrical one as:

A does more: B does more.

In the former, the behaviors are reciprocal and mutually fit, in the latter, the behaviors are competitive. In either, if the behaviors progress to rigid extremes, or if the nature of the relationship is not openly acknowledged and accepted by both parties, dysfunction and eventual breakdown of the relationship will result.

It seems simple to look at an alcoholic interaction and define it as complementary. The alcoholic drinks and is irresponsible or under-responsible and the spouse reacts by "filling in," taking over, being overresponsible. The way an alcoholic relationship evolves over time is that A (the alcoholic) does less and B (the spouse or nondrinker), more.

The Dimensions of Responsibility

It seemed important to focus on the issue of responsibility for self in our treatment of alcohol-affected families precisely because the effect of the symptom (drinking) is that it functions to promote irresponsibility or out-of-control behavior. It was also clear, however, that in an interactional context irresponsibility could not be sustained unless other people in the system acted in ways that permitted, condoned, or maintained it. This is not to assign motivation to behavior, but rather to acknowledge the mutually reinforcing patterns of responses that occur in any relationship, and particularly in a relationship in which one person drinks.

We define self-responsibility as the activity of meeting one's own physical and emotional needs in a way that is developmentally appropriate. A six-year-old is developmentally ready to assume responsibilities at a level that differs from that of a sixteen-year-old. We assume that an adult is fully responsible for self—that is, he provides for his own physical and emotional needs and directly asks for what he wants from others.

Underresponsible behavior is defined as the failure to meet one's physical or emotional needs at an appropriate developmental level. For a six-year-old, underresponsible behavior may mean a failure to dress herself with only the minimal help this task should require. For a sixteen-year-old, it may mean a failure to function optimally in school or a failure to care adequately for his own belongings. For an adult, it may mean the failure to provide adequate financial support for herself or the failure to ask others directly for help or emotional responsiveness rather than expecting it.

Underresponsibility suggests a failure to focus on and act in one's self-interest in a way that maintains physical and emotional well-being. If one is a parent, underresponsibility suggests a greater focus on the child than on self in that the child is overtly or covertly expected to take care of needs that should be appropriately met by oneself.

Overresponsibility suggests a focus on others rather than self in that one responds more to the physical and emotional needs of another person than to one's own needs. If one is an overresponsible parent, one overresponds to the physical and emotional needs of a child—that is one does more than the child really needs to have done. Overresponsibility for others is usually correlated (in different degrees for different people) with underresponsibility for self. While one is busy focusing on others, there is typically a covert expectation that someone else will meet one's own needs. At least there is a tendency to avoid or ignore those needs oneself. Overresponsibility suggests that in most interactions, the needs or expectations of the other are responded to in spite of a potential conflict with one's personal need or desire. The other is always more important than self.

One may be over- or underresponsible in two specific areas: task and emotion. If one is underresponsible in the area of tasks or functions, one may fail to take out the garbage, to pay the bills, to get the oil changed in one's car, or to hand in one's homework. If one is overresponsible in the area of tasks, one does not only one's own chores, but everyone else's as well. Since overresponsibility for function suggests a focus of energy on others, one may not actually perform the tasks for others, but may at least direct them in doing it, or comment on, and criticize how tasks were done. A parent may not actually do a child's homework, but may make endless comments on what the child is or is not doing, should or should not do. One spouse may not perform the other's chore of taking out the garbage, but may focus his energy on describing in detail exactly how the garbage should be packed and where it should be put.

Similarly, in the emotional dimension, the underresponsible person may fail to be direct in dealing with her feelings, she may blame others for her problems or conflicts or she may expect emotional caretaking, sensitivity, recognition, and responsiveness to her feelings without directly asking for them or doing anything to get them. She may fail to negotiate rules or agreements emotionally, leaving the outcome of interactions to "loss by default." She may fail to express what she wants and how she feels, expecting that others are focused on knowing what she wants.

The overresponsible person on the other hand is acutely sensitive to the needs and feelings of others and will often respond to them without being asked. This person has a tendency to be protective of other's feelings and to assume that the other person's feelings are always more important than his own. The overresponsible person always responds to feelings in the other with a sense that he must do something about them. In this sense he always refers the other's feelings back to self. The typical responses of the overresponsible person are:

1. Acting anxious or in some way reactive because the other person has a feeling.
2. Telling the other person not to have the feeling by instructing him or her about it, discounting, explaining, counseling, problem solving, or in some way trying to control the feeling.
3. Having the feeling for the other. For instance, being depressed because the other is depressed, being hurt and angry for one's child because someone called her a name at school.

In the functional (task) dimension, overresponsibility on the part of one person will almost always result in underresponsibility on the part of the other. This type of transaction is directly complementary in that more of A's behavior always leads to less of B's behavior. For example, if a mother performs all the maintenance tasks in a household to the point that she makes all beds, washes all clothes, makes all meals, and cleans all rooms, her husband and children reciprocally make no beds, wash no clothes, make no meals, and clean no rooms. In this transaction she overfunctions and they underfunction. Transactions in the functional domain are usually complementary in that only the two roles are available: that is, if one person in the family performs a particular function, the other people do not, because they don't have to. Complementary roles may be reversed in different areas of function. For instance, a wife may overfunction in areas of house maintenance, while a husband may overfunction in areas relevant to financial support of the family.

Transactions in the emotional domain are inherently more complex because overresponsibility in one person may provoke one of two possible responses. In the first, the other person in the transaction may respond with a symmetrically overresponsible reaction. This type of transaction might look something like this:

Person A is depressed. Person B, being overresponsible, refers the feeling back to herself, that is, assumes that she is responsible for the depression, is angry at the depression, or anxious about the depression. She behaves in a way that is reactive to A's depression. She tries to take care of, counsel, take away the depression, or finally may become depressed herself. Person A, in turn, may respond by being emotionally overresponsible for B. Instead of remaining focused on his own feelings, he may react to B's reaction with anger, guilt, or some other response that suggests a need to take care of B's reaction to his depression. Since both people in this transaction are engaging in the same kind of behavior, that is, focusing on the other rather than remaining focused on self, this type of interaction will typically escalate until the two either fight or reactively distance themselves from each other. To the degree that both are other-focused rather than self-focused, the outcome of their behavior could also be defined as symmetrical underresponsibility for self.

The other potential outcome of a transaction in which one person acts overresponsibly for the feelings of the other is that a complementary acceptance of being "one down" will occur. In this type of interaction, Person A may, again, be depressed and person B may react by trying to "take care of" the depression. Even if B's initial self-referential reactions to the depression are anger or anxiety, A may remain nonreactive to these responses because they essentially respond to his underresponsible role posture which is to have someone else focus on and react to his feelings rather than having to take care of them himself. The configuration of this transaction is, again, complementary, because the overresponsible person focuses energy and attention on the other who then does not have to take care of him or herself. B does more, so A does less. Again, to the degree that B is focusing more on A than on self, both parties in this interaction are underresponsible for self. Their relationship or interaction at this point represents a complementary underresponsibility because the one-up/one-down configuration has been accepted on an overt level.

The complementary and symmetrical forms of interaction described are not the only possible interactional configurations in a family, but they are those that we hypothesize result in the greatest dysfunction. They represent interactions that involve extremes of either over- or underresponsible behavior and, thus, rigid forms of complementarity or symmetry. They essentially define the individual's primary emotional orientation as underresponsible, that is, focused and dependent on other rather than self for one's sense of identity, value, and adequacy as a person.

It is important to note that the categories overresponsible and underresponsible are not static ones. They represent possible reciprocal positions that evolve in response to specific interactional events and they describe generalized presentations of self evolving over time. In certain circumstances, the person generally defined by overresponsible behavior, for instance, may act underresponsible or appropriately responsible. The more behavior falls into a specific category in specific interactional events over time, the more generally defined by that role configuration the person will become. Specific stresses in the family or relationship may also function to shift behavior to one extreme or the other.

A given individual may also shift back and forth between the two categories. The assumption is that the person with whom the individual interacts shifts in reverse order. Since interactions occur between more than two people in a family, all role configurations generally represent responses to the reciprocal behavior of others in the family as well. For instance, a child may become overresponsible for tasks in relationship to the mother's tendency to be a poor housekeeper, and underresponsible emotionally because of the mother's constant overconcern about his feelings. In response to his father's emotional distance, however, he may become overresponsible emotionally, pursuing him by attempting to please or otherwise engage him on an emotional level; the child may also overfunction for tasks in an attempt to please his father. In general, his role orientation over time will become a composite of reciprocal responses to both parents individually as well as responses to the particular demands or constraints communicated by the parental interaction. In other words, role reciprocity results from triadic as well as dyadic interaction.

The child in the situation described may be typically overresponsible for task and underresponsible in the emotional dimension in response to his mother, but overresponsible in both areas in response to his father. If the interaction between the parents tends to be conflicted, the child's dominant role configuration will evolve in a way that best satisfies the demands of the triangular situation. The child may find that acting predominantly overresponsible in both dimensions of task and emotion responds most adequately to the individual relationships he experiences with each parent as well as to the demands precipitated by the conflicts between them. While he may at times allow himself an underresponsible, complementary response to the mother's emotional overresponsibility, in general an overresponsible, symmetrical response resulting in fighting and distance from the mother might best serve the needs of the marital conflict in which the father clearly communicates that he is distant from his wife and seeks an alliance in the child subsystem. Since this child adopts this role in response to the triangular situation, another child may adopt an alternate role because the predominantly overresponsible role is not available. A second child may become predominantly underresponsible both to provide an alternate triangular configuration in the family and to respond to individual interactions with both parents and other siblings.

A family in which members experienced a healthier degree of self-differentiation and self-responsibility would carry out transactions that were less rigidly complementary or symmetrical. The quality of role reciprocity in these families would be likely to be more flexible in response to changing situational and developmental needs, more consensual and overt, and competency-based rather than founded on assumptions or fears of inadequacy or helplessness. The tendency to interact in ways that were either over- or underresponsible for the other and/or self would be replaced by the capacity to be genuinely *responsive to* the needs and feelings of others.

Having outlined a basic conceptual framework for viewing the complementary and symmetrical forms of behavior that may evolve around the issue of responsibility, we can begin to generalize about the predominant patterns we tend to see in alcoholic families. Again, these are clinical observations based on trial and error in evolving clinical interventions and they are not supported by objective research. They are constructs on which we base hypotheses about what will effect change. To begin, the following are some basic generalizations that we make about alcohol-affected families:

1. A predominant theme or question that the family attempts to resolve is who is responsible for and who has power over what or whom? The family never evolves clear answers to these questions.
2. Alcohol serves to regulate the shifting of role behavior along dimensions of over- and underresponsibility from complementary to symmetrical and back again so that family members may avoid overt acknowledgment of responsibility, power, or dependency.
3. Patterns of over- and underresponsible behavior are transmitted cross-generationally. A child who has assumed an overresponsible role in her family of origin, for instance, will perpetuate that role in her own marriage, or will revert to the flip side of that behavior and assume an underresponsible role.
4. The categories of role behavior most likely to produce or to maintain the appearance of alcoholism in a system are those in which over- or underresponsibility exists in both the task and emotional dimensions and, to a lesser degree, those in which the person exhibits a combination of over- and underresponsible behavior.
5. The configurations of over-, under-, or self-responsible behavior that emerge in an individual are always related to the demands and constraints of the particular interactional system within the context of ethnic, life cycle, and sex role factors and as influenced by patterns of stress, loss, and other contiguous events affecting

the system. Behavior may change as changes occur in the system so that individuals may exhibit varying degrees of responsible behavior at different points in time and in response to different circumstances.

6. As a regulator of role configuration in the family, alcohol functions to maintain behavior within extremely rigid parameters. The family interactional process cycles back on itself in the shift from complementary to symmetrical and is increasingly rigid over time so that the degrees of over- and underresponsibility become more and more extreme. The more extreme the degrees, the more the alcoholism is maintained, and the more the alcoholism is maintained, the more extreme the degrees of over- and underresponsibility become.

7. The emergence of over- or underresponsible behavior is always accompanied by shifts in the experience of self and these shifts in turn result in over- or underresponsible behavior. Thus, as alcohol regulates the interactional system, it also regulates the self system. As alcohol distorts interactional processes, resulting in increasing lack of clarity of rules, boundaries, and definitions of power, responsibility, and dependency, it also distorts the experience of self, and as the experience of self is distorted, the reliance on alcohol to correct it is increased.

A Hypothetical Case: The X Family

The following is a genogram (Guerin and Pendagast, 1976), a structural diagram of family relationships, that represents a somewhat "typical" role configuration in an alcohol-affected family along the dimensions of over- and underresponsibility. The clinical chapters of this book will expand on some other types of patterns that commonly occur when alcohol is present in a family system. The analysis of the family that follows is deliberately skeletal and does not take into account important factors such as ethnic background, life cycle issues, family of origin events (deaths, births, losses), etc. that will be elaborated on in the clinical chapters.

In the X family, Mr. X drinks alcoholically, often coming home drunk and frequently getting drunk on weekends. Apart from functioning in his work role, at this time he takes no responsibility for any tasks related to maintenance of the family. He doesn't pay bills, he doesn't work in the yard, and he doesn't help maintain the house, inside or out. He does not participate in school functions or in disciplining of the children. Periodically, when pushed by his wife, he will have explosive rages at his wife and children, particularly his son. He is typically very

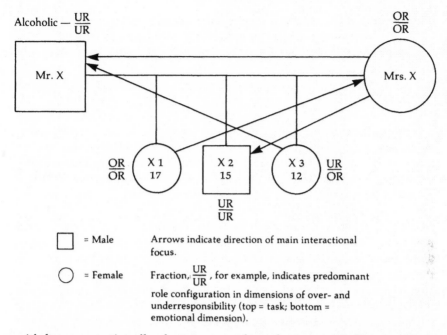

Alcoholic — $\dfrac{UR}{UR}$

$\dfrac{OR}{OR}$

Mr. X

Mrs. X

$\dfrac{OR}{OR}$ X 1 17

X 2 15

X 3 12 $\dfrac{UR}{OR}$

$\dfrac{UR}{UR}$

☐ = Male

○ = Female

Arrows indicate direction of main interactional focus.

Fraction, $\dfrac{UR}{UR}$, for example, indicates predominant role configuration in dimensions of over- and underresponsibility (top = task; bottom = emotional dimension).

withdrawn emotionally, however, and rarely expresses his own feelings, wants, or needs. When he does interact, it is typically to be critical of his wife and children. He continually lets them know that they are inadequate at responding to him and inadequate in general in their functioning.

Mrs. X has begun to assume all responsibilities in the household. Not only does she make an effort to do everything, but she focuses almost exclusively on tasks—on her functions in the household and on doing things "perfectly." Her home is always spotlessly clean, her children are always taken where they need to go on time. She pays very little attention to her own emotional needs except to confide occasionally in her oldest daughter. Her children are reflections of her adequacy as a person. She has many somatic complaints and tends to overeat.

The oldest daughter worries a great deal about the negative interactions between her parents. In spite of this she functions very well at school and has assumed her mother's concern for the care of the house. She has little interaction with her father. She is, however, very family oriented and spends more time at home than she does socializing with friends.

The middle child, the son, has a very conflicted relationship with his father and older sister. His mother tends to dote on him, to do everything for him, and yet he does poorly in school. He prefers being with friends to being at home and frequently abuses alcohol and drugs. The youngest daughter also tends to do nothing around the house, does less well than she might in school and focuses primarily on friends rather than family life. She is a staunch defender of her father, however, and is often the only person with whom he will talk or discuss his feelings. She feels that she "understands" her father.

Comment

The X family is precariously balanced around very complementary over- and underresponsible roles. Mr. X drinks alcoholically and under-functions; Mrs. X overfunctions. Emotionally, however, they are both symmetrically underresponsible for self. This mutual emotional under-responsibility serves as the focus for the many conflicts and fights between them. He blames her for not being responsive to him, for being cold, distant, and overweight, and she blames him for not being an adequate father and husband, and for not functioning adequately around the house. Whenever the tensions in this mutual blaming (symmetrical underresponsibility) mount, he drinks, and the system is restored to a complementarity in which she resumes her role as the over-responsible partner and he resumes his role as the underresponsible partner. In this sense, the alcohol serves to regulate the degree to which either partner looks at issues of power, dependency, or autonomy in the marriage and it serves to help either avoid taking responsibility for his or her emotional needs. Rather than be emotionally responsible for self, she overeats, has somatic complaints, and overfocuses on him and/or her children. The alcohol maintains this underresponsibility, which in turn maintains the alcoholism.

The children evolve supportive and complementary role behaviors in this scenario with the oldest daughter mirroring her mother's over-responsibility, the son his father's underresponsibility, and the third daughter a combination of both. The system is finely balanced so that if any one person in the family begins to step out of role—if, for instance, the father gets sober and becomes more responsible—the focus of energy may shift to the son. The son is the alternate underresponsible member who is at greatest short-term risk of becoming alcoholic in this family because of the predominant underresponsible role configuration he has assumed. The oldest daughter, on the other hand, is likely to marry an alcoholic, because having assumed an overresponsible role she will seek the complementary underresponsible "fit" in a partner, though she may hardly be aware that the characteristics she admires initially in her chosen spouse—the fun-loving, emotionally intense, charming qualities—may eventually evolve into alcoholic behavior. This daughter is equally at risk of becoming alcoholic herself. A flip to the opposite extreme of underresponsibility and alcoholic drinking could become a way of coping with the tremendous strains of the overresponsible role and an expression of her inability to respond successfully to her own emotional needs. A broken marriage, a loss of some figure on whom she was overly focused, a failure to derive a sense of herself as adequate in her functioning in her career or family, or any fear that she was disappointing her own or someone else's expectations might trigger drinking behavior. This outcome is much more likely to occur if there is some figure in the woman's environment who will in some way overfunction for her. In any case, if her overresponsibility continues to an extreme degree, her lack of responsiveness to her own needs will result, like her mother's, in some form of symptomatic behavior.

The youngest daughter is also at risk of becoming either alcoholic herself or the spouse of an alcoholic, but because her role configuration is somewhat less extreme, she also has the better chance for evolving a degree of self-responsible behavior or for finding a life role or marital situation in which her over- and underresponsibilities do not move to the extremes that lay the groundwork for alcoholism. On the basis of the way we conceptualize over- and underresponsibility in its generational progressions, we may assume either that Mr. X was highly overresponsible in both task and emotional dimensions in his family of origin in relationship to one or both parents or in response to the triangular demands of the marital situation (in which case his alcoholism represents a flip to the opposite extreme of behavior), or that he was in a role similar to his son's in which he was doted on by one overresponsible parent and became underresponsible emotionally for self in response to that doting and to the pressures of a conflictual marital situation.

Mrs. X, on the other hand, was very likely the daughter of an alcoholic mother or father or both.

The Under- and Overresponsible Experiences of Self

The constructs of over- and underresponsibility are manifested by specific types of behavior and they are correlated with specific feeling states in the individual. In our clinical work with families, we are constantly impressed by the tremendous power of the particular experience of self associated with extreme degrees of under- and overresponsibility. These feelings almost always represent distortions of what is true about a given individual and they give rise to illusions about the potential consequences of changing one's behavior. In the face of alcohol's power to distort self-experience, coupled with the alcohol-affected person's development of distorted self-perceptions in response to alcohol, both the family and the clinician are indeed faced with powerful resistance to change. As painful and constricting as these illusions about self may be, they function to give both the alcoholic and his co-dependents the only available experience of control over self in an otherwise chaotic and very frightening emotional climate. Any attempt to restore self-control or self-responsibility in an alcohol-affected system is perceived as an attempt to take away control that threatens to bring the individual to an experience of true existential emptiness and collapse.[3] This loss of control must be resisted at all costs, yet paradoxically, the very rigidity of the interactional behavior in the system represents the degree to which alcohol controls the family dynamics by pushing them increasingly to crises that risk dissolution of the system and sometimes death. The individuals in the system experience drinking behavior or overresponsible behavior as measures of control when, in fact, it is precisely these behaviors that lead the individuals and the system to the brink of runaway or of being out of control.

The basic self-experience of the overresponsible or the under-responsible person relates directly to the behavior manifested in each role. Some generalizations can be made about the feeling state accompanied by each role category.

Overresponsible—Functionally and Emotionally

As we have outlined, the overresponsible person has typically evolved his or her behavior in an interactional context in which his predominant pattern has been to act in response to an underfunctioner. Typically, the child who grows up operating in this type of relational pattern (the child of an alcoholic mother for instance) learns some fairly typical things about self:

1. Doing is valued over being—one will be loved or have importance to the other only insofar as one functions well *for* the other person.
2. At times the other is so dysfunctional that it seems clear that unless one takes over, the "world will collapse." The tremendous anxiety and fear registered by the child about the fact that a parent is operating incompetently can be relieved only by taking control and overfunctioning in whatever way the child perceives that he can.
3. The child becomes responsive to the other's emotional under-responsibility and comes to believe that he or she is completely responsible for the other's happiness and well-being. She thus becomes tremendously susceptible to feelings of guilt and inadequacy whenever the other is unhappy or dissatisfied and may often experience tremendous confusion over what exactly will please the other.
4. The intense focus on the other results in inadequate focus on self

and failure to make any demands relative to one's own emotional needs for nurturance or dependency. The child may tend to become "a little adult" who simply assumes and accepts that no self-gratification can be expected from a parent (other) who is totally absorbed in self.

Three predominant emotions result from the set of circumstances outlined:

1. Tremendous anger and sense of deprivation that must always be denied, along with a deep wish to be taken care of that must also be denied because it would directly conflict with the child's sense that his very "being" and sense of worth and adequacy are dependent on taking care of the other. Whenever the anger begins to emerge, tremendous anxiety will result, which will in turn generate more caretaking behavior (or it will generate drinking).
2. A sense of being "special"—of being the person who is at the center of the other's emotional world and a sense of being the "only one" who can understand, take care of, or really make the other happy. If one is displaced from this role by another person in the family, or if the relationship is a marital one, tremendous feelings of betrayal, rage, despair, and competitiveness may result. The person may shift to being underresponsible.
3. A chronic and contrary sense of being inadequate, worthless, and not good enough. A chronic experience of "burnout." Often the overresponsible person has not had the appropriate help she needs to know how to function—she measures her functioning only by her own standards. In fact, she may not be adequate, but she cannot see this. The person typically never feels that she has done enough, been responsible enough. She may feel chronically guilty, depressed, sometimes suicidal. Any situation which calls for self-focus rather than allowing the typical pattern of other-focus to continue creates intense conflict and anxiety.

To summarize, for the person who functions in the role category of overresponsible, "taking care of" the other on an emotional or functional level represents the only viable experience of the self as adequate, worthwhile, and rightfully existing. Functional competence and emotional caretaking are crucial to one's sense of being a valuable, worthy, loved person. However, since one can never accomplish this perfectly enough, in the eyes of oneself or the other, the person is plagued by feelings of self-doubt, guilt, and inadequacy. Since focus on others is tantamount to a validation of self, any tendency toward self-focus is denied, resisted, or accompanied by tremendous anxiety. Anger that one does not experience self-gratification from others must be denied at all costs as it challenges the pervasive belief that one's self-importance resides only in focusing on the other.[4]

The Dilemma of the Underresponsible Person

As the overresponsible person derives his role function and, there-fore, his sense of self in interaction with a predominantly underrespon-sible person, the underresponsible person evolves his self-experience in response to a person who tends always to function *for* him. While the interactional dynamics of his experience are different, some of the net effects in terms of self-experience are similar to those of people in the opposite category.

The following are generalizations about the self-experience of the person in the underresponsible role:

1. As a child, she may have been focused on to such a degree as to experience herself as being at "the center of the universe." She comes to expect to be responded to, taken care of, given to by others. She will typically look to others rather than self for satis-faction of needs, demands, and for response to uncomfortable emotions.

2. The attention of the other is experienced as conveying power and as taking it away at the same time. Undue attention is often experienced as, or has the effect of, control. If another con-tinually does something for the person or continually tells him how to do it, this behavior has the effect of limiting the ability of the person being focused on to evolve his own solutions and his own behaviors. His responses become totally conditioned by the way in which the overfunctioner operates.

3. The less a person is required to do, the less competent he feels and, in fact, the less competent he becomes to handle his own affairs. Gradually he begins to experience himself as in-competent and gradually he will function less.

4. The individual gradually experiences tremendous anger at being told what to do, how to do it, and at having it done, but also experiences tremendous anger at not being done for. Because a true dependency has been nurtured by the overfunctioner, the person is bound by her awareness that she is dependent and incompetent on the one hand, and by the awareness that the only solution to her dependence is to function for self, on the other. However, functioning for self would rob her of her entitle-ment to be given to, and would also raise tremendous anxiety about failure.

5. The underresponsible person becomes accustomed to having all

emotional needs or conflicts anticipated and responded to by the other (either positively or negatively) and, thus, rarely develops inner resources for responding to frustration, anxiety, loneliness, or the common demands of interpersonal relationships. His growing awareness of his inability to negotiate emotional transactions and other demands independently results in intense fear of loss and abandonment by the caretaking other along with an intense resentment over this attachment.

Thus, the underresponsible person pays the price of self-respect and self-confidence both to maintain the requirements of the interactional dynamic—that is, to allow the other to overfunction, and because the offer of constant caretaking is compelling.

She finally experiences herself as an incompetent, inadequate, fear-ridden self who must never admit her inadequacy while still demanding and expecting that others will take care even of this self-conflict—that is, take care of her without pointing out her dependency.

In the same sense that all roads eventually lead to the equator, it becomes clear that functioning in either the extreme range of over-responsibility or the extreme range of underresponsibility may result in different behaviors and self-presentation, but in fundamentally the same experience of self. Consider the following similarities:

1. Both roles result in an illusory feeling of specialness—the overresponsible person takes care of another; the underresponsible person is focused on and taken care of.
2. Both roles result in intense, suppressed feelings of anger—the one because one must always take care of and control and may never be dependent, the other because one becomes too dependent on the other person and is, therefore, controlled.
3. Both roles result in tremendous feelings of anxiety, inadequacy, low self-esteem, worthlessness and fear. The overresponsible person can never be functional enough or perfectly responsible and feels, therefore, never truly lovable or valuable. The underresponsible person has learned to be helpless and incompetent to deal with many aspects of his own life. He therefore feels unworthy and valueless because he is dependent. Neither is emotionally competent at being self-responsible; both are dependent on others for their sense of self.

It is in response to the need to deny these painful self-experiences that alcohol is invited to play its corrective function in a system. Paradoxically, rather than correcting these feeling states, alcohol functions in the end to make them more intense.

The mechanism of denial is at the fulcrum of the oscillating interaction sustaining the alcoholism. The underresponsible person may drink as a way of denying dependency and asserting power, and thus become even more underresponsible. The overresponsible person may overfunction to deny dependency or may drink (become underresponsible) to relieve the pressures of the overresponsible role. The complementary interaction of these two types hinges on another key factor that develops in response to the need to deny the reality of self experience—that is, pride.

Alcoholism and the Self
The Parameters of Pride

THE CONCEPT of pride as it relates to alcohol-affected individuals became relevant to us only after we had experienced some significant failures with interventions designed to reverse patterns of over- and under-responsibility. "Alcoholic pride" was a familiar concept to us and was suggestive of the denial and grandiosity characteristic of the alcoholic who insists that he can have the drink without the drink "having him." Beyond that, it suggests a more general tendency to view the self in arrogant, unrealistic terms, insisting that one owns competencies, skills or personal qualities superior to those of other people, and that, in fact, one does not "need" other people, particularly not in terms of getting help from them. In dealing with the alcoholic we always anticipated the "pride response." We were later to discover, however, that we did not really thoroughly understand it—particularly not as it influenced the interactional components of alcohol-affected relationships. We truly learned about pride as a significant clinical entity primarily from co-alcoholics—that is, parents and children of alcoholics and nondrinking spouses. We were rudely awakened to the fact that often pride is a more important dimension of the co-alcoholic's dilemma than it is for the alcoholic who finally manages to achieve sobriety.

Our first real experience of what we have come to refer to as the "pride system" in the nondrinking member of an alcohol-affected family resulted from our attempts to have the overresponsible person in a complementary alcohol-affected interaction give up overresponsible behavior in the task dimension. This is not a unique intervention. Typically, the nondrinking member of an alcoholic twosome has, during the course of the drinking, gradually assumed the major responsibility for almost all maintenance tasks in the relationship. This overresponsibility maintains the underresponsibility of the alcoholic because it prevents the drinking person from experiencing any of the negative consequences that result from a failure to take responsibility. Often the nondrinking person functions in an almost superhuman manner for everyone in the family. He or she may often work outside the home as well as assume responsibility for all household chores, bill paying, child care, and even maintenance of the house. It is not unusual to meet spouses, mothers, or children of people drinking alcoholically who care for them to the extent that they buy their clothing for them, serve them meals on demand, and in general function for them in every area of their lives exclusive of their jobs. Even there they may operate in a supporting role, agreeing to entertain lavishly for business associates or to "cover" with the boss for the alcoholic when her drinking prevents her from getting to work. Not only do these co-alcoholics "do everything," but they tenaciously may insist on doing it perfectly. They perceive themselves as setting standards of correctness in matters of maintenance and task functioning: these standards assume the significance of moral imperatives. They often reject help from the alcoholic or others in the family because they feel strongly that no one else can do things correctly or well enough. If the alcoholic is emotionally arrogant or prideful, the co-alcoholic unknowingly prides himself on his capacity to function for others.

Again, to intervene with the overfunctioning or overresponsibility of the co-alcoholic is not unique in the beginning phases of alcoholism treatment. Al-Anon has historically coached co-alcoholics to stop doing for the alcoholic—to stop picking up the pieces when his drinking creates problematic situations for him. The concept of "enabling" that appears in much of the Alcoholics Anonymous and Al-Anon literature and in some of the treatment literature, addresses this dynamic of overresponsibility.

On the face of it, it would seem a simple matter to coach a person who presented herself as overwhelmed with work to stop doing so much for everyone else. When we began to work with co-alcoholics on this process in treatment, however, we encountered an intense resistance that indicated to us that the roots of overresponsibility went deeper than simple reciprocity. That is, it was not simply the case that underresponsible behavior resulted in overresponsible behavior. The dynamics of the complementary, reciprocal behavior patterns seemed clearly to be not just behavioral. Given alcohol's addictive physiological and psychological power, it was clear to us why the alcoholic resisted giving up drinking, but it was not clear to us why co-alcoholics so adamantly resisted relinquishing the role of doing too much. Often we found that directly suggesting a shift in this dimension of the relationship prompted our clients to leave treatment abruptly. Often, we coached the client to "stop doing" in some minor way in an attempt to circumvent the very real anxiety involved in being told not to function in very important aspects of the relationship when it was clear that the alcoholic would not immediately take over the task (paying the mortgage, for instance). The client typically found very subtle ways to sabotage the assignment by directing the way someone else did the task or by orchestrating the entire event from the sidelines indirectly.

We decided that "overdoing," the overresponsibility that we had come to view as the crucial dimension of behavioral interaction in alcohol-affected families, clearly had an adaptive function. It seemed clear that anyone who needed so intensely to maintain certain behaviors at what appeared to be his own expense needed to protect some aspect of self experienced as very vulnerable and threatened. It began to appear that overresponsible behavior might have a self-corrective function in the same way that drinking did. Clearly, both behaviors permitted corrective experiences of self that, though distorted, nevertheless became crucial to the person's sense of existential survival. It appeared that the overresponsible person took "pride" in the ability to overdo or function as a way of avoiding some inner, negative experience of self. It became important to us to define exactly what that experience might be and to look at the interactional components of it. It was clear that if we, as therapists, had been managing to offend the "pride" of our clients such that they left treatment, this "pride" must also play a part in the complementary and symmetrical extremes of interactional behavior that took place within the family.

A Definition of Pride: Karen Horney and Gregory Bateson

In attempting to concretize the notion of pride in alcoholic systems, we drew on the work of Karen Horney and Gregory Bateson. Karen Horney (1950) in her work *Neurosis and Human Growth* first suggested the concept of neurotic pride. An apparent elaboration of an earlier concept that she termed the "idealized self-image," the term "neurotic pride" is meant to suggest the construction of an essentially false image of self which "lifts" the person "in his mind above the crude reality of himself and others" (1950:87). Horney theorized that a basic anxiety and sense of helplessness experienced in childhood coupled with a lack of appropriate appreciation, validation, and encouragement of self by significant others results in the child's need to construct for himself an "image" of a self that would render him lovable and acceptable to others. The constructed or idealized image typically bears little resemblance to the true self, but the person begins to pride herself on the ownership of these false attributes and feelings.

The neurotic "problem" that develops within the person has essentially to do with a set of false premises about self that the person needs to defend against contrary feedback from the environment. Horney believed that in Western culture people are particularly vulnerable to the need to construct false images of self because of the particular cultural values that condone competitiveness and one-upmanship rather than cooperation and community. Horney believes that the person who develops a neurotic pride structure sees the world as a basically hostile one in which he must constantly strategize ways to acquire power in order to protect himself from anxiety. His behavior tends to become rigid and reactionary in direct proportion to the degree of his real, but unacknowledged, feelings of powerlessness, vulnerability, and worthlessness, and his increasingly distorted perceptions of reality.

Bateson similarly views alcoholic pride as embedded in a cultural context which is defined by the assumption of the individual's ability to dominate his environment, self, and others. The prideful assertion of control over alcohol ("the fictitious other" as Bateson refers to the bottle) arises out of a sense of one's actual helplessness to accomplish this expected domination at many systemic levels. The relationship with alcohol metaphorically represents a symmetrical insistence that one is not smaller than, weaker than, or the same as persons or events in the larger interactional field, but rather equal to or dominant over people or things at all levels.

Fundamentally, alcoholic drinking represents a drive to create a shift in one's state of existence. The drinker seeks a godlike control over herself, others, and over the alcohol itself.

The Interactional Dynamics of Alcoholic Pride

The presence of alcohol in any relationship tends to rigidify the pride structure of both partners or all family members because alcoholic drinking eventually results in negative emotional consequences that impair both self-esteem and the capacity for realistic self-appraisal. The pride structures of family members become more rigid and intense, the nature of their interactions reflects this rigidity, and, in turn, the increased rigidity sets the stage for more drinking.

Different people take pride in different aspects of self—they develop false or idealized images of themselves depending on messages they have received from their particular family and social environment. In alcoholic relationships, however, it is predictable that certain specific pride issues emerge. The alcoholic predictably and basically takes pride in emotional independence and in control over drinking, while the co-alcoholic takes pride in the ability to function competently for others. In other words, he takes pride in his ability to control the environment.

The principal rule that exists in a relationship in which pride is rigidified is that one person should always validate or confirm the idealized image of the other. Whenever the interaction in the relationship begins to challenge the idealized self-image of either partner, drinking on the alcoholic's part is one result. Drinking functions to help avoid a definition of the real rules and power hierarchy of the relationship and it functions to avoid an acknowledgment of the truth of one's self-status. Equally, the alcoholic's drinking functions to help the co-alcoholic to avoid acknowledgment of her own feelings of inadequacy and worthlessness.

Again, the corrective or adaptive function of the alcohol results in a circular process that occurs over time. As the alcoholic experiences a discrepancy between his image of self and his real experience of self, he drinks more and more. The more he drinks, the more discrepant feelings intensify. The more he drinks, the more those around him feel powerless and inadequate and the more they defend against these feelings with rigid, pride-based behavior. This sets in motion a process of feedback to the alcoholic that results in his drinking more, and so on.

In order to describe the structure, power hierarchy, and interactional processes of an alcoholic relationship, it is necessary to return to Bateson's concepts of symmetry and complementarity.

Bateson describes the structure of alcoholic pride as symmetrical in the sense that the alcoholic's relationship with alcohol represents a challenge to the notion that "I cannot." The alcoholic insists that she can be in control, be powerful, be equal to the alcohol. The alcoholic drinks to assert her own power in the face of the bottle, whose intensifying power over her she must deny.

In interactional terms, then, drinking also represents an assertion or an activating of the symmetrical pride system in that it is a statement of denial of complementarity. In the context of the other, I cannot be controlled; I will do as I please; I will have power over that which renders me powerless. Drinking makes a statement to the other— an employer, parent, or spouse—that "I will do as I please; you cannot control me." Its symmetrical intent is a denial of complementarity, a denial that one is part of a relationship in which one is not necessarily "on top" or "one-up" or "the same as." It represents a denial that one is "a part of" a mutually fitting relational structure.

However, the effect of drinking is paradoxically the opposite of its symmetrical intent. In the dimension of responsibility, the more one drinks, the more underresponsible one becomes and the more overresponsible the other becomes. The complementarity that the alcoholic seeks to deny is in fact enhanced by the drinking.

The "drunken state," in Bateson's thinking, represents the ultimate complementary surrender both to the alcohol and by extension, interactionally, to the other. When drunk or en route to drunkenness, one feels "a part of" one's social group, one feels warmly towards others, and, finally, if one is drunk enough, one becomes totally dependent on the other to care for one's drunken, disempowered self.

The alcohol benefits the alcoholic's pride system, finally, in that it permits complementarity or dependency on others without the need to acknowledge it to self. As Joseph Kellerman (1976) has noted, "The alcoholic is a dependent who behaves as if he were independent, and drinking makes it easy to convince himself that this is true. Yet, the results of his drinking make him even more dependent on others."

One might make the broad generalization that for the alcoholic, or the person in the underresponsible role, pride takes the form of self-aggrandizement—a tendency toward arrogance, grandiosity, direct pursuit of power and control, and open denial of dependency.

What then of the pride system of the co-alcoholic, or the person who relates to the alcoholic? To the person in the overresponsible role in the alcoholic relationship, *doing for others* comes to represent the basic behavioral foundation of the pride structure and represents a covert form of grandiosity. The nondrinker finds self-value and self-affirmation in a sense of goodness, or rightness, in a sense of willingness to do for others at one's own expense. The denial inherent in this role is the denial of the fact that doing for or caring for others has the covert effect of controlling them.

The overresponsible person avoids feelings of dependency and denies any desire for power because he takes pride in selfless behavior. That is, he seems to want a complementary relationship. To suggest that the overresponsible person give up doing for others is tantamount to confirming his worst fear—that his existence is fundamentally empty and that he is inherently "bad," or worthless. The overresponsible person feels helpless and powerless to "be" a self except insofar as he can be or do *for* another. Thus, the alcoholic's pride system is typically self-focused while the nonalcoholic's in relationship to him tends to be other-focused.

Figure 3–1 suggests some of the reciprocal pride responses that characterize alcoholic interaction. The attitudes described and their corresponding behaviors are never actually fixed in one person, but rather may exist to different degrees in both. The important point is that any extreme of behavior in one person elicits its opposite in the other. The two extremes of attitude or behavior actually represent "two sides of the same coin" in terms of actual experience of self. Alcoholic and co-alcoholic are, or become, mirror images of one another.

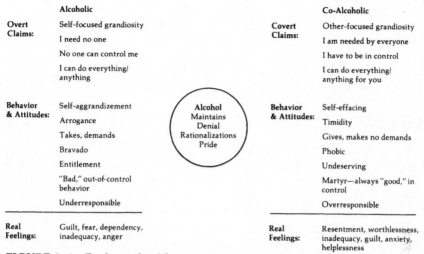

	Alcoholic		Co-Alcoholic
Overt Claims:	Self-focused grandiosity	Covert Claims:	Other-focused grandiosity
	I need no one		I am needed by everyone
	No one can control me		I have to be in control
	I can do everything/ anything		I can do everything/ anything for you
Behavior & Attitudes:	Self-aggrandizement	Behavior & Attitudes:	Self-effacing
	Arrogance		Timidity
	Takes, demands		Gives, makes no demands
	Bravado		Phobic
	Entitlement		Undeserving
	"Bad," out-of-control behavior		Martyr—always "good," in control
	Underresponsible		Overresponsible
Real Feelings:	Guilt, fear, dependency, inadequacy, anger	Real Feelings:	Resentment, worthlessness, inadequacy, guilt, anxiety, helplessness

(Center circle: Alcohol / Maintains / Denial / Rationalizations / Pride)

FIGURE 3–1   Reciprocal pride responses

The interactional flavor of a relationship in which people operate in these two reciprocal roles thus becomes more clear. The primary rule for both is denial—the expectation is that one's perception of self as defined by one's pride system should be maintained. For the alcoholic this means "never tell me that my relationship with you *is* complementary— that is, that I am dependent on you, that I am underresponsible, that I am not in control or not powerful." For the co-alcoholic it means "never tell me that my relationship with you is not complementary—that is, that I am *not* more self-sacrificing, more responsible, less self-seeking, more "right", competent, and perfect; that is, less dependent and more powerful. Never tell me I want power for myself."

The interaction between two people who bind one another to this sort of communicational rule will always be symmetrical—in other words, a continual struggle to force the other to maintain one's preferred and prideful view of self. The marital "quid pro quo" looks something like, "I will protect your image of you if you will protect my image of me."

The true equilibrium in the relationship, however, is a complementary one with the co-alcoholic in the one-up position. In other words, the co-alcoholic operates in the role of good, responsible, independent person, while the alcoholic operates as the underresponsible, dependent, "bad" person. The rule is, however, that this complementarity should never be directly acknowledged because the alcoholic takes pride in never being "one-down." To be one-down is to be dependent, to be "wrong," to be the "sinner." Conversely, the co-alcoholic takes pride in never being "one-up." To be one-up is to be powerful, to be controlling, to be the "self-righteous saint." Each struggles symmetrically for control of the definition of the relationship. The alcoholic insists that the co-alcoholic is wrong, powerful, controlling, and self-righteous. The co-alcoholic insists that the alcoholic is dependent, wrong, bad, or out of control. Each attacks the pride system of the other.

Thus, the relationship operates on a complementary basis—in other words, one does more and the other does less—but it is always framed or defined verbally as a symmetrical relationship in the interests of protecting distorted self-images. The relationship cycles back and forth as complementary modes of behavior are interspersed with symmetrical verbal struggles that deny the complementarity.

When the symmetrical battles to assert the false image of self dictated by the pride system become too intense and threaten schismogenesis or runaway, the best protection that can be had in the system is for the alcoholic to drink, thus setting in motion a sequence of interactions which will short-circuit the symmetry and return the relationship to its true complementary balance. When the complementary balance becomes too extreme, threatening to force an open acknowledgment of the truth of the relationship—that is, the true extremes of under- and overresponsibility, the real dependency of the alcoholic and the control of the co-alcoholic—the best protection for the system is, again, for the alcoholic to drink. The drinking reignites the symmetrical struggle that constitutes the denial of the relationship. In a dry system, the equivalent of drinking may be a rage or some other out-of-control behavior.

Pride and Paradox

The act of taking the drink is perhaps one of the most paradoxically complex behaviors that can occur in any system. To take the drink is for the drinker to frame the relationship between the two people involved as symmetrical. It is a statement that "you are not one-up to me, you cannot control me; I am your equal." This, of course, represents the rigidifying of the alcoholic's assertion of the idealized self-image in the face of evidence to the contrary; that is, the realization that within the complementary frame of the relationship, he is, in fact, one-down and she one-up. The typical response of the spouse is to attempt to maintain the complementary frame by trying to control or telling him he needs help or is "bad," thereby remaining "one-up". The alcoholic's response is to drink more, to escalate the symmetrical struggle. The system is then in a state of schismogenesis or runaway until the point that the alcoholic's dysfunction is so severe that the old, comfortable complementarity is restored in a face-saving way because, finally, the alcoholic becomes incapable of functioning for himself. The paradox exists in the fact that the alcoholic engages in a symmetrical behavior designed to assert his control, the effect of which is to guarantee that he will lose control and thereby reestablish himself in a dependent, one-down position.

The dependency of the alcoholic and the control of the co-alcoholic which are reestablished by the alcoholic's drinking, and the subsequent sequence of behaviors are both denied by the act of drinking. The alcoholic can hide his dependency because he was independent enough to drink. The spouse can deny any need for power or control because she is only taking charge because she has to, not because she wants to. Thus, drinking protects the pride systems of both.

Even after sobriety has been achieved, this oscillation between symmetrical and complementary behavior is likely to continue in the relationship; the alcoholic will continually insist that he is not "one-down" at the same time that he behaves in such a way that he is. Often, the spouse will invite the drinker to be in the one-down position because the complementarity maintains his own tenuous sense of self. The alcoholic's position is the typical stance of the adolescent, for instance, who insists he is grown up and independent when, in fact, he refuses to take responsibility for the most minor functional tasks. In most instances, the parent who cannot tolerate separation will subtly reinforce the complementarity by functioning for the child. Once again, it is to the advantage of each member of the system to maintain the complementarity of the equilibrium between over- and underresponsibility.

Thus, the interaction cycles back and forth between symmetrical and complementary, but it is always "framed" as symmetrical by both spouses: two people compete to be in control of the definition of the relationship. The alcohol functions to prevent the interaction from cycling too far in either direction. As drinking progresses over time, the pride systems of both rigidify and the oscillations between states become more frequent and intense. Schismogenesis may finally occur on the larger relationship level in that the spouse may "throw in the towel" and leave the relationship, the alcoholic may "throw in the towel" and get sober, or the alcoholic may die. Infrequently, the alcoholic may leave the relationship, but typically this occurs only if another relationship has existed, so the interactional dynamic simply shifts to involvement with a different person.

The Morning After Phase

In the cycling between complementarity with the nonalcoholic in the one-up position and the symmetrical battling phase, some relationships may experience a kind of interregnum or "timeout" period during which the relationship may exist in a state of complementarity predicated on the alcoholic's admission that he was "bad" or on the co-alcoholic's giving in and "loving him anyway." This phase represents a degree of "correctness" or "truth" in the relationship in that, because the alcoholic has remorsefully acknowledged his shame and guilt, the nonalcoholic's pride structure can be relaxed and the two can share a degree of emotional intimacy that is never possible in either of the two other phases. Couples report that in this phase typically they were able to make love or engage in some other enjoyable activity or to communicate honestly or otherwise be close. "The morning after" thus represents a truce of sorts in the relational struggle to deny the reality of self. In certain phases of drinking in certain relationships, drinking may function to produce precisely this possibility of closeness. Alcohol, however, is still the only factor powerful enough to produce the shift to mutuality, so that the underlying pride dynamics in the relationship continue to hold sway and the mutuality is tenuous at best. As drinking progresses, this phase tends to wane and eventually disappear as the pride structures and extremes of over- and underresponsibility rigidify.

The Reciprocal Effects of Alcoholic Interaction: Saints and Sinners

The interactional processes set in motion by alcohol are uniquely paradoxical. In a marriage they represent the struggles of two people who basically feel helpless and powerless to assert unequivocally that they are in control of themselves and the relationship. Each needs, however, to deny both helplessness (dependency) and power. Both partners insist that they behave as they do because of the behavior of the other, not because of any self-motivated intention. In this sense, the behavior of the one partner becomes a regulating and limiting mechanism for the behavior of the other.

The underresponsible role of the drinker evokes tremendous guilt that is balanced and limited by the moral superiority of the nonalcoholic. As pride rigidifies, it becomes impossible for the alcoholic to "do anything right." The co-alcoholic will counter any attempt at "good" behavior on the alcoholic's part with a "yes, but" or "not quite good enough" response that both assuages the drinker's guilt and evokes anger that sets the drinking cycle back in motion. The co-alcoholic is reestablished in the one-up position.

Similarly, the co-alcoholic's self-control and overfunctioning counterbalance the alcoholic's out-of-control behavior. The more "in control" the co-alcoholic becomes, the more out of control the alcoholic becomes. The more out of control or irresponsible the alcoholic becomes, the more in control the co-alcoholic is until the interaction reaches a point of runaway when the co-alcoholic may feel that "out of control" rage, anger, resentment, or anxiety is justified. The one always "blames" the out-of-control or irresponsible behavior on the other.

Finally, the alcoholic typically pursues the co-alcoholic emotionally and the more she pursues, the more the co-alcoholic distances himself on the pretext that the alcoholic is too "bad" to get close to. Alternatively, the co-alcoholic may pursue the alcoholic, who is viewed as keeping to herself, or as being depressed or withdrawn, only to be verbally attacked or abused. Either cycle results in drinking behavior or an excuse for continued distance in the relationship.

The War of the Pride Systems

The following short transcript presents a segment of a therapy session in which a symmetrical battle between husband and wife is being reported. In this relationship, since both partners are alcoholic, the complementary over- and underresponsible reciprocity tends to shift back and forth from one partner to the other at various times and around various matters. What is more at issue in the relationship is the ongoing verbal struggle to maintain the pride systems of each—in other words, a struggle to maintain control of the definition of the relationship. The transcript provides some flavor of this symmetrical battle.

Bob and Sandy are both recovered alcoholics. This is the second marriage for each. Sandy initiated their entry into Alcoholics Anonymous and is active in the program. Bob occasionally goes to meetings, but is less certain that he is an alcoholic. In the reciprocal role relationship between the two of them, Bob plays the role that the co-alcoholic typically plays. That is to say that he is the "saint" in the saint-sinner dynamic. In the following he is reporting his latest fight with Sandy to the therapist. Sandy has become very angry at some things he has done.

BOB: I said, "You don't trust me. You just don't basically trust me. You haven't trusted me for years . . . and I don't know what to do about that, Sandy. That's *your* problem."

THERAPIST: When she gets into one of these things, what happens in your stomach, what happens in your gut?

BOB: I literally get so upset that I get a headache and I don't have them very often, but I get a huge tension headache and I have that all day long and I said that to her, I said, "I feel rotten." Physically and emotionally I am just whipped.

The therapist continues to explore with Bob why he gets so upset, since he says it is Sandy's problem.

BOB: When I'm going through this I get more and more frustrated and I get more and more resolved that I am not wrong and I get more and more saying my position and I just don't back off. Sandy plays twenty questions and I say, "I tell you why I do it and you don't believe that really is my feeling. You think I'm giving you a lot of baloney but I'm telling you *this is the way it is!*"

THERAPIST: O.K., tell me more about that, that resolve deepening that you are not wrong.

The therapist pursues this for awhile and then says:

THERAPIST: Why do you have to keep reassuring yourself that you are not wrong?

BOB: If I don't keep my position, don't keep it, then I will go totally to pieces because I don't know how to answer any of her questions which are this angle now, this angle there, constantly "Why do you do this?" "Sandy, I am not doing what you think"—and then she'll come back at it a different way, "You did this!" "Yes, I did, but you're telling me what I did and that's not what I did."

THERAPIST: . . . You tell yourself that this justifying is irrational and you say that these issues go back to Sandy's childhood, but behaviorally you act as if these are real accusations, you are in a court of law and you must answer them.

BOB: Yes, that's a great analogy.

THERAPIST: And you have to muster your evidence. And what's so curious to me . . . it's like you don't let the judge think you're guilty when you know you're not. There's something about it you just can't stand.

What is at stake here is Bob's image of himself, his pride system. When he says "Sandy, I am not doing what you think," he is saying that her accusations paint a picture of him that is totally inconsistent with his picture of himself. It is intolerable to him to let that picture stand. It is equally intolerable to her for him not to see the picture she sees, and if he tries to end the interaction by walking out of the room, she follows him to make her point. It is intolerable to her for him to imply that her feelings are irrational, or "wrong," so she needs to continue to point out to him that he "caused" her feelings. She is invested in a picture of herself as reasonable. He is invested in an image of himself as trustworthy, "good," and above reproach. The two are now engaged in what we call "Star Wars" or the Battle of the Pride Systems.

Both partners in this interaction need to be taught ways to short-circuit this negative interaction now that drinking is not an option. When both drank, getting drunk together made them equal, and it helped to circumvent precisely this type of pride battle.

However, on a long-term basis each has to be helped to recognize his own idealized image of self and to differentiate enough not to have to defend it totally. Once this can be accomplished, a less extreme, more comfortable complementarity can evolve in the relationship and the need for symmetrical battles will be reduced.

The Concept of "Correct" Complementarity

Ernest Kurtz (1982) describes the person who drinks alcoholically as one who seeks to achieve both absolute control of his environment and absolute independence from others at the same time that he is becoming absolutely out of control and absolutely dependent on alcohol. As the alcoholic seeks a sense of transcendence from human limitation through drinking, it is clear that the person who interacts with him comes to seek that transcendence from limitation through experiencing him or herself as "better than" or "in control of" in the context of his or her focus on the alcoholic.

Kurtz defines the critical problem for the alcoholic as a fundamental inability to accept essential human limitation because the failure to achieve perfectibility or absolute power and control results in intense feelings of shame at one's inadequacy. This sense that one can or should be "God," as opposed to the conflicting feedback of reality which tells the person that he is "not God" (Kurtz, 1979) results in what we have defined as the development of the pride system—that is, the erection of a false set of self-images that protects one from the awareness of his limitation and finitude. The alcoholic, thus, responds to his need for others and his humanness (i.e., limitedness) by denying it, and hence he becomes alienated from self and others. The co-alcoholic participates in this process with the drinker and moves with him over time down a path defined by alienation, shame, and powerlessness. Paradoxically, the alcohol as solution becomes the problem or, in effect, it becomes the problem enhancer.

It is this need to deny "essential limitation" that results in the symmetrical and incorrectly complementary interactions of an alcoholic system. The complementarity is "incorrect" because it is based on essentially false premises about the relationship and on the false premises of each individual about oneself. It is a complementarity based on a denial of dependency and on a denial of the need to dominate. Inasmuch as both parties need to deny dependency and control, it is essentially a relationship in which each is almost helplessly dependent and in which each is absolutely controlled. The ultimate rule of the relationship is that this reality should never be acknowledged by either.

Figure 3-2 depicts the cycle of internal self-experience and of interactional experience that occurs as pride rigidifies. Based on Kurtz's notion that the alcoholic seeks to deny that she is not God, the chart represents the extremes of behavior and feeling that occur when the

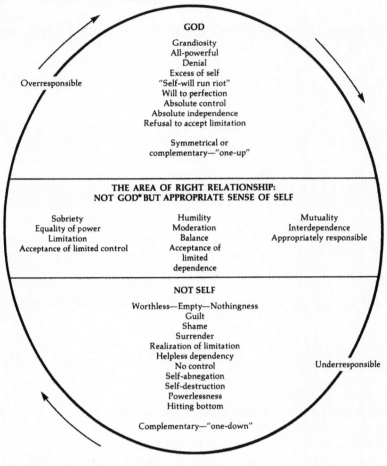

GOD

Grandiosity
All-powerful
Denial
Excess of self
"Self-will run riot"
Will to perfection
Absolute control
Absolute independence
Refusal to accept limitation

Symmetrical or
complementary—"one-up"

Overresponsible

THE AREA OF RIGHT RELATIONSHIP:
NOT GOD* BUT APPROPRIATE SENSE OF SELF

Sobriety	Humility	Mutuality
Equality of power	Moderation	Interdependence
Limitation	Balance	Appropriately responsible
Acceptance of limited control	Acceptance of limited dependence	

NOT SELF

Worthless—Empty—Nothingness
Guilt
Shame
Surrender
Realization of limitation
Helpless dependency
No control
Self-abnegation
Self-destruction
Powerlessness
Hitting bottom

Complementary—"one-down"

Underresponsible

*Concept based on Ernest Kurtz's work (1979).

FIGURE 3–2   Pride cycle

person does, in fact, pridefully define herself in godlike or grandiose terms, as well as the counterbalancing reaction when she fails to maintain her sense of "godness" or grandiosity—in other words, has the experience of her pride being "hurt."

Interactionally, two partners, alcoholic and spouse, oscillate between the two positions of extreme dominance and extreme dependence. When one is at the top of the wheel, the other is at the bottom.

The middle range of the chart represents a "normal" state in which the person accepts that she is "not God" and is able to achieve a "correct" interactional complementarity with herself and others in which she acknowledges mutuality, limitedness, and dependence.

Therapy should serve to keep the alcoholic and her family in the area of right relationship or correct complementarity. Acceptance of limited control and of limitation refers primarily to the alcoholic's relationship to herself and to the universe. Acceptance of limited dependence refers primarily to her interaction with others. The various phrases in the midrange of the chart are descriptions of right relationship or correct complementarity.

Horney's thesis is that all neurotics oscillate between feelings of grandiosity as represented by the idealized self-image and countervailing feelings of worthlessness generated by a recognition that one has failed to live up to the dictates of the idealized image. For the alcoholic, these oscillations are more intense. The efforts to sustain grandiosity lead to more rigid pride. Ultimately, in the face of realistic feedback and challenges to that pride, grandiosity may have to be maintained with the aid of alcohol. The end result of alcoholic drinking is a return to a state of being out of control, a return to an experience of powerlessness. Drinking then becomes necessary to cover self-loathing, deny powerlessness, and an attempt to reassert grandiose claims occurs. The cycle can continue indefinitely unless it is interrupted by a recognition of the need for "right relation" to self and others.

AA and the Concept of "Correct Complementarity"

Harry Tiebout (1954) and Ernest Kurtz both believe that the therapeutic power of AA resides in the fact that its "fellowship" breaks the vicious cycle of denial of need for alcohol and for others. In "surrendering" to the acceptance of his alcoholism, the drinker at once acknowledges both her own limitation or powerlessness (thus her shame) and her need for others. Step 2 of the AA program[1] speaks of being "restored to sanity" and fundamentally suggests the establishment of a correctly complementary relationship both with self and with the larger system; the alcoholic acknowledges that he is both limited and dependent and that it is mutuality and shared dependency, rather than control and independence, that result in transcendence of one's own limitations. AA helps to foster acceptance of the fact that reality is synonymous with limitation and in this sense it directly addresses the false pride of the alcoholic who must insist that he is "God" in order to avoid or deny the reality that he is not.

In systemic terms, the ritualized program of AA helps the drinker to put his thinking about himself into a new context so that he can function on a more realistic basis with himself and those around him. Many of the steps and slogans of the AA program specifically address the alcoholic's erroneous expectation that he should experience mastery over himself and others in the environment.

To refer back to the pride chart, the alcoholic entering AA has to experience "hitting bottom" at some point in order truly to recover from the damage of alcoholism. This surrender, or experience of powerlessness, renders one "teachable," vulnerable, accepting of help. In Bateson's words, it destroys "the myth of self-power" (1972:313). It is an experience of utter ego-deflation, a recognition of being dependent on something outside oneself. Through the acceptance of this outside help, the individual begins to get well until she reaches a point where she not only takes help from AA, but also gives it back. In other words, she achieves mutuality, or complementarity. This mutual interdependence is fostered early on by the encouragement the newcomer is given to pick up the ash trays after the meeting, to put the chairs away, make the coffee. In the very beginning these tasks represent aids to ego deflation and are the only ways the newly recovering person can give back. As she begins to get healthier, she can engage in "12th Step" work, making calls on newcomers and sharing the message of the program, sponsoring new people, speaking at meetings. The person is now in the realm of "correct complementarity" in which she experiences a renewed sense of self-esteem, but still knows that she is not God. This is the realm of humility, which has been defined as the "true and honest estimation of one's own worth." It is a state in which one takes appropriate responsibility for self without being overresponsible or thinking one can control all things. However, this is also a danger zone. Such is the nature of alcoholic *hubris* that a taste of power is intoxicating. Unless the individual continues actively to keep herself in this realm, the old subtle false pride begins to assert itself, and she begins to confuse limited control with absolute control, begins to attribute her growing health to her own doing rather than to the corrective interpersonal context of the AA program. At this point, an inevitable movement up the scale toward grandiosity occurs with a reassertion of claims reflecting an "excess of self" as well as an inability to recognize limitation. The "excess of self" triggers, again, a trip down the pride cycle to renewed feelings of powerlessness and self-loathing. A drink could be the outcome.

The AA program provides a constant availability of corrective experience, however, to help the alcoholic counter his impulse to drink in the face of this predictable reactivation of pride. Sometimes alcoholics do manage to stay "dry" without the AA program or a similar support situation, but the relentless cycle from grandiosity to self-loathing typically continues to manifest itself in other areas of behavior such as "workaholism," extremes of dependence or control in personal relationships, cyclical rages or depressions, and so on.

Co-Alcoholism: The Bedrock of Inadequacy

While the alcoholic sets out in brazen denial of his limitation with help from the alcohol, the co-alcoholic typically feels called upon to become godlike because others in her world are not. Her need to deny limitation and dependency is often based on an intense fear that if she can't take care of things, no one else will. Thus, the alcoholic is often a person who has been raised to believe that there are, or should be, no limits to self-will, while the co-alcoholic has typically learned to feel that the demands on her to function are limitless in the vacuum left by others' lack of function. The co-alcoholic is also vulnerable to indulgence in alcoholic drinking as a way of avoiding this intense sense of pressure and as a way of reacting to it. She adopts a "to hell with it all" stance in which she reacts to what appears to be an overwhelming situation in which her resources must certainly fail to keep the world operating perfectly. Thus, grandiose pride operates in both cases, on the one hand, in the belief that the world should "dance to my tune," and on the other, in the belief that either "I alone must keep the world running," or "since I can't keep the world running perfectly, to hell with it."

Paradoxically, the co-alcoholic's pride in functioning for others is a reaction to her intense experience of complete inadequacy at functioning for self. Realistic limitation is experienced as absolute helplessness and inadequacy. Confronted with the need to focus on self, the co-alcoholic experiences an existential sense of emptiness or nothingness that is intolerable (Fogarty, "On Emptiness and Closeness").

Just as AA provides a correction for the extremes of alcoholic pride, Al-Anon may offer a structure in which the co-alcoholic may learn to develop a more correct relationship with herself and others.

Implications for Treatment

Bateson's and Kurtz's views on the existential and spiritual issues represented by alcoholism provide a strong argument for the position that AA and systemically oriented therapy offer treatment for alcoholism at different contextual levels, and that both may be necessary for effective recovery. The AA program provides a corrective context that directly addresses the fundamental erroneous self-premises that result in addiction to alcohol. Individually oriented therapy may tend to substitute one form of incorrect complementarity for another. Fundamentally, it moves the alcoholic from an interactional system in which she is in a one-down position with both self and other, to one in which she is alternatively one-down to the therapist. By definition, the context of individual therapy is one in which the therapist is more expert, more in control, more "right" or correct in his perceptions, and more powerful than the client. This complementary relationship precisely mirrors the complementary interaction that evolves with others in the alcoholic's environment and is more likely to perpetuate drinking than to stop it.

Alcoholics Anonymous and its related groups function to keep their members within the "not god" zone of correct complementarity where one is responsible for self, responsive to others, and acknowledges one's human limitation and need for others. Once this has been accomplished, the major contribution of systemic family therapy lies in its potential for restoring and maintaining that same correct complementarity between spouses and family members. This aspect of complementarity within the family is a crucial issue which AA cannot address, focused as it is on the individual's relationship to self and alcohol. The sad reality of many families recovering from alcoholism is that each family member may live alienated from the others, focused on his or her own separate "program," without a more satisfying, intimate, or mutual pattern of relationship ever evolving. AA and family therapy both have crucial contributions to make in the treatment of alcoholism, the one in restoring the alcoholic to "sanity," and the other in restoring the family interaction to "sanity."

Finally, beyond the personal, interactional, and spiritual issues that are implicated in alcoholism, it is important to confront issues in the larger social system that determine the need for alcohol as a self-corrective mechanism. This chapter has focused on the concept of pride and the interactional dynamics of alcoholic pride within a relationship. One of the major aspects of self on which pride may be focused is one's sense of masculinity and femininity. The next chapter focuses on the notion that sex role stereotypes in our culture serve as a foundation for the evolution of dysfunctional patterns of relatedness that result in or maintain alcoholic drinking.

CHAPTER 4

Alcoholism and Gender
Correcting the Socialized Self

THE CULTURAL NORMS that define power hierarchies in our society cannot be separated from the reality of gender role definitions elaborated by traditional sex role socialization. Social norms defining gender-based behavior are a significant context in which to view the self-corrective function of alcohol, because one's predominant sense of the adequacy of self is based on one's perception that self-presentation is consistent with the prescriptions surrounding maleness and femaleness. In most systems, and predominantly in family systems, rules relating to power and to permitted forms of autonomy and dependency are directly linked to gender. One's maleness or femaleness carries with it both overt and covert prescriptions regarding how powerful and competent, dependent or autonomous one is permitted or expected to be.

There have been many attempts made in the alcoholism literature to link the issue of gender and sex role socialization with drinking behavior. Sex role conflict or discordance between self-perception and perceived social role requirements appears to many researchers and clinicians to be related to the eventual outcome that an individual drinks alcoholically. To date, however, no clear or conclusive statement about the way in which these factors relate to alcoholism is available.

Different studies have reflected different biases in the sense that some studies operate within a framework that defines traditional values regarding gender behavior and sex role stereotypes as normative, so that drinking is perceived to occur essentially because the person is "not normal" and knows it. Drinking is thus seen as a response to failure or conflict in living up to prescribed role expectations.

If one approaches the gender issue from a different perspective, however, and suggests that perhaps it is traditional values regarding sex-typed behavior that are, in fact, the problem, then with regard to issues of gender as a context in which the individual plays out his life, alcoholism could be viewed as behavior that has the function of allowing the person to operate within a set of imposed assumptions about self that are inherently constricting and not consistent with the person's true experience of self. If we put together in a family system a man and a woman who both experience an incongruity between who they think they should be and who they really are in the context of gender role behavior, tremendous confusion, discordance and dysfunctional patterns of reciprocal feedback will result. Drinking is likely to become an attempt to self-correct and the adaptive behaviors it permits may represent a more consistent picture of who the person experiences himself to be. Drinking may function to permit a man dependency and emotional intensity while it may allow a woman to be competent, powerful, and aggressive. Both of these role behaviors or characteristics have traditionally been assigned to the opposite sex. Not only the drinker, but the co-drinker too can benefit from the corrective power of the alcohol since one will evolve a complementary role in relationship to the other. If one partner expresses more "masculine" behavior in the "wet" phase, for example, the other may compensate by expressing more "feminine" behavior in response.

Alcoholism may be a marker of the inability to achieve an androgynous integration of sex role behavior within the individual and within the relational system. It is also a marker of the constriction imposed by a larger social context in which such integration has been explicitly defined as nonnormative.

Such a movement toward androgyny for both sexes would represent a true challenge to the patriarchal definitions of power hierarchies in our society. So it is not surprising that within the larger social context, alcoholism is a symptom of a power imbalance that finally disempowers the individual and, thus, helps to maintain the status quo. It is a symptom that at all levels prevents the system from moving on to newer forms of sex role integration and newer, more balanced expressions of power and dependency.

Literature on Alcoholism and Sex Roles

In reviewing the literature on sex role conflicts as they relate to alcoholism, one thing that is notable is that issues related to an inability to accept without conflict one's assigned gender role is consistently studied as a problem for women, but almost never suggested as a problem for men. The implication of this peculiar bias in the literature is that clearly a woman might experience the desire, consciously or unconsciously, to behave in traditionally masculine ways (that is, to participate in male power), but that it is (apparently) inconceivable that males could experience conflicts having to do with a conscious or unconscious desire to be more female. Older, more psychoanalytic views of male alcoholics suggest that latent homosexuality underlies alcohol addiction and more recent studies (Blane, 1968) suggest that men may drink to satisfy dependency needs in response to social sanctions against their expression. But it has almost never been suggested that men drink because of a conflict between the mandate to be male and the unconscious desire to be feminine.

This bias reflects, within the mental health professions themselves, the need to perpetuate the male power hierarchy around which our cultural norms are structured. Women may experience conflict and are hence "pathological" if they attempt to acquire power (be masculine), but certainly no male would be troubled by a desire to give up power by being feminine. If that appeared to be the case, he would then be defined not as a man with conflicts surrounding the constrictions of his sex role, but as latently homosexual, that is, pathological in a feminine way. For men there are two options: either one's maleness is defined by the assumptions of power or one must be homosexual, that is, feminine and pathological. There is a similar tendency to define women who do acquire more independent assertive qualities as "masculine," and therefore lesbians.

Statistics belie this assumption that alcoholism represents underlying or repressed conflicts about homosexuality. Despite a paucity of research on alcoholism in the gay community, available data (Fifeld, Latham & Phillips, 1978) estimate that 25 to 30 percent of homosexual men and women living openly gay lifestyles are alcoholic. Since rates of alcoholism in the population at large are estimated at between 4 and 8 percent, (Royce, 1981) this indicates a significantly higher incidence of drinking among those who are openly gay. It is not clear that these figures represent a cause and effect relationship between alcoholism and homosexuality; rather they may represent a statement about the pressures experienced in the larger culture relative to one's lifestyle preference. Certainly homosexuals experience many of the sex-role related conflicts to be discussed in this chapter, probably to a more intense degree, since gay relationships lack a socially sanctioned context for defining appropriate role behavior. If heterosexuals experience a need for self-correction based on their perception that they fail to meet social requirements for adequate maleness or femaleness, this conflict may be significantly intensified in a gay relationship where no clear rules exist for defining who operates in what role. It is beyond the scope of this book to address issues specific to alcoholic lesbians and gay men, but it is important to acknowledge in a discussion of sex roles that differences and similarities in role conflict between heterosexual and gay people do exist.

One notes in the literature on alcohol and gender role behavior a progression reflecting changing attitudes about more traditionally defined social requirements for masculinity/femininity versus more currect awareness and acceptance of androgynous sex role behavior and identification as normative. In other words, sex role conflict, particularly in women, was viewed essentially as an etiological factor in drinking—a cause of pathology rather than an effect of constricting role definitions.

Sharon Wilsnack in her early studies (1973, 1976) on the issue distinguished between conscious and unconscious femininity and masculinity, suggesting that women who drink experience conflict between conscious identification with the female role and unconscious identification with the male role. In general, she found that drinking enhanced feelings of womanliness in women who tended to be more masculine in sex role style prior to drinking. It is interesting to note that most of these studies used instruments that were coded for masculinity/femininity along exceedingly traditional lines, suggesting that traits such as assertiveness and independence were exclusively "masculine" while childlikeness and gentleness were exclusively "feminine."

As late as the early 1970s, the literature tended to reflect a highly sexist bias characteristic of prevalent mental health attitudes. Women alcoholics were found to be more pathological in general than male alcoholics (Pishkin & Thorne, 1977; Blane, 1968; Curlee, 1970). They were viewed as having deep-seated sex role conflicts that gave rise to the intense anxiety that precipitates drinking (Kinsey, 1966). The message of the literature suggested a curious "catch-22." Not only were women socialized to be more dependent and, therefore, "less adequate" than men, but they were indicted for failing to succeed at it. In most cases, they were viewed as "not as good as" men even in their alcoholism, which in itself was viewed as resulting from their failure to be adequate women—that is, less competent than men.

As for male alcoholics, two etiological theories, besides the more psychoanalytic views (Blum, 1966), were in vogue before the mid-1970s. Curiously, the two views are almost polar opposites and to a great degree reflect an attitude not that males have conflicts about "unconscious femininity," but that alcoholism represents an attempt to maintain (male) integrity (Blane, 1968). In Blane's theory, dependency is seen as a key factor in male alcoholism. Dependent feelings are handled either through relinquishing of adult responsibilities or surrender to dependency behavior, or by the assumption of a "counterdependent" stance in which alcoholic drinking proves that one is manly. A third type of alcoholic is thought to fluctuate between both extremes of behavior. Blane's contention is that the alcoholic drinks to "preserve himself" in the face of the threatening dependent wishes.

McClelland and associates (1972) posed an opposite theory which suggested that "a heavy drinker is an impulsive person who has a strong need to think of himself as powerful. This need is unfulfilled and this man's drinking represents a way to gratify temporarily his quest for personal power." Note the difference in tone between the female and male versions of etiology. A woman drinks because she is inadequate at and conflicted about being a woman. A male drinks to sustain and enhance his male integrity.

In the mid-1970s, S. L. Bem (1974) developed a scale for assessing psychological androgyny—that is, the possibility that one person could integrate both masculine and feminine sex role characteristics despite his specific gender. She suggested that an integration of sex role behaviors and characteristics might produce greater role flexibility and a more healthy personality integration (Bem, 1975). Gradually, some of these concepts related to androgyny began to appear in the alcoholism literature.

In another study, Linda Beckman (1978) found that the problems alcoholic women have in the area of sex role identification tend to be characteristic of problems of disturbed women in general. She found alcoholic women to be more undifferentiated and less androgynous than normal women. Her research did not support Wilsnack's earlier contention that alcoholic women had strong unconscious masculine identification. Instead, Beckman found that their masculinity scores tended to be rather weak. She interpreted these findings to mean that a lack of *integrated* masculine and feminine characteristics may be associated with maladaptive behavior. She did agree with Wilsnack's view that drinking might function to help persons with "one-sided personalities to recapture a sense of wholeness or integration" (Wilsnack, 1976). Beckman suggested the importance of assessing masculinity and femininity as separate dimensions relevant to both sexes rather than as a bipolar continuum defining "either/or" characteristics.

Vasanti Burtle (1979), using S. L. Bem's sex role inventory, concluded one study by indicating that there are many individual differences among women in sex role style and that these differences must be addressed in treatment if an alcoholic lifestyle was to be reversed. Sex role conflict increasingly came to be viewed as an interpersonal as well as intrapsychic process. Wilsnack and Wilsnack (1979) studied the relationship of sex roles to adolescent drinking in males and females. They determined that sex role performance is part of a social context for drinking behavior and that drinking functions to help adolescent males display traditional masculinity while for girls drinking represents an attempt to disregard traditional femininity. They suggest education or social change that reflects more androgynous sex role orientations so that drinking becomes less important as a symbol of or rebellion against traditional role orientations.

As the 1970s progressed, inconsistent research evidence[1] began to undermine earlier theories that sex role confusion in women was a definite correlate of alcoholism. In a review of the sex role issue Gomberg (1981) made the point that a major problem with sex role research is a lack of clarity about what is being studied. Sex roles as they are learned and experienced intrapsychically differ over time and they differ from the expectations of behavior perceived interpersonally. Social norms change and, consequently, definitions of sex role behavior change. Gomberg concludes that the variability and contradictory nature of the research is a result primarily of assumptions that masculinity and femininity can be accurately studied on the basis of stereotyped images of traditional adult male and female roles.

Clearly, there is tremendous variability and inconsistency in the way women (Wilsnack, 1982) and presumably men experience themselves in terms of maleness and femaleness, and it is important not to assume that traditional, stereotyped applications of sex role definitions are applicable and useful for all individuals. The more recent literature clearly suggests, however, an increasing recognition of the need for role flexibility. Very rigidly held notions of traditional stereotyped maleness or femaleness appear to be more highly correlated with alcoholic drinking. The suggestion is that a more androgynous individual adjustment to sex role demands, as well as a social context in which gender role behavior is defined as appropriately androgynous, may alleviate some of the variables that make alcoholic drinking functional to correcting one's sense of self.

Some new directions for study in this area are suggested by the growing recognition of the concept of androgyny. Very little work has been done that assesses the development of sex role awareness and socialization within specific family contexts. One might assume that the conflicting data gathered relative to the sex role issue might be accounted for by the fact that people may assume different roles and behaviors in different families and that there may be considerable conflict between the prevailing social norm defining gender behavior and the actual behavior expected from a given individual within a given family. Studies of cultural and ethnic variations in sex role patterning are also conspicuously absent.

Finally, the alcoholism literature suggests very little in the way of a more feminist analysis of the politics that define the way sex role issues have been raised for study. For the most part, very traditional standards have been used to evaluate sex role patterns, and the bias that women alcoholics are "sicker" than men tends to prevail. Women alcoholics are presumed to have more sex role conflict than men because they are sicker and not because the female role, as traditionally defined by society, may be inherently more untenable as a model of mental health. Equally, it is never assumed that the male role, as traditionally defined, is a constricting and untenable one—men supposedly drink only to reinforce their masculinity, to have more power, not because they may find "masculinity" an unmanageable burden or because instead of more power they may really want less.

Taking into account the strengths and weaknesses of the work that has been done relating sex role conflict to alcoholism, we would like to propose some new ways of approaching the sex role controversy. On the basis of the conflicts that we see arising in families and among married couples in our clinical work, it seems apparent that in many, if not all, families in which alcoholism is a factor, an inability to acknowledge or act on feelings that run counter to traditional sex role expectations is always present to a greater or lesser degree. Further, these conflicts regarding sex role behavior cannot be separated from the patterns of over- and underresponsibility that emerge in the family and they cannot be viewed separately from the specific pride issues that determine the nature of the symmetrical and complementary interactional dynamics for which alcohol becomes the fulcrum. Finally, it seems clear to us that no lasting effective clinical work can be accomplished with families unless family members are helped to develop an awareness of the constricting nature of sex role stereotypes, and are also helped to negotiate new expectations of self and others within the family context.[2]

Sex Roles: A Definition of Terms

For purposes of this discussion, the term "sex role" is used interchangeably with the term "gender role." It is meant to suggest a set of feelings and behavior assumed to be characteristic of an individual based on broadly stereotyped generalizations that are generally accepted by society as normative given the individual's gender. Fundamentally, we are referring to sets of *learned* behavior and attitudes as opposed to those qualities inherent in the self-experience referred to as "gender identity" in which one knows oneself to be male or female.

If one experiences gender identity conflict, one feels confusion as to whether one is actually male or female in a biological, genetic sense. This type of conflict may be characteristic of the transsexual, for instance. One who experiences gender or sex role conflict experiences a discrepancy between what one has learned one is supposed to feel or do because of one's gender, as opposed to what one is inclined to do or feel. For instance, a woman may experience gender or sex role conflict if she believes strongly that a primary function for a woman is to be a mother, and yet strongly feels that she prefers not to have children. Sexual identity conflict, as a final distinction, refers to concerns regarding sexual preference. Since heterosexuality is assumed to be a norm in our society, if one experiences a sexual or emotional attraction for the same sex, one may question one's sexual identity—that is, does one prefer to be or experience oneself as predominantly hetero- or homosexual in inclination?

In treating families, it seems important not to assume that their attitudes have necessarily been influenced strongly by recent changes in social expectations of female behavior. To make a broad generalization, families who have successfully negotiated changes in attitudes and behavior relative to sex role expectations are typically not those who appear in treatment, and if they do, it is important to assess the degree to which changes in attitudes about sex roles have really been internalized in family members as opposed to having been simply verbalized. Traditional sex role attitudes are a deeply ingrained part of our psychological makeup and even for those of us who feel and act as if we have been "liberated" from those stereotypes, there may still be lingering doubts, guilt, questions, and uneasiness that we try to intellectualize away. In some families, no such shift in attitudes or behavior has even begun to occur. One client reports being astounded at an encounter she overheard between a mother and her four-year-old son one Sunday afternoon at a park. The family had been picnicking and fishing together near a brook and the mother left to talk to friends at another spot. Realizing his mother was leaving, the son became upset and started crying and calling for her. Finally, in exasperation, the mother turned back to the boy and insisted that he stop crying. "For a boy, you sure make a good little girl," she told him.

It is tempting to assume that this sort of attitude has all but vanished from our social scene, but in fact, the reality one encounters in working with families is that these stereotyped attitudes are still very much alive and well. One has only to look at the powerful display of reaction against passage of the Equal Rights Amendment to be aware that homeostatic pressures are very much alive and in support of the sexual status quo. Had social pressures upholding these traditional sorts of values not begun to change, families might be in less upheaval than they presently are. As it is, family problems, and particularly alcoholism, may represent symptoms of two kinds of problems: the constriction and inequities of traditional family roles and structures and the difficulties inherent in making a transition to new ones. In other words, the symptom—in this case alcoholism—may suggest the inability of the system to shift to a different pattern of integration and may also function as a signal that old patterns are unworkable.

In working with families within the dimension of sex role socialization, we make a number of general assumptions from which we can build more specific hypotheses tailored to the individual family.

Over- and Underresponsibility

Women are typically socialized to be overresponsible in the task *and* emotional dimensions related to the maintenance of a home and family. They are or have been raised to be *for others*. Their function is to foster and care for the growth of their spouse and their children and to find their own satisfaction and growth in this activity. Sociologically, or in group theory, this is often defined as the expressive function—maintenance of concern for the emotional needs or feelings of others.

Men are typically socialized to feel that they must be overresponsible in the instrumental dimension. They must be somebody or do something in the world—in competition with others. Competition denotes survival—the more effectively one functions in the world, the better one is able to provide for the survival and material comfort of the family. Men are taught to believe that women are responsible to them and for their physical and emotional comfort. They are typically socialized to underfunction for self in these areas.

Women are taught to overfunction for others and, thus, to underfunction in their own self-interest; men are taught that someone else is to be responsible for them and, thus, they too underfunction for self. However, they also learn to be overly responsible for the well-being of their spouses in the "instrumental" dimension. They feel constantly called upon to "make a woman happy" and their assumption is that this means to provide material goods.

Dependency

Women are or have been socialized to be economically dependent; however, paradoxically, they are expected to assume the entire responsibility for the emotional and physical needs of their families. While they are permitted to depend economically on a spouse, it is expected that they will meet their own emotional needs or look to female friends for the support and nurturing that they provide to spouses and children.

If a woman makes emotional demands on her husband, or expresses her dependency, she is defined as "nagging," demanding, hysterical, or crazy. Thus, she is to act vulnerable and weak so that the "stronger" one—the man— may justify his competitiveness in the work world by "taking care of" her, but she is never to express emotional needs. She is to be strong emotionally, but never in a way that makes her spouse look weak or makes him feel inadequate.

Men are socialized to believe that they are perfectly independent and have no emotional needs. They are raised to be self-sufficient and to believe that their role is to take care of the weaker sex by achieving mastery in the outside world. They learn to believe that their physical and emotional well-being is a woman's responsibility and that they are entitled to nurturing and caretaking without having to experience themselves as needing or being dependent on it. They learn that feelings and particularly dependency of any sort are "female" and are to be avoided or denied at all costs.

Both men and women learn *not* to be responsible for their feelings and needs and never to ask directly or acknowledge directly that they want, feel, or need anything.

Power

Society has prescribed a complementary relationship for males and females in which the male is one-up. Males hold the formally acknowledged power in male-female interactions by virtue of their status as economic providers and competitors in the affairs of running the "outside" world. Because their instrumental power is accorded higher status than expressive power, they often feel entitled to assert their power over women and children and they expect that power to be acknowledged.

Females have been taught that men, therefore, are more important and that their own complementary role is one of dependent, subservient service-provider to the male. Although they may also have needs for power and control and may seek to establish greater symmetry in a relationship, they are never to do this in a direct way. Females learn that they must assume power covertly by undermining male power rather than by directly asserting their own. Consequently, they may become guilty of emotional "blackmail." Using the tactics of the expressive domain, or "feminine wiles," they may try to subvert male power or authority, the rule being that they are never directly to take power for themselves. Power struggles that arise in most marital relationships may be defined as symmetrical struggles that take place within the frame of a complementary relationship. The male is acknowledged as being one-up while the female may attempt to be one-up by wielding the covert power of the victim.

Pride

Males take pride in being "masculine"—and for each man this may mean some different aspect of maleness. For some it is physical strength, for others, power and prestige, for others, sexuality, and for still others being a good provider. (Typically, pride in one's prescribed sex role attributes becomes an integrated and balanced part of one's experience of self.)

Females may typically take pride in being "feminine," that is, being physically or sexually alluring, good mothers, good homemakers, good "wives" to their spouses, and, in general, prideful about being for others.

False or inordinate pride may develop in one area of sex role functioning if one feels deficient or inadequate in another area based on the particular norms internalized in family or social settings. If one is male and feels emotional and dependent, one may develop inordinate pride in being independent. If one is female and feels aggressive and competitive, one may take pride in acting self-effacing and compliant. The feelings of inadequacy that give rise to rigid pride structures always lead to extreme forms of the particular behavior in which one is invested, so that if a man feels dependent and this is unacceptable to him, he may go to extreme lengths to prove to himself that he is independent. If a woman's aggressiveness is unacceptable to her, she may go to extreme lengths to convince herself that she is not at all interested in power or control.

Interactionally, extremes of behavior in one person pull for extremes of behavior in another. Rigid pride structures, thus, set the stage for symmetrical struggles predicated on the need to deny the reality of the experienced inadequacy underlying certain types of behavior.

Anger and Control

Inordinate anger and excessive attempts at control are frequent results of sex role socialization dillemmas. Aspects of the traditional patterns of socialization suggested above have allowed little room for either males or females to learn that they are entitled to ask for what they need directly. Consequently, a sense of being at the mercy of hostile, withholding powers has led to rage and frantic attempts to control others as well as one's environment. Males learn that they are, in fact, dependent on an all-powerful mother for their emotional survival so that they must assume at once the dual roles of little boys and rulers of the world. A man is taught to take power aggressively and to fight physically with everyone but a woman, and this because she is weak and needful of him, not because in fact he needs her. Males assert power and control over women precisely because of their need for them. When the wife, as mother substitute, fails to come across with the expected, needed emotional goods, a male's rage may overwhelm him enough to push him to physical violence or it may go underground and express itself as an incestuous relationship with a daughter. Finally, it may express itself in passive resignation or hostility.

Females learn that they must be the nurturers who never ask for nurturing. Their anger comes to be expressed in more appropriately "feminine" ways such as somatic complaints, hysterical symptoms, eating disorders, and the like. Since a woman must acknowledge her second-class status and must tell herself that her own needs pale in importance beside those of a man or children, she expresses her anger and attempts to control her environment quietly—she becomes expert at taking care of her home and silently withholds the emotional responsiveness at which she is expected to be expert. At worst—and this is most common—she becomes depressed. For both men and women, angry, controlling behaviors have their roots in a deep-seated experience of being inadequate in terms of the social structures and mores that define how one is to be male or female.

The Function of Alcohol

It may be helpful to summarize here the assumptions we find to be implicit in our sex role socialization as they relate to the constructs we work with.

Women are socialized to be emotionally overresponsible; men to be emotionally underresponsible. The typical power balance expected in a relationship is a complementary one with the woman in the one-down position and the male in the one-up position. Messages about appropriate, adult dependency needs are contradicting and paradoxical—women are to be both dependent (one-down) and primary emotional caretakers, but are never to express their own emotional needs. Men are to be taken care of by women emotionally, but neither they nor their caretakers are to acknowledge that they have needs. For either party to directly acknowledge or take responsibility for emotional needs would challenge the power balance in the relationship (the male would be assuming a female role if he became an emotional caretaker, the female would be assuming a male role—that is, being powerful and one-up—if the male acknowledged his need).

To the degree that a person of either gender experiences impulses, needs, or feelings that contradict the prevalent stereotypes regarding what makes one truly masculine or truly feminine, that person begins to exaggerate and take pride in behaviors that support an image of self as being totally masculine or totally feminine. To the degree that one must operate at an extreme of "masculine" behavior to prove that one is not feminine, or at an extreme of feminine behavior to prove that one is not "masculine," any integration of personality along the axis of masculinity/femininity, in other words, a more androgynous integration of personality factors, is blocked. Consequently, the interactional dynamics of a relationship in which this process occurs become constricted, rigid, and either complementary or symmetrical to an extreme, dysfunctional degree.

The functional utility of an alcohol problem both for the protection of the sexual self-image and the interactional processes that support and sustain that image can be considered in light of the behaviors that alcohol either permits or helps suppress.

In the case where the male is the alcoholic, the presence of the alcoholism permits him to be emotionally dependent and taken care of without having to acknowledge dependency. As a symmetrical gesture of independence, maleness, and power, taking the drink eventually permits the male to be totally emotionally dependent while appearing to be acting in a very masculine, independent manner. It heightens the emotional underresponsibility while at the same time enhancing the illusion that the male retains control of the relationship. The alcohol in effect permits the expression of more stereotypically female traits. The drinking alcoholic may become highly emotional, irrational, overly sensitive, and is typically the emotional pursuer in a relationship. Alcohol provides a face-saving way for him to express his more female qualities. Not only does it permit the expression of opposite sex feeling, but it provides punishment for it as well.

For the co-alcoholic who is a woman, alcohol serves a similar function. As the alcoholic drinks more and becomes less and less responsible, the woman gains power by virtue of being so needed. As he becomes less competent, she becomes more so. As he acts less the "man," she becomes more and more "male" in her ability to handle the functional demands of the relationship. As he becomes more emotional, she becomes less so. Indirectly, without ever having had to acknowledge a desire for power, she has gained it. She has been able to become more "masculine," to assume the male one-up role, to be complementary in a female way (that is, as his caretaker) without having had to acknowledge it and, thus, without any affront to her feminine self-image. She is also punished for her departure from her true role, however, as she begins to pay a terrible price by virtue of the damaging and destructive effects of the alcoholic interaction. The stress of constant denial of the self and the dynamics of the relationship constantly erode the self-image and self-esteem that they were meant to protect.

In other types of relationships, the drinking male may already experience himself as "one-down" to his wife in some way or he may consciously envy her dependent role. In this type of relationship alcohol becomes a vehicle for the suppression of anger and feeling, but in the end the effect is the same—the appearance of the status quo or stereotypical power structure is maintained while the reality of the relationship is avoided or denied. He really desires dependency—she gains independence and power without having to own or acknowledge it.

In the relationship where the woman is the alcoholic, the dynamics are very similar. As she becomes more underresponsible and begins to act more "male" in terms of such behaviors as spending time in bars and being overtly angry, aggressive, belligerent, and "independent," he gradually assumes more of the female caretaking role. Alcohol thus provides her with a face-saving way to be more masculine, and him with a face-saving way to be more nurturing and feminine. This view is corroborated by studies of males married to female alcoholics in which the men have been found to be nurturing, protective, overresponsible, and to have a feminine self-concept (Busch, Kormendy & Feuerlein, 1973; Altman, Crocker & Gaines, 1980).

Alcohol may permit either suppression or expression of undesirable feelings. It may allow the woman to suppress anger, aggressiveness, or her distaste for the one-down position in the relationship. Or it may allow her, while drinking, to express anger, aggressiveness, and her dislike of her role. When alcohol functions to suppress her anger or her dislike of her role, the woman's pride is not assaulted by having to acknowledge these "male" feelings. When alcohol functions to permit expression of the "male" feelings, it also acts as a disqualifier so that she does not have to acknowledge that her sober self feels that way. In either case the status quo is maintained in the relationship, but only because alcohol prevents any *overt* challenge to the power structure from erupting.

When Dependency Equals Power

In relationships where both people drink alcoholically, there is often a highly competitive, symmetrical struggle for the dependent role. To the degree that females have been socialized to be girls who mother and males have been socialized to be boys who rule the world, all power struggles in relationships have to do with questions that might be posed as, "who will take care of whom," "who will be the parent" (the responsible one), and "who will be the child" (the powerful one)? Some people have experienced themselves as powerful while they were being cared for. In fact, they have had great power as children in their families of origin in that they were doted on, given to exclusively, and made to feel that they were the center of the universe. They were essentially overindulged either materially, emotionally, or functionally. A covert claim that emerges in marriage is that they are to be the dependent (powerful) person in the relationship. When two people are both making a bid for the dependent, powerful role in the relationship, alcohol may mask the real nature of the game or struggle. The female cannot overtly demand dependency. Both may drink for a while, and during this phase of the relationship the two will appear to be equally in the "child" mode—often defined as "having a good time together". Eventually, it is typical for one or the other to stop drinking, or for them to take turns being sober, so that the power struggle becomes more overt as one decides to be the good child, while the other is the bad child. The power (dependency) struggles often take the form of arguments about who drinks more or who drinks less, or who can stop and who can't. Again, alcohol helps avoid an overt definition of the real nature of the relationship.

Thus, to the degree that it helps to maintain the appearance of the sex role status quo in relationships, alcohol functions to mask any assault on the idealized sex role image because it permits one to express the other half of one's nature in a way that does not contradict the image.

Alcohol and Sex Role Behavior

The drinking "environment" and the social contact fostered by drinking serve to enhance the male's sense of masculinity. Men whose habit it is to spend time in bars, clubs, firehouses, or other male-dominated environments after work often talk about the positive experience of being "one of the boys"—drinking often fosters an identification and a sense of companionship with other males as well as hostility and aggressiveness toward females which may be expressed in the form of inappropriate sexual advances.

The other dominant pattern for male drinkers is the "loner" stance. This type "clings" more overtly to his home. He often drinks at home, is typically withdrawn, morose, and depressed, and spends most of his time at home sleeping, watching television, or in some way maintaining a rigid distance from his spouse and the family. This type of drinker is often viewed by his family as very passive and "just not there." Family life often goes on around him as if he simply didn't exist, though outwardly his physical needs are responded to with impeccable care.

Often, the two behaviors are mixed—the drinker may spend significant amounts of time out of the home drinking with male friends, and return home only to be distant, withdrawn, and depressed. More typically, the more "extroverted" drinker returns home and is likely to unleash a barrage of hostility and aggressiveness in openly bullying, badgering, and fighting with his wife and/or children. Sexual dysfunction or complete absence of sex tends to be equally present in both types of interaction.

What is the characteristic of both situations is the extreme polarity of the two spouses along lines of sex role functioning. The male operates almost exclusively in his "masculine" world of work activity and its related social networks. The female tends to be focused solely on home and children. Neither has any interest or involvement in the "territory" of the other. Each typically takes great pride in his or her functional ability in those two areas, and each is very sensitive to any perceived "intrusion" on his or her domain of control by the other. Emotional distance in the relationship is extreme, except when the interaction focuses on drinking.

In this situation the dominant complaint of a male about his wife is that "she does not respect me or treat me the way she should. I am the man and she doesn't seem to recognize that." All the male's complaints finally boil down to an intense experience that the prerogative and entitlement of his male role are being violated: "You don't respond to me as you should sexually; you don't protect my feelings; you don't nurture me adequately; you don't respect or acknowledge my power and achievement." This attitude may be particularly pronounced in relationships where the wife works.

One man in treatment was able to verbalize these feelings very explicitly. He described how in the beginning of the marriage the two used to talk about their fantasy that he was the "white knight." The beginnings of the marriage were "romantic" and sexually satisfying. Both acted "in role"—he was her provider and protector and she catered to his needs. Gradually, however, she began to define interests and needs outside the relationship. She went to school, became a teacher, and discovered herself to be a very competent, independent, and capable person in her own right. The marriage slowly deteriorated and alcoholic drinking became more pronounced. The husband began to feel very intensely that his role was being violated. He found it intolerable that she now often questioned his financial decisions, that often she was involved in her own activities in the evening and not around when he came home—in general he felt that she no longer recognized that he was the male and should have the primary responsibility for making decisions. Their sex life had deteriorated and he had become involved in an affair with a woman who "makes me feel like a man—she depends on me, will always be there for me, and needs me to take care of her and teach her certain things." For her part, the wife had begun to feel that she was not a real person to her husband and that sexually he didn't "make her feel like a woman." His affair was preceded by her own affair with one of her professors that allowed her momentarily to recapture a sense of romance and sexuality—he was "dominant" sexually in a way that her husband wasn't. This affair could be viewed as her own retreat to sex role conformity in the face of her growing autonomy and self-definition.

When the woman is the drinker, sex role issues are equally evident. Often, women experience themselves as sexually "adequate" or responsive only when drinking. Various studies[3] have indicated that female reproductive or physiological dysfunctions often precede the onset of problematic drinking, so that, again, drinking may correct for a pronounced sense of inadequacy or anxiety about sex role status.

One alcoholic woman in treatment began drinking problematically when menopause ended. She was a highly overresponsible woman who experienced menstruation as an "excuse" to relax her own perfectionistic standards related to her role as a woman—menstruation essentially allowed her a "day off." Once menopause occurred, she no longer had permission to relax her overfunctioning so that drinking provided both a means to relax and, eventually, a punishment as well.

For both males and females, sex-role related issues figure heavily in resistance to attending Alcoholics Anonymous. Men tend to resist the perception of themselves as needing help from anyone else. Fighting Alcoholics Anonymous becomes another aspect of the assertion of independence represented by their drinking.

For women, sex role stereotyping carries with it an added burden of shame and stigma associated with being guilty of the "male" behavior of drinking too much. Whereas resistance to AA may represent a denial of dependency for the male, who may be embarrassed and remorseful but is on some level proud of his drinking, for the woman a deep sense of shame coupled with intense feelings of lowered self-worth make her feel in some way unworthy of the very help she needs. She tends to avoid help in the form of other people to a greater degree because she feels worthless and somehow "untouchable." These feelings are reinforced by a society in which people reorganize around, tolerate, and almost condone drinking behavior for men, yet condemn the same behavior in a woman. A male who drinks to excess is merely being manly. A female who drinks too much is looked on with scorn and derision, and is seen as morally weak or bad. Men who drink are rarely taunted or abused by other men. Women who drink are frequently abused, raped, or rejected by men because their drinking renders them more vulnerable. Women who drink are frequently perceived as sexually loose or aggressive, while a male's sexual aggressiveness when drunk is perceived as "normal" for a male.

Ultimately, the blame most frequently leveled at a woman who drinks is her failure to be adequately nurturing to her family. For years the mental health profession has maintained the myth that the "bad mother" is somehow the root of the psychic ills of all of us, male or female. The father who may have already had his three or four martinis on the way home from work, or who may walk in the door and proceed to become abusive to his wife or his child, or who may never arrive home until well into each evening because he needed to "relax" at the local bar with his friends will never be perceived as sharing as much in the responsibility for child neglect and abuse as the mother who silently sips from a camouflaged wine glass all day as she goes about being a housekeeper, or who likewise stops off for a drink on her way home from work.

One has only to watch much of the television advertising for various brands of beer to understand why this double standard continues to perpetuate itself in our daily lives. The commercial for one well-known brand of beer portrays two male friends walking eagerly into a bar presumably after a hard day's work. The message from the beer maker: Only this brand of beer can truly reward you for the hard, man-sized job you've done today. Needless to say, the beer is served by an attractive, smiling female waitress. Such are the inducements against which people struggle to be sober, much less more balanced in their standards of sex role equality.

Sex Roles and the Family of Origin

Just as patterns of over- and underresponsibility may be traced generationally, messages about sex role identification may be traced in family of origin patterns. While all families operate within a larger social context in which appropriate sex role patterning is defined, each family is unique in terms of the roles and functions each family member is asked to play. On an overt level, maleness or femaleness is defined by biological status. However, each child assumes a different significance for the parent and often the emotional demands or constrictions of the role a child plays in a family may belie the traditional expectations of his gender. For instance, in a family where there are only daughters, depending on birth order, or patterns of losses and deaths in the grandparents' generation, one of the siblings may unconsciously begin to fill the role of a male child in terms of becoming very achievement oriented, involved with sports, and acquiring a sense of competitiveness, competence, and independence. While in and of itself this is not problematic, abnormal, or dysfunctional, it may become so if at the same time this particular person experiences herself as different or abnormal because she is unlike other girls. Often, an oldest or a youngest male in a family assumes the role of the mother's emotional caretaker in the face of a distant, absent, or abusive father. This role means two things for him: first, his socialization or role function has been more "female" in that he has learned to be overresponsible emotionally for his mother, and second, his own dependency needs have probably been unmet. While there is nothing dysfunctional in and of itself about a male being emotionally responsive and feeling dependent or needy, this experience is in direct contradiction with the dictates of the male role. The role that was functional and rewarded within the family becomes abnormal and dysfunctional in the context of the larger society and creates dissonance in the individual's experience of himself.

If we make the assumption that all people encompass the ability to be both male and female in all aspects of personality and behavior other than reproductive function, it becomes questionable why the polarization of masculinity and feminity has been so necessary to our cultural life. The roots of this polarization have undoubtedly been economic and political, but to some degree they have been mythical and based in primitive fear as well. One might define it as the fear of the female—the discomfort with that side of our natures which is submissive, vulnerable, soft, encompassing, nurturing. In what is perceived dualistically as a hostile world, the vulnerable don't survive. Consequently, we pit the strong against the weak, and we pit one part of our natures against the other. The result is that males are pitted against females in a relationship that is overtly defined as a cooperative partnership, but covertly becomes the emotional equivalent of war.

Larry Feldman (1982) talks about the concept of androgyny in families and equates "normal" or optimum family functioning with an androgynous integration of sex role behavior and identification. It is precisely this type of integration that is at issue and that is not achieved in families where alcohol is a problem. People in alcoholic families tend to play out the destructive extremes of one type of sex role behavior while allowing themselves to believe that they are actually engaged in the other.

It is these extreme polarizations of behavior and of self-experience that alcohol maintains and is meant to address at the same time. The alcoholic drinks to move from the experience of himself at one extreme of feeling and behavior only to find himself at the opposite pole. For both individuals and families, health is represented by a meeting in the middle—not polarization, but integration—the creation of a context in which it is safe to own all aspects of the self and in which relationships may be established by patterns of mutuality rather than hierarchies of power.

Intervention

5

Assessing Alcohol Problems and Setting Treatment Goals

THE FIRST CHAPTERS of this book outlined the elements of what constitutes for us an evolving but workable map of the territory of alcoholism. To recapitulate the major landmarks:

Alcohol is a substance whose physiological effects are such that the user experiences an alteration of his sense of self.

This experience of self-correction potentiates her further use of the substance.

Changes in the drinker's behavior affect the self-experiences of those around him. Their self-corrective reactions prompt him to experience a further need to self-correct which in turn reaffects the self-experience of the others. This process becomes cyclical and repetitive and locks the entire family into a rigid immobility that erodes the well-being and self-experience of all members.

The most repetitive and rigid of the interactional dynamics that occurs in the family is an incorrect complementarity in the dimensions of over- and underresponsibility.

Because the emotional climate of the family is one of anger, distrust, fear, and a sense of worthlessness and inadequacy, people develop pride structures that serve to help them avoid painful feelings of worthlessness. The pride structure represents erroneous and grandiose images of self that are supported either by drinking or by other forms of compulsive, controlling behavior. This pride structure represents the single greatest obstacle to sobriety and to change in the family.

The social context in which alcoholism develops is one in which the "correctness" of self is defined primarily in response to traditional stereotypes of masculinity and feminity. The impulse to self-correct is intimately linked to sex role socialization and this socialization constitutes one element of the pride structure that alcoholic drinking supports.

Finally, we base our work on an additional set of theoretical and clinical assumptions suggested by the work of family therapists and researchers David Berenson and Peter Steinglass and their colleagues (Davis, Berenson, Steinglass & Davis, 1974; Steinglass, Weiner & Mendelson, 1971; Steinglass, Davis & Berenson, 1977).

Much of their model evolved as a result of studying the interactional patterns that occurred between spouses who were hospitalized together in a controlled environment where drinking was prescribed or permitted at specific points within the daily schedule. Their observations were of particular significance in that they incorporated perceptions of the dynamics that occurred between couples during intoxicated states so that shifts in the behavioral and communication patterns from "drunk" to "sober" states could be identified. These observations resulted in the following theoretical and clinical constructs regarding the relationship between alcoholism and family theory:

1. Drinking behavior may be of secondary importance to other stresses or problems in the family so that treatment of the primary problem will moderate or stop the drinking behavior. However, drinking behavior may also assume a central position in the life of the family so that it becomes the primary focus of interactional sequences. In these cases, the family may be labeled as an "alcoholic system." The presence or absence of alcohol in such a family becomes the primary variable determining interactional patterns, feedback, and behavioral responses among all members of the family. The family may be viewed as "organized around" alcohol. In this type of system abstinence from drinking is an inadequate therapeutic goal. Intervention must address the distorted and dysfunctional interaction of the family. Interactional sequences must be changed to incorporate greater flexibility and more optimal functioning of family members.

2. It is important to focus on behavioral patterns that reinforce and maintain drinking behavior rather than to look for the causes of drinking behavior. Drinking behavior has adaptive consequences that serve to reinforce continued drinking regardless of underlying causes. These adaptive consequences differ for each individual and for each family. A primary goal of treatment based on this model is to help the family to

permit the adaptive behavior that emerges as a result of drinking to become a normal part of the family's functioning without the need for alcohol to trigger or permit it. This focus for treatment requires a thorough understanding of the behavior that occurs during drinking states as compared to that occurring in the family during sober states.

3. The unique characteristic of the alcoholic system is an oscillation of interactional behavior between what Berenson describes as "the overresponsible, nonexperience of dryness" and the underresponsible, intense experience of "wetness'" (1976b:288). Different behaviors and feelings are expressible in different states. The oscillating shift to the wet state from the dry state and back again is viewed as necessary to stabilize the family in the face of stresses that may exist on an intrapsychic, interpersonal, or societal level. The adaptive responses of the family to these stresses are incorporated in the cyclical expressions of behavior around the use of alcohol such that alcohol use becomes the family's major mechanism for problem solving. Steinglass (1980) goes on to suggest that this cycling between wet and dry states occurs both day to day and over time in the life cycle of the family and that the family in which there is a pattern of chronic alcohol use is organized in cyclical fashion. It tends to double back on itself, repeating old adaptive patterns over time rather than moving ahead to deal with progressively more complex stages of the normal developmental life cycle. Alcohol creates an inflexible stability in the family both in the here and now and over time that "blunts" the normal developmental progressions of the family and its members.

Based on this outline of the general nature of the territory, the following chapters will focus on suggested techniques for developing specific maps for specific families. This chapter will focus on assessment, and the following chapters will describe in more detail the clinical realities of families in treatment as well as the interventions we use to move in the direction of change.

The Process and Techniques of Therapy

The framework for the treatment principles we present in this book is systemic family therapy. As a generalization, it could be claimed that all systemically oriented therapy with families involves a process of helping to restructure the family's dysfunctional patterns of organization and communication. Families with alcohol problems are assumed to be organized in certain dysfunctional patterns around the abuse of alcohol, and assessment is geared toward outlining the current patterns of organization so that specific interventions can be directed at shifting and restructuring that organization.

While most systemically oriented family therapy focuses on interactional process and tends to downplay the importance of the content material that arises in family sessions, we believe that it is crucial to direct assessment and treatment toward content issues that are specific to alcoholic families. The following guideline to assessment is intended to suggest the specific content as well as process information necessary to the diagnosis and treatment of alcoholism within a family system.

Systemic family theory embodies a number of different techniques or approaches to treatment. While it is not within the scope of this book to address them all, it is relevant to mention the three major schools of thought and their specific techniques as they might relate to assessment. We believe that any approach to alcoholism treatment must involve an integrative use of these three approaches as well as incorporating the clinician's skills in other treatment modalities. The treatment techniques presented later in this book call on specific approaches at different points in the treatment process. They should be used judiciously with attention to the particular needs, style, and phase of treatment identified by the specific family. Our discussion in this text is meant to "add flesh" to the bare bones of family therapy technique as it relates to alcoholism; thus our discussion is often issue or content oriented. Our purpose is to help family therapists and other clinicians to understand the family dynamics specific to alcoholism and to provide useful systems-oriented techniques for those whose backgrounds already include an extensive understanding of alcoholism.

The three major approaches to family therapy relevant to this text involve *structural* techniques as developed by Minuchin (1974) and Haley (1963), *strategic* techniques as developed by Watzlawick, Weakland, and Fisch (1974), Haley (1976), Selvini-Palazzoli, Cecchin, Prata, and Boscolo (1978), Madanes (1981), Hoffman (1981), and Papp (1983), and a more *intergenerational* approach to treatment as developed by Bowen (1978).

The structural family therapist is concerned with the hierarchical patterns of organization in the family and with mapping the roles, rules, and boundaries that mark the interactional patterns among family members. He assumes that certain patterns of family organization are more functional than others and seeks to reorganize family structure. In his process of assessment he is likely to seek information about the family using the following techniques:

1. He "joins" with the family—he enters the family and becomes a part of its specific organization by relating to each individual family member in a way that validates each person's self-experience and perspective on the problem.

2. He is careful to elicit the families' definition of the problem.
3. He has the family enact a typical behavioral sequence in the session.
4. He assigns a task for the family to carry out.

These techniques enable him to map the rules and hierarchies implicit in the family organization. He watches for coalitions among family members, for triangular interactions in which two people align to exclude a third, and he looks for evidence of impaired boundary marking such as a parent aligning inappropriately with a child against a spouse, or a grandparent functioning inappropriately in the role of parent surrogate. He notes whether the family is overly involved or overly distant. He is aware of who does what when in the family. His style is to be directive and involved with the family and to give specific instructions or suggestions as to what to do and how to do it.

The strategic therapist is concerned primarily with dysfunctional sequences of behavior and communication among family members. Her goal is also to become part of and intervene in the family organization in a way that makes it possible to alter sequences of behavior and communication that are dysfunctional. The strategic therapist works with communication patterns that are both apparent and implied or covert. Her techniques, consequently, involve strategies such as the use of paradox or reframing that address the several levels of meaning on which the family communicates, and the contradictions inherent in their attempted solution to their problem.

In assessment, the strategic therapist may utilize a process of circular questioning from which she draws a hypothesis that relates the problem in the family to each of its members. In other words, she assesses how the symptom functions for each member of the family and how each member contributes to sequences of interaction that maintain the problem. She begins to change those sequences by reframing specific communications or perceptions, by the use of paradox, and by the use of behavioral prescriptions to the family that at once challenge their cognitive "set" with regard to the problem and disrupt dysfunctional sequences of behavior. For instance, if the therapist tells the family to do more of the same with regard to their approach to a problem, this prescription addresses the family's dysfunctional cognitive "set" on two levels. It contradicts their overt perception that they need to change while sustaining the homeostatic mechanisms in the system that operate to resist change. The introduction of this new communication forces the family to find different solutions and to shift to a different level of operation. For instance, if a family problem is defined as the father's controlling behavior and the therapist suggests that the father control more, the family is forced to shift its cognitive assumptions about the problem. Furthermore, the normal resistance inherent in the system may now operate to help lessen rather than increase control—in fighting the therapist the family acts out a different solution and shifts its behavioral sequences. The style of the strategic therapist is cognitive, analytic, and questioning. The use of prescription becomes an assessment tool in that the family's response to a prescription or paradoxical statement gives the therapist further information with which to build a fuller hypothesis regarding the function of the symptom.

The Bowen therapist focuses more than the structural or strategic therapist on intergenerational patterns and individual levels of functioning within the nuclear family. The primary goal of Bowen therapy is to facilitate the differentiation of individuals in the family from what Bowen refers to as the "undifferentiated family ego mass." Bowen assumes that current levels of individual functioning in the family are directly related to intergenerational patterns, and that levels of "fusion" or undifferentiation in the nuclear family reflect dysfunctional patterns and lack of differentiation in the extended family. Consequently, in assessing family problems, the Bowen therapist views it as crucial to construct a genogram that charts at least three generations of family chronology. When constructing the genogram, the Bowen therapist looks for the major triangular relationships in the family and he determines where major cutoffs in relationships interrupted a process of differentiation among family members. He helps individuals in the family to step down emotional reactivity and encourages a more cognitive approach to problem resolution. He may coach individuals within the family to reverse behaviors or change role behaviors that block differentiation. He specifically encourages family members to take clear positions about how they will or will not behave in response to other family members. His style is the calm, questioning stance of the researcher who seeks to help the family unfold information about itself. To this end, it is typical for the Bowen therapist not to encourage interaction between family members in the session, but to deal directly himself with each individual member's perspectives, positions, and extended family patterns.

Whichever approach a given therapist uses with a family at whatever point in time, it is crucial to elicit some content information in the treatment of alcoholism. Specific techniques can be adopted as functional depending on the number of family members who appear for treatment and the stage of treatment indicated. In all families where alcoholism is suspected to be or has been acknowledged as a problem, however, certain information must be elicited regardless of one's preferred therapeutic technique.

Assessment—Mapping the Present Territory

The clinician's first task in assessing an alcohol problem is to answer for himself two basic questions:

1. Is alcohol a problem in this family?
2. In what way and to what degree is alcohol a problem at this point in time—in other words, what place and function has alcohol assumed in the organization of the family?

It cannot be emphasized enough that a lack of knowledge and understanding of alcoholism has resulted in misdiagnosis and misdirection of treatment in many families who define the presenting problem in any one of the myriad ways that families perceive problems. Common presenting complaints that often mask alcoholism are depression, marital discord, sexual dysfunction, sexual acting out, other compulsive disorders such as overeating or prescription drug abuse, physical violence, incest, and school or behavioral problems in one of the children.

Given the growing awareness of the pervasiveness of alcoholism as a social and medical problem, it does not seem extreme to suggest that the clinician should rule out alcoholism as a factor in all family problems before pursuing any set course of treatment.

An alcohol problem may be an active one in which the drinker is presently drinking (presobriety), the drinking may be untreated but not occurring in the present (dry) or the alcoholic may already have achieved sobriety (postsobriety) but may experience continued problems in family interaction or within other interactional contexts (work, school). In other words, the "traces" of the alcohol may still determine the functional organization of the family and its interactions. The alcohol problem will either be openly identified or alluded to by the family or family member or it will be suspected by the clinician, but denied by the family. Of the two types of cases, that in which the alcohol problem has been identified or acknowledged is the easier to assess.

Assessment When the Alcohol Problem Is Acknowledged

Problem assessment is most effective when it is based on the kind of clear generalized conceptual map of the problem that we have discussed. The process of assessment, when placed within a specific conceptual frame, becomes the first phase of treatment because one gives information to the family by the way one obtains it from them. The clinician's questions and comments communicate to the family new information and a new approach to viewing their problem. Assessment can be viewed as the first step in the corrective process represented by the therapeutic situation.

In cases where alcoholism or drinking behavior has been identified as a problem it is usually within the context of one of a range of potential situations:

1. The drinker comes in for "help" with her problem, often as a response to pressures from others in the family. She may be actively drinking or dry at the time.
2. A family member other than the drinker—usually the spouse, sometimes a child—identifies an alcohol problem that is either current and denied by the drinker, intermittent and denied, or in the past, denied, and untreated. The interaction between the two or within the family as a whole is still problematic.
3. Both drinker and other family members acknowledge a current drinking problem (this is rare) but the drinker resists treatment.
4. A couple comes in to deal with the drinking behavior of a child or to discuss a marital problem, one aspect of which is drinking, but the drinker resists treatment.
5. One or more members of a family presents postsobriety problems (the drinking has been treated).

To clarify our use of terms presobriety, postsobriety, dryness, and treatment, it is important to note, again, that we do not consider family therapy a treatment for alcoholism but rather a treatment for the family affected by alcoholism. It is our assumption that alcoholism "treatment" takes place only in rehabilitation centers that rely heavily on Alcoholics Anonymous, in AA itself, or in other types of treatment programs designed specifically for the chemically dependent. Thus, sobriety refers to arrested drinking within the context of some ongoing association with AA or other formal treatment. It is our personal bias that for most alcoholics, AA provides the best context for encouraging a shift in self-perception that constitutes sober *thinking* and, thus, maintained sobriety. "Dryness" refers to arrested drinking with no association with any alcoholism treatment context. While an overall treatment goal is a family organization that permits lasting sobriety for the alcoholic, family therapy alone does not cure alcoholism or result in achieving *lasting* sobriety for the drinker.

Assessment, then, is directed at determining the family's position in the sequence of events that constitutes a predictable alcoholic process. Our treatment approach assumes that the state of the individual and the family presobriety and postsobriety form a continuum and can only be understood in relationship to one another. An understanding of the problematic postsobriety family organization requires a thorough understanding of the family interaction before sobriety and during active drinking. To intervene effectively toward helping the family achieve an organization that can sustain sobriety, one must understand clearly what factors contributed to an organization that sustained drinking. To that end, in our assessment we attempt to answer the following questions:

1. Where is the alcoholism? In other words, who drinks—one spouse, both, a child, a parent? Who drinks with whom? When and under what circumstances do they drink? How much do they drink? What changes occur as a result of the drinking?

2. Who is most affected by the drinking? Is a son or daughter more anxious than a spouse? Is one parent more upset by a child's drinking than another?

3. Is it "really" alcoholism—is the drinker "really" an alcoholic? This question is always in the back of the family's mind and in the back of the drinker's mind, and while only the alcoholic can finally make this determination for himself, the clinician must make this assessment for herself and use her decision strategically (see Chapter 7). Crucial to making this assessment is an understanding of the accepted diagnostic indicators of alcoholism approved by organizations such as the National Council on Alcoholism, the World Health Organization, and the American Medical Association.[1]

4. Remembering the concept of alcoholism as a *sequence* of events occurring over time, in what *phase* is the drinking behavior at the time the family appears for treatment? It is helpful here to refer to Jellinek's concepts of the phases of drinking behavior.[2] Treatment planning and interventions will always be focused on the particular time in a sequence to which the drinker and family members have evolved.

5. What phase is the family in—how organized are they around the behavior of the alcoholic? Do family members overreact or underreact to the drinking—is the drinking member the sole focus of concern for the rest of the family or is she apparently peripheral to the family's concerns?

6. What phase of the life cycle is the family/drinker in? For instance, is the drinker an adolescent facing tasks of separation or a widow facing problems of bereavement and readjustment? In what phase does the family locate itself in defining when alcohol became a problem? What developmental tasks have been accomplished by the drinker/family and which seem to be arrested by the drinking? (Carter & McGoldrick, 1980)

7. How does the family "think" about the drinking—do they deny that it is a problem, or think that it is the only problem? ("If dad/mom/sister/brother would stop drinking, everything would be all right.") Who denies and who doesn't? Be particularly aware of differences in perceptions because these tend to provide clues to either

overt or covert alliances among family members. It is helpful to become familiar with the concept of the "preferred defense structure"[3] both for the alcoholic and the family. Be certain to survey grandparents, employers, and friends either directly by inviting them in or indirectly by asking the family how those others see the problem.[4]

8. What solutions have already been attempted by the family? Those might have included consultations with ministers or priests, moving to a new town, changing jobs, and "controlled drinking"—taking prescription or other drugs to help avoid drinking. Often the drinker has tried AA or the spouse Al-Anon and felt that "it didn't help; its not for me." These responses often indicate that attendance at either program has offended the pride system in some way and it is important to understand what the issue of "pride" was for that particular individual. If one spouse attends a program and the other does not, an assessment of the attitudes conveyed between the two about this can provide important information about the nature of the interactional struggles around which the marriage is organized. Finally, have there been attempts at detoxification, failed rehabilitation programs, marital separation? Has the alcoholism previously been diagnosed as something else? *What brings the family into treatment at this point in time?*

9. Make a secrecy map—who knows and who doesn't about the drinking? Does the spouse know, but try to hide it from the children, in-laws, friends? Do the children try to avoid talking about it or bringing their friends home? This is basically an assessment of the degree to which the family has begun to isolate itself. The greater the isolation, the greater the feelings of humiliation, fear, low self-worth. The secrecy map also serves as an intervention technique because it conveys the message that the secrecy surrounding the problem is making the problem worse—that everybody will feel better as they let more people know about the problem. The family is asked to begin to break down its collective pride structure by asking for help and support from the larger community.

10. What is the family history of alcoholism? It is crucial to make a family genogram[5] that extends back at least three generations (to parent's parents) tracking alcoholism in other family members and determining how the alcoholism was perceived, dealt with, and responded to by the alcoholic and by the family as a whole. How did those persons solve their drinking problem (AA, stopped for medical reasons, didn't stop, sobered up "on his own," detoxes, rehabs)? Experiences and attitudes of other members of the family relative to drinking will strongly influence the present family "thinking" or "ethic" about the problem. Has anyone in the family died of alcoholism? Include a history of other compulsive or mental disorders—problems with weight control, gambling, prescription drug use. It is often effective to ask the alcoholic at

this point in a gently humorous way about the spouse's "compul-sions"—for instance, overconcern with housecleaning, money manage-ment, and so on. Even children may be asked about compulsive habits. This is actually an interventive technique that allows the clinician to join with the alcoholic in a way that also begins to address the saint/sinner organization that is predictably true of the relationship. This type of questioning conveys that the alcoholic is not the "villain" in the family and suggests that the spouse or other family members may also engage in dysfunctional behavior. It must be accomplished gently in a way that does not alienate the spouse. The therapist might, for instance, begin to reflect out loud at this point on some of her own "crazy compulsions," or she might talk about the way her husband is "driven crazy" by some behavior of hers that is hard to live with.

11. Make a detailed and careful assessment of the patterns of over-responsible and underresponsible behavior in the marriage/family. Who does what for whom? Who takes care of whom? Who worries about and is overly reactive to whose feelings? Who is particularly unresponsive to feelings or is particularly unemotional, uninvolved? What is the emo-tional tone or climate of the family? How do people handle and ex-press—or not express—feeling? Is there an extreme of deadness, lack of feeling, or is there explosive, abusive behavior, or both? Is one family member overtly very controlling and intimidating? Do some family members function to express all the feeling in the family while others are withdrawn, quiet? Which spouse takes the major responsibility for par-enting? Who is most demanding—who gets things without having to ask? Be very specific in questioning for concrete details such as who takes out the garbage, who makes sure Johnny gets up on time, who pays the bills. Extend the questioning to the larger system—ask about the parent's roles in their family of origin. Who did what for them— what were they required to do? Who did they worry about and take care of emotionally? Who took care of their feelings? What about functioning at work, with friends, extended family, other organizations? It is impor-tant to keep in mind that the dynamic of over- and underresponsibility is the most critical aspect of the family organization to be addressed ini-tially in the process of "unbalancing" the patterns that help maintain drinking behavior. Except in the rare instances when the alcoholic comes in asking for help with his drinking, a typical first intervention will be to reverse the overresponsibility of others in the family.

12. What is the perceived power structure in the relationship? In other words, who is the boss? Responses to this question are either quite tension-producing or quite humorous, but revealing. Everyone, includ-ing children, should be asked to respond. Ask who makes decisions about specific situations. Who usually agrees or disagrees with whom? How do disagreements get resolved among siblings?

Careful assessment of under- and overresponsibe behavior and of the perceived power structure in a family will reveal a great deal of significant information regarding the power hierarchy and structure as well as the covert and overt alliances forming the major triangular relationships in the family.

Such questions should help to determine what boundaries are being violated in the family. In other words, are children forming alliances with one parent to act in a parental role and, thus, exclude the other parent? Is one parent identifying more with a son or daughter than with a marital partner, or relinquishing the parental role in order to achieve a close relationship with the child? These types of boundary violations are extremely typical in alcoholic families and result in a breakdown of family functioning.

More importantly, however, this line of questioning reveals a good deal about the sex role assumptions on which the family operates and by which it is constricted. It often reveals a major source of the contradictions inherent in the differences between the way the family believes or says things should work and the way that, in fact, they do work.

Often a spouse may be functioning highly competently in almost every aspect of the relationship and yet perceive herself as powerless. The male may be the supposed head of household, yet may abdicate all responsibility for decision making. It is often the case that one spouse has most of the responsibility, but none of the perceived power, while the other has most of the perceived power (often achieved through intimidation or abuse or incapacity), but none of the responsibility. Children are often very astute in commenting on the discrepancies in stated and actual power arrangements unless it is important to them to retain any power that they may have gained themselves by virtue of an alliance with one of their parents, or unless they fear retaliation from a hostile parent for speaking the truth.

Assessment When the Alcoholic Is Already Sober

In cases where one or more family members seek treatment after the alcoholic is sober, it is helpful first to recognize that this, not the drinking phase, is the most unstable and tenuous in terms of family organization and is the period during which divorce or separation is most likely to occur. Alcohol has served an important, stabilizing function in the marriage or family and the task at this point is to assess what that adaptive or corrective function was.

The postsobriety family is in a state of rapid, accelerating change which represents a stark contrast to the state of sustained crisis it experienced during drinking. The drinking has, in fact, allowed a blocking of the developments that may emerge once sobriety is achieved. The family is characterized by shifting, ambiguous roles, a residue of bitterness and resentment, and weakened capacity to achieve more flexible role functioning as a result of the energy that went toward coping with chronic crisis. The family has been accustomed to a climate of deadness, or wild and explosive events, or both. The relative evenness of sobriety now becomes a problem in and of itself. Along with a shifting in the emotional climate, as recovery progresses, family members experience a loss of role that feels threatening and uncomfortable. While often negative, the self-experience each family member has evolved as a result of playing his or her particular role during the drinking phase is at least familiar—change threatens a forced correction of self-perception that the individual experiences as out of his control.

All the assessment information suggested for the presobriety family should also apply to the postsobriety family. A sense of the continuum of family experience must be developed. While the process of postsobriety assessment may be shortened, it should help the clinician to achieve an understanding both of the adaptive or corrective function of the alcoholism before sobriety and the consequences of drinking, particularly for the marriage. In other words, what behaviors and self-experience did the alcohol permit without requiring their direct acknowledgement? What balance did the relationship achieve through drinking? What self-truth or reality did alcohol help distort? For instance, did alcohol permit a male to be dependent without having to acknowledge it; a female to be powerful without having to acknowledge it? Did it permit an escape from feelings of loss or anger at the same time the person told himself that he had accepted the loss? Did it permit two people to avoid intimacy with each other or to avoid the truth that they had entered a relationship based on false premises about what they wanted or felt and now realize that they are "stuck" with each other? Did alcohol permit people to have fun, be sexual, be loose, when their premise about self was that they must be self-contained, controlled, and "moral," or did alcohol permit the person to be relieved from the responsibility to take care of everyone but herself when her socialization had been to caretake?

In short, how did alcohol bridge the discrepancy or gap between the person's belief or premise about who or what he should be and what he really feels or wants. And how did alcohol help to maintain this myth for everyone in the family?

Concrete questions to be addressed in the postsobriety phase are:

1. What is the presenting problem right now? Potential issues might include problems with the children, marital difficulties, inability of the spouse to overcome anger, bitterness, and resentment toward the drinker, or inability of the family to adjust to

the drinker's reentry into the family. The drinker may want to leave the marriage because the family doesn't trust him instantly. The spouse may want to leave the marriage because of intense resentment of the alcoholic's new demands on her and because she can't bring herself to trust him. The shift in roles feels intolerable. Frequently, both parties now have to acknowledge unhappiness with the marriage that was masked by a focus on drinking.

2. How have roles in the family shifted since sobriety or how have they not shifted? What factors are preventing roles from changing in a way that helps the alcoholic reintegrate himself in the family in her appropriate role?

3. What is the length and quality of the alcoholic's sobriety? Is he attending AA meetings? How often, and for how long? Does he have a sponsor, a home group? Does he go for himself, or to keep his spouse "happy"? Does the spouse attend Al-Anon or the children Alateen? If not, why not?

4. Does the problem appear to be one that will ensure the alcoholic's return to drinking if it goes unresolved? (This is not to suggest that "something else" is responsible for the alcoholic's drinking, but rather that the conditions within the family that potentiated the drinking behavior previously have not been resolved or reversed.)

5. Is the immediate problem related to maintaining a sober environment for the family, or is it a more immediately serious one such as physical abuse, incest, suicide, or drug or alcohol abuse in the children?

6. Does the problem involve sexual dysfunction or issues related to the power structure in the marriage?

Assessment When the Clinician Suspects Alcoholism, but the Family Denies It

As mentioned before, many of the problems families typically present on entering treatment are actually manifestations of a nonsober family climate. When alcohol is, in fact, a problem in the family, but the family denies or minimizes it, the clinician can make the assumption that both the drinker and the family are operating in a different phase in the alcoholic sequence than is the family who either identifies or has begun to suspect that drinking may be a problem.

The information or evidence needed to substantiate a drinking problem may not evolve in the initial assessment phases with the family in denial, but may become more evident as the clinician tries to work with the family to effect change. What may be experienced as an elusive

"resistance," a chronic relapse, or a repetitive cycle or sequence of behavior that resists interruption may often provide the best clue that
another factor is operative in the system.

The clinician can make early hypotheses about the possibility of a
denied alcohol problem based on responses to routine questions such as
the following:

Is there any history of alcoholic drinking in your family?
Is drinking a problem for anybody in this family right now?
Does anyone worry about anyone's drinking?

Each question can be asked in several ways during the session.
Typical responses to these types of questions from the family in denial
include:

"Well, I don't know what you mean by alcoholic. He drank a little,
but I wouldn't call him an alcoholic."
"What do you mean by a problem? Sure, I take a drink now and
then, but nothing that's a problem."

The use of the terms alcoholic and "problem" are tactical here because they will typically elicit defensiveness or uneasiness if the family
and drinker feel they have something to defend. They also provide the
clinician with an excuse to continue the discussion of drinking behavior
with the family since she now has an excuse for talking about her perception of what a drinking "problem" is. A discussion of the various
aspects of a drinking "problem" such as blackouts, personality changes,
auto accidents, drunkenness, argumentativeness, will elicit various reactions from family members that are usually diagnostic. Often different
members of the family will voice different reactions to such a discussion
and it is important to take note of any dissent or conflict in family
perceptions. Not infrequently a child in the family will be the one to
make a comment such as, "But Dad, what about the night you came
home from the party and got sick because you drank too much?"

The most diagnostic response from the family in denial is often a
rigid nonresponsiveness to questioning—the clinician may literally experience a "wall" of resistance from the family as he talks about the
importance of ruling out drinking as a problem. It is important to be
aware that a spouse, parent, or child of an alcoholic in treatment is as
likely as the alcoholic to deny the problem drinking.

Another useful question in this type of assessment is, "What do
you do to relax?" or "How do you handle stress?" Frequently, the
response will include mention of some drinking-related activity: "I stop
off at a bar with friends after work—I'll sit and watch TV—have a beer—
a drink when I get home from work—a drink before dinner—a nightcap
to help me sleep—I like to go to parties—I like wine with dinner." All

these behaviors are typically considered "normal" and the client may mention the fact that he "takes a drink" without being clear about how often, how much, or how compulsively.

The clinician faces two dilemmas in this assessment process. She may overreact to information that is elicited about drinking, or she may elicit too much information that she can't make use of and in the process alienate the family by failing to give attention to their perceptions of their problem. It is important to use the information gathered about drinking within the context of other verbal and nonverbal information that the family conveys about its interaction and it is also important not to make overassessments initially. Again, the determination that an alcohol problem is present is one that may require a good deal of time beyond an initial assessment and one that may reveal itself more in the behavior of the family than in what they say about drinking.

For instance, one family came to our treatment center because the husband had left home and was having an affair with another woman. When the distraught wife was asked if drinking was a problem she very innocently said, "Oh no—no." She focused entirely on her hurt, anger, and jealousy about the other woman. When asked the same question, the children also seemed to deny very genuinely that anyone drank too much—the "problem" was the "other woman." In a subsequent session, the woman described an incident in which she chased her husband, who was a truck driver, half way down Route 95 to Florida while he was on his way to visit the "other woman," because she was so worried about him. The therapist, finding it curious that she described herself as "worried" rather than angry or jealous, asked what she was worried about. "Well," she said, "he was drinking as usual when he left and when he drinks he swerves all over the road, so I followed him to be sure he didn't have an accident." "Well, does this happen very often?" the therapist asked. "Oh yes—he always drinks when he drives and I worry about him constantly. If only that woman didn't live all the way in Florida. . . ."

After further sessions, it became questionable who in the family had the drinking problem; it appeared that it might be both the client and her husband. The children began to report that when dad did come home to visit, everybody kind of "partied"—they all sat and drank beer and had pizza. On occasion, even the children drank beer. When it was suggested that drinking might, in fact, be a big part of the family's problem, the client again looked genuinely bewildered. Drinking was such a normalized part of this family's experience together that it never occurred to them to think about it as a "problem." Their response to the therapist's initial questioning could not really be called "denial"; rather, their "thinking" about drinking totally precluded any awareness that their experience might not be "normal." The only "problem" as they defined it was the other woman.

Other "clues," perceived by the treatment team, however, had produced uneasy suspicions about alcoholism in this case long before it could be definitively diagnosed. Any incidence of sexual acting out, for example, can be regarded as potential evidence of an alcohol problem. The children were very much the overfunctioners in the family and the mother clearly looked to them for help and emotional support. Their perceptions and comments about the family were often more adult than hers and there was a strong sense that parent-child roles were completely reversed and that neither parent really assumed a parental role. A younger child acted out in school and had learning problems to which the mother responded inadequately and with a sense of helplessness. The husband often wrote his wife long letters, attesting to his deep love for her on the one hand, and insisting that he "needed" the other woman on the other. His thinking tended to be grandiose and his emotionality overly effusive and unrealistic. The children felt almost unanimously loyal to their father and denied any anger about his behavior.

The biggest diagnostic clue for the team was the lack of a sense of coherence in the family structure, interaction, and thinking. The family had an elusive, vague quality about it that typically left the therapist feeling confused and "off balance." Behavioral sequences were difficult to track and the family members' perceptions of themselves were unclear and constantly changing. The family's boundaries were rigidly diffuse. It could be said that alcohol had rendered the family structure, as a whole, incoherent. It was, in fact, a "drunk" family, and for this very reason the evidence of alcoholism was not easily pinpointed in the early assessment session.

Setting Treatment Goals

General goals for treatment relate directly to an assessment of the phase in which the family presents itself for treatment. The three stages of treatment and, therefore, stages in assessment, may be characterized as follows:

1. Attainment of sobriety—unbalancing the system
2. Adjustment to sobriety—stabilizing the system
3. Long-term maintenance of sobriety for the whole family—rebalancing the system

In Phase 1, presobriety phase, it is generally useless to address any but actual crisis situations until the drinking is acknowledged as a problem. The primary goal then becomes moving the family toward a set of interactions that will result in the drinker going either for detoxification and rehabilitation or to AA. In other words, the goal in Phase 1 is that the drinker stop drinking. This goal is typically most effectively approached through the spouse or other overfunctioning family members.

In the early stages of sobriety, Phase 2, a stable family adjustment to sobriety is a primary goal. In this phase therapy is often contraindicated for the alcoholic or should be attempted only with a clear contract regarding Alcoholics Anonymous and Al-Anon attendance. Treatment of family members other than the drinker may be the more appropriate course. The emphasis should be on "cooling down" the system and on education about the predictable feelings and events of this period. The spouse in particular can benefit from support and individual help in dealing with his bitterness, anger, and loss of role. While AA is the primary context for maintained sobriety at this point, and while the alcoholic is always considered responsible for her own sobriety, it may be helpful to work with the spouse to avoid the possibility that his reactions to sobriety, or those of the children or of relevant family members, will have the effect of undermining the drinker.

In Phase 3—the rebalancing phase—maintenance of a climate for sobriety and prevention of symptom substitution or symptom reemergence in other family members is an ultimate goal. The changes that will constitute a sober climate for each family will differ depending on the functions the alcohol served in the presobriety phase.

Goal setting in postsobriety treatment is difficult and depends heavily on an accurate assessment of the solidity of the alcoholic's sobriety. Immediate serious difficulties such as physical or sexual abuse, suicidal behavior, or crises with the children must be dealt with on a crisis basis.

However, if the alcoholic's sobriety appears tenuous as evidenced either by relatively new membership in AA (less than one year—in some cases, less than two years) or by inconsistent attendance coupled with considerable rationalizing about the need for it, or by actual slips or recurrences of drinking, the real treatment issue becomes one of reestablishing and maintaining a sober environment, in other words, a return to Phase 1. Intervening with the marriage around highly charged issues such as sexuality or power imbalances may cause a relapse to drinking behavior.

If a postsobriety family comes into treatment in the adjustment phase and the sobriety phase has not been solidly resolved, working on adjustment issues may result in relapse. However, if adjustment issues are not resolved, the potential for relapse is equally great. The same holds true for movement to Phase 3. Rebalancing the system to address issues that resulted in the need for self-correction initially will always rekindle that need. Solid sobriety is always necessary for approaching this phase, yet maintained sobriety is dependent on resolving issues in this phase at the same time.

This again, underlines the need for a supportive system outside the family to provide a context for sobriety while the family dynamics that became a part of the drinking context change. The alcoholic is a person who has learned one response to any challenge to his sense of self, and that is to drink. As the family recovers and as newer self-perceptions and newer levels of feedback begin to emerge within the family interaction, the alcoholic and other family members must have an outside source of feedback that is consistent and conveys the same unchanging message: You are an alcoholic; even if the events occurring around you raise anxiety, anger, resentment, unhappiness—no matter what happens—don't drink.

Armed with this stable set of messages about self, the alcoholic can begin to refocus the interpersonal sphere of his relationships and roles within the family. The potentially positive effects of these changes will reinforce the "sober self-image" that has begun to evolve in AA.

The clinician's goal in treatment may not always be the client's initial goal, but with the exception of the presobriety phase, the two are never mutually exclusive. While the client may define the "problem" as marital dysfunction or a child's behavior, the clinician will be accomplishing his larger goals of stabilization or rebalancing by the way in which he works with the specific problem. In other words, he works with the client's specific goals within the context of a larger framework in which the problem is always viewed in terms of its occurrence within an alcoholic process.

In the presobriety phase, the client's goals and the clinician's may decidedly clash, since we feel that the clinician, responsibly, must always address the alcoholism before any other goals can be lastingly achieved. This clash can be used strategically, however, to enhance the possibilities that sobriety will result, though ultimately sobriety is the client's choice and responsibility and not the clinician's. This problem will be discussed more fully in Chapter 7.

Pitfalls in Assessment

1. Do not assume that assessment stops after the first few sessions. Information gathering is an ongoing process which continually directs concrete intervention. "First impressions" or hunches often have to be revised based on new information or on evolving changes in family dynamics. Different pieces of information recede or emerge in importance at different points in the treatment process.

2. Too much information can be a dangerous thing and can inhibit

effective therapeutic action. Only the information that is needed at a given point should be elicited. The twelve-question outline is meant to be used as a tool for focusing information gathering, not as an exhaustive questionnaire to be completed in the first session. With experience, the clinician can often acquire this "information" without directly asking for it, simply by virtue of being aware that she is looking for it.

3. Be particularly alert to the problem of distortion in alcoholic systems. Because alcohol has distorted the perceptions of all family members and because the family's pride is invested in avoiding the truth, what they report about interaction or behavior or themselves is not necessarily accurate or true. Don't be afraid to express mild skepticism or to enlist the aid of other family members in clarifying what happens in the family. Is it really two drinks that Mrs. X has every afternoon, or is it sometimes four or five? Does Mr. X really get over his anger quickly or does he tend to hold grudges and take things out on other people in the family? The clinician's gentle probing to find out what is most accurate about the family constitutes the beginning of a process of restoring the family to a healthier, more real perception of itself.

4. Documenting a suspected alcohol problem should not be more important than remaining "joined" with the family. In initial sessions with families suspected to be in denial, too much probing about alcohol is both threatening and disruptive because it conveys the message that the clinician is refusing to see things the way the family sees them. Timing is crucial in the process of alcohol assessment. Questioning should be initiated only when the family or individual has begun to express confidence and trust in the clinician's ability to help them and when the clinician feels he can convince the family that no further progress can be made in working towards their goals until the issue or potential issue is addressed. With some families, or individuals, this point may be reached in the first session and in others it may not occur until much preliminary work with the family has been done.

5. Never directly "argue" either with the drinker or co-alcoholic about their views regarding drinking or any other aspect of the family's interaction, even though you know or suspect that their thinking is erroneous, distorted, or inaccurate. The alcoholic is typically eager to defend or rationalize his behavior and may be very skilled at verbally engaging and then "putting down" his opponent. The resistance of the co-alcoholic will be less direct and sometimes more intense. When conveying your perception of a situation or your understanding of alcoholism with a highly resistant family or individual, either take a very direct, strong, and confrontative position (particularly with the alcoholic) that conveys, "Come on, we both know what you're telling me is nonsense," then back off and move on to other issues, or take a "one-down" position (particularly with the co-alcoholic) in which you convey

no particular investment in being "right." "I could be wrong about this," or "I'm sure you know yourself better than I do," or "I've been told I'm a bit compulsive on this issue, but . . ." are all statements that convey no particular investment in challenging the family's resistance. Often it is effective to do both—"I think that drinking is very definitely a problem in this family, but I could be wrong." "I think what you need is AA (Al-Anon) right now, but AA is a program for people who want to stay sober, and I'm not sure you really want to get sober. In fact if you did, it might create a lot of problems for you, so, on second thought, maybe you'd better skip that suggestion right now." These types of responses are strategic and paradoxical and address the family's need to deny and resist definition of the problem as well as the intense pride that has evolved to protect each family member's image of self.

CHAPTER 6

Intervening in Alcoholic Systems Before Sobriety

INTERVENING EFFECTIVELY with an alcoholic family is not an easy task. As much knowledge as the clinician may gain about the nature of the disease and its function within a particular family, as many therapeutic skills as the clinician may have at his command, the primary requisite for working with the family is an acceptance of one's own limitation. When one works with alcoholism, one is primarily doing battle with a very powerful drug—one that has the power to influence the client's experience of self much more profoundly than the therapist does. The secondary effects of this altered self-perception on both the drinker and others in the system become so self-reinforcing that a solid wall of defense shields the people in the family from any feedback that would contradict their prevalent views about who they are and what they are doing.

The task of the clinician is to help the family to dismantle the wall slowly, painstakingly, and to permit a new repertoire of behaviors and, consequently, self-perceptions to evolve. No therapist can do this singlehandedly—he is no match for the powerful resistances that alcohol and "alcoholic thinking" set in motion. Part of the clinical task in treating alcoholism, then, is to muster reinforcements from the larger system—to use any and all resources in the community and within the treatment context itself to provide alternate experiences from those the family typically associates with itself. It is important to keep in mind that the alcoholic family is a system turned inward against itself—it continually feeds on negative and distorted information about itself. It is isolated and closed to outside influence. A primary therapeutic task is to engage the family or its individual members with groups such as Alcoholics Anonymous, Alateen, and Adult Child of Alcoholics, who understand the experience of living with alcoholism and who can provide accurate feedback that will correct the distorted perceptions the alcoholic and his counterparts have lived with over time. To the degree that the clinician can accomplish this, his treatment is more likely to be successful. To the degree that he cannot, he must accept that the family will not recover fully; that he as an individual and/or therapy alone is not enough.

With this awareness of her "essential limitation" in mind, the clinician can base intervention strategies on goals formulated in the assessment phase. Primarily, intervention must address the phase or stage of the process of dealing with alcohol at which the family presents itself. As outlined in Chapter 5, those phases are:

1. Presobriety—unbalancing the system
2. Adjustment to sobriety—stabilizing the system
3. Maintenance of sobriety—rebalancing the system

The next two chapters will suggest specific therapeutic goals for each stage, describe typical interventions helpful in addressing these goals, and discuss the clinical issues relevant specifically to alcoholic families based on the constructs outlined in Part I.

While we operate theoretically within a framework that is primarily defined by the work of Bowen, we make frequent use of structural or strategic family therapy techniques and concepts to accomplish Bowen goals. Within the general frame of Bowen theory, our underlying goals always involve reducing the overfunctioning in the system, shifting the major triangular interactions so that people deal with one another directly rather than through a third person or issue (in this case alcohol), and finally, encouraging increased differentiation and appropriate self-responsibility in the system. To that end, Bowen techniques that will be mentioned frequently in the intervention sections include coaching, direct teaching of concepts, family of origin work, and asking the client to take direct "I" positions. The assigning of tasks or homework is a technique shared by Bowen, structural, and strategic therapists, while examples of strategic technique include prescribing reversals, prescribing the symptom, telling the client not to change, paradoxical injunctions, and reframing. (The term overresponsibility as it is used here refers to the positive reframing of controlling behavior, for instance, as too much of a good thing.)

Different techniques may be more applicable to one phase of treatment than another. When working with the adjustment phase, in which it is crucial to address changes in role behavior, structural techniques such as enactment or boundary marking may be crucial to the process of restoring appropriate rules, hierarchy, and parental functioning in the family. In maintenance phases where restoration of communication and intimacy are primary goals, Bowen techniques for conjoint marital therapy such as directing the flow of conversation between therapist and spouse rather than between the two spouses themselves may provide an initial nonreactive context for increased differentiation while more structural interventions such as asking partners to interact with one another directly in the session may be the technique of choice as the couple develops the ability for more sustained and intimate interaction. Strategic techniques are always useful in helping to shift the perceived power balance in a system and to undercut resistant pride responses. For instance, if the therapist asks one spouse to focus and comment even more intently on the other spouse's perceived negative behavior, the one-up/one-down nature of the interaction between spouses is disrupted because by permitting this behavior to occur, the therapist prevents a self-directed attempt at being one-up on the spouse's part. The meaning of the behavior and thus its power to confer status in the interaction changes.

In the presobriety phase, very directive coaching and teaching as well as more strategic approaches to denial are indicated. In general, the therapist is attempting to help the family achieve a more functional structure which eliminates the need for alcohol as an interactional fulcrum. A more functional structure will provide a foundation for more optimal differentiation of family members, but some differentiation must be facilitated by the process of therapy so that a more functional structure can be achieved and maintained.

More in-depth material on the process of family therapy in its different approaches can be located by referring to the bibliography and chapter notes in this text.

Phase 1: Presobriety—Unbalancing the System

In this phase drinking is occurring in some part of the system in a way that appears, on assessment, to be compulsive and problematic either for the drinker or for other family members. Drinking appears to be closely associated with dysfunctional behaviors such as acting out, abusiveness, job loss, marital conflict, school failure, generalized depression, and anxiety. The drinking is either acknowledged overtly as a problem or else denied as a problem or as a factor in the problems that the family presents.

Treatment Goals

1. Anticipate and deal with denial.
2. Work toward the drinker's achieving abstinence through involvement with AA, Al-Anon, a rehabilitation program, and/or detox depending on the stage and severity of the drinking.
3. Begin the process of interrupting patterns of over- and underresponsibility.

Drinking Denied

Treatment in presobriety is the treatment of denial. Even when a family acknowledges that drinking is a problem, they are rarely ready to acknowledge the degree to which alcoholism affects the continuum of their life together and family members other than the alcoholic tend to deny their part in maintaining alcoholic behavior. Most important, the family denies the need for sustained and incisive change in their lifestyle. Their dysfunctional patterns of interaction have become so ingrained over time that a certain numbness to pain blocks recognition of the degree to which family life is "abnormal."

Members of alcoholic families develop a high tolerance for living with chronic tension and stress. The effects of the disease are so insidious that the disease patterns themselves begin to represent normalcy. If an immediately traumatic event were to occur, such as an accident, the sudden potentially fatal illness of a family member, or their house burning down, the family would find it impossible to deny the need for immediate action. The irony of alcoholic processes is that the family tends to work hard to sustain the very behaviors that make the situation worse. Any change represents an unthinkable, traumatic event that must be accomplished with tremendous support and skilled intervention from sources outside the family system. As an example, one woman who always drove her drunk husband home from parties was asked to attend social events in a separate car so that she didn't have to be responsible for getting him home. She was horrified at this suggestion and told the therapist she couldn't possibly do it because she would consider herself responsible if he drove and had an accident in which he injured someone else. She was incapable of seeing how her willingness to be responsible for the driving made it possible for him to keep drinking with impunity.

This denial and capacity for progressive and sustained tolerance for stress, again, relates to the inconsistent nature of alcoholic behavior and experience. One bout of drunkenness is easily tolerated and between bouts events in the family may return to "normal." In most families the progression of drinking occurs over time in small increments so that adaptive changes are incorporated rather than reacted to. High degrees of anxiety may be raised by each isolated drinking event, but the tension will be relieved as soon as the "drunk" is over. Both the drinker and other family members thus receive intermittent doses of tension alternating with release from tension. This inconsistency traps the family within a chronic, ongoing pattern in which no one isolated event seems to represent a serious, out-of-control situation because the immediate crisis is never sustained enough—sobriety is only a hangover away. One client reported that she came home one evening to find that her husband had fallen from his commuter train as it pulled out of the station. He had been so drunk that he had almost missed his stop. He was cut and badly bruised, but two nights later talked about the event as if it were a humorous incident that had given his colleagues at work a good laugh. Car accidents, entire nights spent sleeping in a car because one was too drunk to navigate, or any of the other potential occurrences resulting from being drunk are perceived as isolated events that can be forgotten once the drinker is in a sober—that is, controlled—state.

The degree of denial may differ from family to family and in different family members at the point that they present themselves for treatment. In one family, a child may be the one to have the most intense reaction to her father's falling off the train while the spouse may term it "just an accident." In other families, it may be the spouse and children both who recognize that "this behavior is abnormal and something's really wrong here." If the drinking family member is an adolescent, parents may minimize the seriousness of the child's behavior, or their denial may take the form of resistance to relating incidents of unacceptable behavior to alcohol or drug abuse.

Families typically present all of the common resistances to defining a problem as alcoholism that have been enumerated in AA or National Council on Alcoholism literature.[1] These include: he doesn't drink every day, she goes to work every day, he is a "problem" drinker but not an alcoholic, my child was always a behavior problem even before she started to drink or use drugs, and so on.

Once the assessment is made that alcoholism is a primary problem in the family, the therapeutic task is to shift the family's perception of its problems and motivate a corresponding change in behavior. The recognition that alcoholism is affecting a family immediately imposes parameters on treatment. It is rarely possible to intervene effectively with other presenting problems until alcoholism has been addressed; often, when alcoholism is treated, other problems are resolved in the process. The therapist is faced with the task of convincing the family to see its problem differently when the entire mode of being of the family has been to operate in a way that denies acknowledgment of alcoholism. The family will fight to maintain the very rigid interactional patterns that have evolved in response to alcoholic drinking, and the therapist must find a way to destabilize and shift those patterns so that sobriety can be achieved.

The family's denial of alcoholism and the therapist's need to redefine the problem may be approached either directly or strategically.

A direct approach is indicated when at least one key family member is highly motivated and likely to be receptive to acknowledging a drinking problem. The clinician's assessment of his own skills is also important in deciding on a course of action. If strategic techniques are unfamiliar or uncomfortable, than a more direct approach is likely to be more effective.

Strategic techniques are useful when only one intensely resistant member of an alcoholic family is involved in treatment, or when an actively drinking alcoholic attends family sessions and is highly defensive about drinking. The most effective method for confronting denial probably involves a combination of both approaches, but for the sake of simplicity and organization, each is outlined here separately.

The Direct Approach

To confront denial directly, the clinician first takes the position that alcohol appears to cause a problem for the family, *whether or not the alcoholic agrees that she has a drinking problem*. The statement is made that alcohol is obviously affecting the family's behavior and interaction and that no progress is likely to occur with other problems while it continues to do so. It is important that the problem be defined as existing within the family or relationship rather than within the drinker.

Secondly, the clinician must present cogent and persuasive arguments that prove the point while managing never to engage in direct argument or debate. Using whatever information the family has communicated about its interactional or perceptual style, the clinician can use actual events reported by the family to point out the relationship between drinking and their chronic problems. She should use whatever definition of alcoholism fits the particular family situation best. She must be able to cite statistics and offer dramatic evidence of the results of allowing the situation to progress—in other words, she must provide information about alcoholism that directly challenges the family's inaccurate understanding of what alcoholism is and the way it is or isn't directly affecting their own experience. Then she must ask the family to take specific steps to address the problem.

The drinker at this point may or may not leave treatment. The family should be assured that work on the problem can continue even if the drinker will not attend sessions, and in fact it is often helpful to predict that this will occur.

Finally, the family should be asked to make the choice to continue with treatment based on the assessment that the problem is alcohol. The clinician may indicate a willingness to continue treatment temporarily if the denial is still strong, with the understanding that any progress that is made will eventually be undermined by drinking, or he may indicate that without an agreement on the drinker's part to stop drinking and attend AA, or on the family's part to attend Al-Anon, no further work is possible.

The latter decision should be based on the clinician's sense that there is no readiness on the family's part to change behavior even though there may be minimal acknowledgment that drinking might be a problem. If the client directly states, "I don't want to stop drinking," or "I won't go to Al-Anon and I won't stop doing what I feel needs to be done for her, then the family is not ready to change. If the family is skeptical, uneasy, and not sure what they are willing to do when first confronted, but seem receptive to seeing the problem differently, more work on the denial is indicated and the clinician should convey that she is willing to give them more time to make a decision, but that, again, progress on their presenting problems will be limited. A short-term contract might be agreed to. Work during this time may consist primarily of education about alcoholism, referral to community education programs, suggestions for reading, suggestions of trial attempts to stop drinking, or arrangement for a "consultation" with an alcoholism counselor.

Other Specific Interventions with the Direct Approach

Ask family members to attend AA, Al-Anon, Alateen meetings. Get a firm commitment to a specific number of meetings for the purpose of helping the family to "educate" themselves about alcoholism.

Ask the drinker to stop drinking for ninety days to aid him in deciding whether he is truly alcoholic. Avoid direct arguments with the drinker. Put the responsibility on him to make a decision about his drinking, but define drinking as a problem for others in the family even if he does not feel that it is one for him.

Families who will cooperate with these initial types of interventions to any degree usually can be expected to make slow progress toward a recognition of the centrality of alcoholism in their lives. If their denial is too intense or if the family truly is not ready for change, the clinician should pride himself on the ability to let go when the family terminates treatment.

Paradoxical or Strategic Approaches

Denial in family members or in the alcoholic may be addressed more strategically by restraining the family from change or reframing the alcoholism in a way that is more easily accepted by the client because it is more consistent with the client's view of the problem. Another approach is for the clinician to indicate that he has no investment whatever in the client's decision to address the alcoholism while suggesting at the same time that although things are likely to get worse, perhaps that is preferable to having to think about a drinking problem. When things do, in fact, get worse, the therapist has greater leverage to make some statement to the effect that he was certain that might happen but that he really didn't think anyone in the family was ready to deal with alcoholism. One client was told that there were things that she *could* do to address her husband's drinking problem, including stopping her own drinking, but that because things would change so radically in the family if he stopped drinking, she should think seriously about any decision to do anything at all. This was a highly intelligent woman who fully understood the therapist's explanations of the effects of drinking on each family member and the systemic dynamics maintained by the drinking. Faced with a clear understanding of what alcohol was doing to the family, she was disturbed by the therapist's continuing observation that it was not clear that the client really wanted her husband to stop drinking because things would change too much. She was told it might take her a great deal of time to make the decision. This intervention immediately mobilized her to stop her own drinking and very quickly led her to a confrontation with her husband.

In another example of a more strategic approach to denial, the spouse of the alcoholic began a supervised session by talking about her husband's affair. As is often the case, the affair, not the alcoholism, had been the precipitant of therapy. Our goal in the session was to elicit a firm contract with this woman to attend six Al-Anon meetings. Fifteen minutes into the session, and after the client had said "I don't know why everything began to bother me three or four years ago," the therapist was called out and instructed to go back in and tell the client that her consulting team knew for certain why the client had begun to be bothered. She was to say it was at that point that the husband had begun a passionate affair with his mistress, one in which he could never be without the mistress. The therapist was to emphasize and reiterate this theme.

As she carried out the intervention, which she did in a particularly dramatic, creative way, we on the team could see the client struggling to understand. Finally, she connected. Alcohol was the mistress. At the point of this realization she began spontaneously to offer the twenty-year evidence of alcoholism and her efforts to cover it up. The contract to attend Al-Anon was agreed to.

In another situation we sidestepped the issue of the alcoholism. In this case the male alcoholic's pride and denial were very intense, but he had already made statements that he would do anything to help his wife feel better. He was told, "Look, Jim, we are not even going to discuss whether or not you are alcoholic. But it is clear that we both know that your wife watched her father die of alcoholism and that it hurts her a lot when you drink. Therefore, we want you to help her by quitting drinking." He readily agreed to this because he was now in a bind. If he did not manage to quit drinking, there would be additional leverage to get him to AA and to confront his drinking problem more directly. If he did quit, and constantly reminded his wife of it, we could confront him about his putting responsibility on her; and if he were able to quit easily and happily, then perhaps it was her sensitivity that set an "alcoholic interaction" in motion. In any case, the cycle would be interrupted.

When employing strategic methods, the clinician should continue to convey information about alcoholism at the same time that he restrains the family, spouse, or drinker from making hasty decisions or from moving into action too quickly. Whenever the client tries to focus on other issues, however, the clinician may talk about working toward a "dead end" since the drinking will always interfere with the process ultimately. If this approach is not successful, the clinician may either shift to the more direct approach, or suggest that the family take a vacation from treatment.

Working with denial takes time and judgment and interventions must be geared to the specific family or individual. No hard and fast rule can apply in all cases except the premise that to continue to treat a family who flatly denies the alcoholism or resists dealing with it over an extended period of time is to enable the alcoholism and is therapeutically irresponsible.

Treatment Once a Drinking Problem Is Acknowledged

When a family, an individual, or any part of a family finally acknowledges that drinking is a problem and agrees to a contract to focus and work on it, a number of potential steps may be suggested, depending on which family member is or remains in treatment.

It is important to remember that while drinking may be acknowledged as a problem, another aspect of denial reveals itself in the family's unwillingness to take specific steps to do something about it. Simply to acknowledge "Yes, drinking is a problem and I'll try to stop," or, "yes, he has a drinking problem and it really affects us," does not indicate complete willingness to address the problem behaviorally. Unless the family makes a commitment to *act*, denial is still operating.

Specific Interventions for the Drinker

Once the severity of the drinking and level of physiological addiction have been assessed, and if the client agrees, she can be referred to a hospital rehabilitation or detoxification unit. The initial assessment that rehab or detox will be necessary to achieve sobriety should take into account the level of physiological addiction as indicated by other failed attempts to stop drinking as well as medical complications that might now accompany the drinking or might occur in the attempt to stop. If the alcoholic is drinking daily, is drinking large quantities, and has had a history of withdrawal symptoms when stopping, a rehab program is almost always necessary to interrupt both the physiological and psychological addiction and is medically indicated for treatment of the withdrawal.

A second option, if hospitalization does not appear to be required, is to refer the client to AA. If possible, contacts should be provided through the National Council on Alcoholism or local alcohol treatment programs who will take the client to his first meeting. If the client slacks off in AA attendance and begins to drink again, referral to a rehab program would be appropriate. This procedure applies to both adult and adolescent drinkers.

Often, though the drinker acknowledges her problem with alcohol, she resists the notion that AA attendance is a treatment for the problem. At this point in therapy, the client typically becomes argumentative and takes the "Philadelphia lawyer" approach, insisting that AA is not for everybody and certainly not for her. The potential arguments against AA attendance are typically quite varied and creative. They usually represent the client's fear about giving up drinking as well as the pride issues involved in seeking help from "ordinary people" whom the drinker typically perceives as much sicker or more "drunk" than herself. Most people find it much more palatable to seek help from a professional than to acknowledge their commonality with others. The therapeutic relationship represents a tolerable complementarity to the client's pride system which is precisely why the therapeutic relationship alone cannot address the pride issues represented by chemical dependency.

It is important for the therapist not to argue with the client nor to be highly invested in his final decision about AA. The therapist's task at this point is to define or describe the nature of AA and its purpose in a way that is most palatable to the particular client. It is helpful to use metaphors that relate directly to some aspect of the client's life or to mirror the client's particular defensive style in approaching a discussion of AA. For instance, if the client is highly intellectualized in his approach to problems, it is helpful to discuss AA in highly intellectual, rational terms. One client talked about a fear of being "brainwashed" by AA. In his need to rationalize, he had defined AA as a religious cult whose purpose was to take over and control his life. Rather than argue that this is not, in fact, the reality of the AA program, the therapist pointed out that at present alcohol controlled the client's life and that his brain was being "washed" every time he took a drink.

Finally, reframing the drinker's perceptions, acknowledging her fears, mirroring her defense processes, and using any other sophisticated clinical skills that the clinician may have in his possession are typically not sufficient to get the drinker to AA. They may help, but ultimately only a change in the interactional system coupled with the drinker's increasing panic at her awareness that both her life and her drinking are, in fact, out of control will prompt a real commitment to AA.

The therapist's role is to continue to take a very simple position: "AA is one of the best treatments that I am aware of for a drinking problem. However, AA is a program only for people who want it. Therefore, I would certainly not encourage you to go if you feel you don't want to. However, I really can't be of much more help to you while you continue to drink." If the client is assessed as highly resistant and not likely to make a commitment to AA at this time, treatment should be terminated with the understanding that he may always return after a stable period of sobriety in AA. If the client is wavering and has attended one or two meetings, it is helpful to suggest a vacation from therapy in which the client will be able to make up his own mind and then reassess the need for counseling at a later time. We believe it is important to convey that given a choice between therapy and AA, AA is a better choice under those circumstances.

Specific Interventions for Other Family Members

Treatment of the presobriety phase may occur over a much greater time span when family members other than the drinker come for treatment and when the drinker continues to deny his problem. The immediate goal is to help other family members, particularly a spouse or parents, to shift their role behavior significantly both in the interest of their greatest well-being and with the expectation that a change in their part of the systemic interaction will eventually lead to the drinker's sobriety.

A Crisis-Oriented Approach

In families where drinking has progressed to its final stages and serious behavioral, medical, or financial consequences are occurring, when physical abuse is frequent, job loss has occurred, or when others in the family are symptomatic, the clinician does not have the luxury of time required to change family patterns.

A crisis-oriented approach involving direct confrontation of the alcoholic through use of the Johnson Intervention Technique is indicated.[2] The therapist may either arrange and conduct the intervention herself or refer the family to a facility where personnel are specifically trained in this confrontative method. The therapist's task in this situation is to help the family acknowledge to itself the seriousness of its situation and the need for immediate and intensive intervention.

Attempts should be made at this time to involve all significant family members, friends, and employers who might provide support in convincing the primary family members of the need for direct action. The therapist must convey a calm assurance and certainty that this technique will help and that the family has the strength and competence to follow through with it. The therapist may use the principal person's pride constructively by suggesting extreme and "heroic" lengths to which that person would resort in the cause of helping the drinker and acknowledging that this intervention is ultimately the most difficult thing that she might be called on to do. Fear may be reframed as fear of the intervention failing or the fear of putting the family through such a difficult process because the therapist is aware that the ultimate motivation is to protect the family from more hurt. Eagerness or willingness on the part of other family members should be used to advantage in convincing a hesitant party to proceed.

If the family or family member is unwilling to make use of this option, work can be focused on responsibility issues, in either individual or group treatment, or both. The therapist should continue periodically to suggest the need for intervention while working with the pride issues and fear that are resulting in resistance to this move. Frequently, the natural course of events that typically occurs when alcoholism has progressed to its end stages will ultimately be the precipitating factor for an agreement to participate in an intervention. A car accident, legal crisis, a child's suicide threat, or an ultimatum from the drinker's employer will finally hold enough sway to prompt the client into action. Ironically, if a male alcoholic becomes involved with another woman, this may push the spouse into action faster than the drinking. Likewise, parents can often be motivated to take action if the therapist stresses the damage alcohol is doing to the children.

Shifting Patterns of Over- and Underresponsibility: A Rationale

The primary work of presobriety treatment involves shifting roles in the family along the dimensions of functional and emotional responsibility. Whether or not the alcoholic is present for treatment, and in spite of the degree of denial operating in the system, the primary basis for intervention is the assumption that the parent's, spouse's, or adult child's overfunctioning in both the emotional or functional dimensions has been a dominant factor in maintaining the alcoholic's underresponsible drinking behavior.

The goal of treatment, then, is to unbalance the rigid complementarity of the system such that the principal overfunctioner is no longer taking inappropriate responsibility for other people's feelings or doing things that are developmentally inappropriate for the underresponsible person. It is important to be aware of substitute or secondary overfunctioners in the system and to intervene at as many levels of the family as possible to insure that the overresponsible role is not vacated by one person only to be assumed by another.

The therapist cannot stress too emphatically the importance to the family of changing this dynamic in whatever way a given family is able to "hear" the prescription. The therapist can predict with certainty for the family that unless these behaviors change, the alcoholic will continue to drink or return to drinking, that the marriage will fail, or that one of the children will develop an addictive problem. One makes these statements with a clear understanding of the difficulty the overfunctioner will have giving up his role, the pride that has been invested in maintaining that role, and the resistance that the rest of the family will mount when the overfunctioner does begin to change. The process of therapy becomes one of confrontation coupled with support—the therapist must be "joined" with the client in terms of her recognition of the serious and damaging consequences for the client and the family of a failure to change, coupled with confidence and conviction that change is possible.

The Concept of "Hitting Bottom"

The overfunctioner in an alcoholic system must "hit bottom" in the sense that she accepts her powerlessness over the alcoholic. For the drinker, the notion of "hitting bottom" implies a surrender to the reality that his drinking behavior and therefore his life is out of control. In part the goal of work on the responsibility dynamic in families is to help the co-alcoholic to achieve a similar surrender with regard to her focus on the alcoholic. Once people around the alcoholic have "hit bottom," the likelihood that the alcoholic will reach this state is strengthened.

The co-alcoholic's overresponsibility represents a focus on the other that is motivated in part by a conviction that "if I just do this correctly," "if I take care of this problem," she will change and be the person I need her to be. For the co-alcoholic, "hitting bottom" represents a process of acceptance that the attempt to change another person is doomed to failure, and that one is powerless to mold the other person's behavior in a way that represents an idealized notion of what that behavior should be. Recognition of that powerlessness implies a process of grieving over the loss of the hoped for gratification the other person was expected to provide. Just as the alcoholic who hits bottom is forced to confront his own powerlessness and a distorted view of himself that may plunge him into despair, the co-alcoholic is faced with acknowledging the degree to which she has spent immeasurable energy attempting to gain self-validation and self-definition through dogged overfocus on an unchangeable other. Once the futility of her position becomes clear, the co-alcoholic must face her own despair with self—that is, the confrontation with emptiness mentioned in Chapter 2.

Work on the responsibility dynamic should be undertaken in a context in which this surrender and grieving process can occur. Clients can be helped to "hit bottom" if the therapist persistently points out both the degree of overfocus on the alcoholic, as well as the degree to which that overfocus has not worked to bring about any change.

In describing interventions for working with the responsibility dynamic in families, our primary focus is on marital interaction, but the principles apply equally to parent-child interaction.

Specific Interventions with Patterns of Over- and Underresponsibility

A context for discussion of responsibility is set in the assessment phase where a careful inventory of over- and underresponsible behaviors is made for both the functional and emotional domains. The following questionnaire is useful in helping the individual, couple, or family distinguish between functional and emotional responsibility for self versus responsibility for others. The client is asked to identify which statements are true for her.

1. When someone I love feels depressed, it tends to make me depressed too.
2. People who know me ought to know how I feel without my saying so.
3. There are certain tasks at home that simply won't get done unless I step in and do them.

4. If anyone else has a problem I feel obligated to solve it.
5. When I have a lot of time alone I tend to feel somewhat empty or I fill it with chores.
6. There are factors that make it impossible for me to change my life situation.
7. It is hard for me to pursue any pleasure for myself unless I can see a benefit for someone else in the family.
8. I tend to be the one to raise issues for discussion with my spouse.
9. People ought to be as sensitive to me as I am to them.
10. There are certain life tasks I couldn't handle alone.
11. I have to mediate between the kids and their father.
12. My spouse owes me certain things for what he's put me through.
13. My life would be pretty meaningless without my children.
14. I could do less for my parents if my siblings did more.
15. If someone expects something of me and states it directly or indirectly I get angry, but I usually do it anyway.
16. I wish some of the people around me would change.
17. Things are better now than they used to be so I have to be careful not to rock the boat.
18. If I had a day planned just for myself and a close friend said he needed help, I would usually change my plans.
19. I often feel that life is unfair.
20. If people important to me treated me differently, I would feel better about myself.
21. I vacillate between being superwoman and wishing that someone would just take care of me for a change.
22. My parent/spouse/child can make me feel very guilty.
23. It is tough to set limits with the kids because of what I (or my spouse) put them through in the past.
24. One of my kids tends to understand me better than my spouse does.
25. I have to mediate between my family and my spouse, child, etc.
26. Someone else has the answers.
27. I often feel feel that I have been the innocent victim of the alcoholism in my family.
28. I feel I must give people whatever they want.
29. If someone gets angry with me, I feel guilty.
30. If someone else feels inadequate, I feel responsible.
31. It will be difficult for me in this group to decide what my fair share of air time is and claim it.
32. If I really let my parents know who I am, it would kill them.

This work may be done in the session or the couple/parent/spouse may be sent home with homework. Often, spouses are asked to work on listing their responsibilities separately and to discuss those lists in the sessions. The list on p. 109 represents one woman's perceptions of her responsibilities as they involved her emotional and task functioning for her husband.

Emotional

Encourage relationships with his family and keep them smooth

Tried constantly to reassure when impotence was a problem

Try to encourage good relationships with children

Functional

Make all appointments; make other calls—dentist, doctor, etc.

Plan for all vacations, weddings, birthdays, holidays

Wash, cook, clean, iron, call repairmen, drive kids, make rules for kids, enforce rules, deal with school problems

Take car to get repaired

Buy clothes, groceries, household items

Decorate house, paint, wallpaper

The differences in perspectives about who does what or who is responsible for what provide very useful information for both the clinician and the spouse about the clarity of rules regulating the relationship. If a parent is asked to outline an adolescent's responsibilities, and the adolescent is asked to do the same, the two lists frequently differ so significantly that inconsistency about expectations and responsibility becomes quite clear to all family members even without the therapist pointing out that this could be a problem.

A first behavioral step toward self-responsibility for nondrinking family members is to attend Al-Anon or a related support group such as Adult Children of Alcoholics or Families Anonymous. The family member's willingness to do this is diagnostic. Unwillingness is an indication of the intensity of the family's pride. Spouses, parents, or adult children who are unwilling to take this step are sometimes best referred for group treatment at this point since individual work with the therapist will tend to be a long-term process usually netting little gain in terms of actual shifts in the interactional processes in the family. (See Chapter 9 on group treatment models.) The client's relationship with the therapist will often replicate the kind of control struggle that occurred in the interaction with the alcoholic. Group interaction thus tends to be much more effective in terms of circumventing pride issues.

Other steps in the process of working with the responsibility dynamic include a careful didactic discussion of alcoholism as a "disease of responsibility" in which the therapist describes the ways in which somebody doing too much can set up a situation in which somebody else does too little. The therapist points out that if one person always takes care of another person's feelings, the other person never really learns to do it for herself. The use of the term "overresponsible" is very deliberate and is meant to convey that someone is doing too much of a good thing. Again, it is an attempt to form a positive alliance with the client's pride system by suggesting that the person is being too good, rather than somehow bad, wrong, or inadequate. Such terms as "enabling," "controlling," or "overfunctioner" are avoided. It is important to convey that the client is assumed to have good intentions and that, in fact, she has probably exhausted herself trying to do everything and take care of the other's feelings. Most important, the therapist must indicate an understanding that in spite of the person's overwork, the other continues to be a problem. Often the therapist will comment, "Gee, it must be very frustrating to you. I know that you are doing what you're doing for her out of the best of motives [love, worry, concern, desire to be helpful], but the ironic thing is that whenever you are overresponsible for someone else, no matter how good the motives, the other person somehow ends up feeling controlled and will fight you." If the other person is in the session, she will typically nod vehement agreement to the statement that she feels controlled. The further statement is made to the overresponsible person, "It isn't fair to you that you're so misunderstood, but this just seems to happen in families. You take over out of caring and you end up being perceived as controlling." This intervention simultaneously conveys sympathy to the overresponsible partner for being misunderstood, maligned, and misused and acknowledges the underresponsible party's feeling that she is being controlled.

The most direct form of intervention is to coach the client or family members to stop overdoing in very specific ways. Spouses or parents must be coached to stop being overresponsible in functional ways such as the following:

Stop shopping for her clothes.
Stop calling his mother for him.
Stop making her doctor/dentist appointments for her.
Stop making excuses with his boss when he can't get to work because he's been drinking.
Don't clean up the mess when she comes home drunk and gets sick.
Stop running to school to talk with the teacher everytime he has a problem.
Let her find her own misplaced belongings.

In the emotional dimension, some specific coaching might involve:

Don't tell him how to do something.
Don't criticize how she does something.
Let him make his own decision.
When she is upset, just listen; don't try to solve it, comment on it, advise about it.
Don't protect his feelings.
Don't nag or question her about drinking—it's her problem.

The specific content of coaching will depend on what issues the client raises in sessions and it will also depend on the clinician's knowledge that certain types of overresponsibility *always* occur in alcoholic systems.

Whatever the issue that is raised for discussion, it is always framed within the context of over- and underresponsibility so that the client begins to see the interaction in the family within that framework. Clients will manage some changes and not others—the process is ongoing and cumulative.

As an example of one client who shifted a pattern of overresponsibility in a very effective way, Mary reported in a session one day that not only was her husband's alcoholic drinking obviously progressing, but he had just borrowed $20,000 for a boat that he couldn't afford. An assessment of her "overresponsibility history" showed that she had always taken all the responsibility for finding money to pay the bills. The first move the therapist made was to support her in deciding to turn the books and bills over to her husband—in short, to turn the responsibility over to him. She anticipated that the money would not be there for the kids' shoes and resolved that she would instruct the kids to go directly to their father for the money.

Finally, a technique of David Berenson's (1979:238) often helps the spouse of the alcoholic to justify to himself the necessity to give up overresponsibility. Berenson, when treating a despairing spouse who is confronting a partner's alcoholism, tells her that she has three choices:

1. She can keep doing whatever they're already doing
2. She can detach emotionally from the drinker
3. She can leave physically

Since the first and third options are usually never palatable, the spouse typically chooses the second, which can be elaborated on by defining "detachment" as the necessity to give up overresponsibility.

A Brief Case Study: Roger and Susan

The following transcripts are excerpts from presobriety work with Roger and Susan. Susan's drinking appeared to become particularly problematic at menopause. The couple sought marital counseling when Roger retired. The excerpts are from a two-month period of initial therapy during which most of the therapist's efforts are directed toward short-circuiting Roger's perfectionism and overresponsibility and in which attention is also paid to Susan's overresponsibility. It was the assumption that Roger's overresponsibility for Susan in conjunction with her own overresponsibility also led to the irresponsibility of alcoholic drinking. Family-of-origin work accompanied the segments presented here as the patterns of responsibility were traced to their sources.

ROGER: This furious activity and wanting to help and wanting . . . is I think partly because I feel responsible for the drinking. . . . I think I must have done something wrong. You know . . . what did I do wrong? If I can't identify what I did wrong, I can't stop doing it and I haven't been able to identify it. . . .Maybe I'm not doing enough of this . . . maybe I'm not paying enough attention . . . maybe I'm not spending enough time. Because I have a big life of my own and I go off and live my own life, so maybe I'm being inconsiderate and maybe I'm not helping enough around the house and, you know . . . I know that Susan doesn't have the physical stamina that I do.

THERAPIST: [interrupts] At the point that Susan wants to drink, she doesn't want you to do the right thing. She wants you to do the wrong thing so she has an excuse to drink. [to Susan] Do you know what I'm saying?

SUSAN: Yeah.

THERAPIST: Don't you ever feel in drinking . . . like you're just spoiling for a fight? And you want that fight . . . you want that release?

SUSAN: I want that release.

THERAPIST: [to Roger] And so, the more you try to be perfect, the more aggravating it is to her. [to Susan] When does Roger make mistakes?

SUSAN: [Surprised] Mistakes? What kind of mistakes?

THERAPIST: Any kind of mistakes. Big ones.

SUSAN: I don't know whether he does or not [laughs]. I never thought of things as mistakes.

THERAPIST: He's so competent, isn't he?

SUSAN: Yes he is.

THERAPIST: It must be very hard to live with such a superior being.

SUSAN: Sometimes it is.

THERAPIST: Can you tell me about that? [to Roger] And I don't mean you're acting superior. [Roger looks deep in thought.]

SUSAN: Being superior . . . just being.

THERAPIST: How is that hard?

SUSAN: I don't know why it is hard. You know, maybe it's because I feel I should be that good. . . .

THERAPIST: Maybe.

SUSAN: Well, I do know that if anything, if one little thing he does goes wrong, he thinks it's horrible. . . .If he doesn't put something together right or something he really goes into almost a tantrum [chuckles].

[Roger got the point and made quite an effort to back off.]

Here, a session or two later, Susan has stopped drinking but is giving her reasons why she doesn't want to go to AA. For example, she has other things she wants to do at night, such as knitting. The therapist says she can knit at a meeting.

SUSAN: I want to read my paper, and I want to read my book before I go to bed.

THERAPIST: A whole book?

SUSAN: Some. If I go out at night then I'm up till two o'clock because I'm keyed up.

THERAPIST: I understand that.

ROGER: But, you know, it does have something to do with what you're interested in too, because you know that other night a couple of weeks ago, whenever it was, I'd been working on something during the day and I got interested in it and I—I don't know where the devil I had to go, but I no more felt like it and I got home at nine and worked steadily till midnight and I wasn't tired at all; I felt wonderful. I sat up until almost two reading. Now I was exhausted the next morning, but I had no problem with it because I really was interested in what I was doing . . . I really wanted to do it. . . .

SUSAN: That's what I said.

ROGER: [talking over her] But, you can get interested in the other things too. It's just that at the time you have to make a decision. You know you're interested in the knitting and the reading. [shaking his finger emphatically, explaining] I'm not all that enthusiastic about going to Al-Anon but I also know what things have gotten better in the last two weeks and I don't want to let them slip back and . . . in fact, I want them to get even better.

THERAPIST: Roger, I want to ask you a very personal question. Did you ever want to go into the ministry?

[silence]

ROGER: Funny, I don't answer you right off. Maybe there's a powerful answer in that. No, I don't think I ever thought seriously about it.

THERAPIST: You know why I ask you? Before you get insulted, because you'll be a little insulted about what I'm going to say, but I want you to hear me . . . you enjoy preaching.

ROGER: Yeah.

THERAPIST: You're preaching at Susan right now. [Susan has a smile.]

ROGER: Yeah, that's right.

THERAPIST: She probably doesn't enjoy your preaching.

ROGER: That's a good observation.

THERAPIST: But, that doesn't mean you're not a good preacher. I'm a very good preacher too. I'm a very good preacher as you know [Susan chuckles], but you pay me to preach.

[Later in the session, the therapist says that all this preaching makes her want to drink.]

In the next session, they report that they have done beautifully and Roger attributes it to his having backed off. The therapist asks Susan if he really has backed off, and she says that yes, he has. The therapist congratulates Roger and says that she has a new job for him anyhow; she has been reading an article about "motivators" who get paid $10,000 an assignment by industry to motivate people, and Roger could always consult. . .

ROGER: I don't find it easy.

THERAPIST: [to Susan] How did you notice his backing off? Was it really obvious to you?

SUSAN: It was very obvious to me, yes. He wasn't constantly saying this, and this, and this, and he wasn't getting that long look everytime when I used to feel, you know, that I'm not doing what he wants so he has this long sulky look. Which allowed us to talk some and to have some lovemaking.

THERAPIST: Lovemaking? Really?

ROGER: How about that?

[Susan has also stopped drinking, with the exception of two drinks, and has gone back to AA at the beginning of the week. The therapist expresses pleasure, but adds that she had not expected Susan to go to AA.]

SUSAN: "I didn't know whether I was going to or not, but no one was pushing me."

[later on]

SUSAN: The problem that I saw there is gone, because it was a problem that was in my mind.

THERAPIST: You've been less focused on Roger.

SUSAN: You're damn right.

THERAPIST: And lo and behold you discovered lots of things that you want to do.

SUSAN: [almost defiantly] Yes!

THERAPIST: But, they aren't necessarily the things he thinks you should want to do.

SUSAN: There's a big difference in the attitude. I say, "You know I want to go there." Roger will ask me in the morning what I'm going to do that day and I say, "Don't bother to ask me," because when I get up in the morning, I don't know what I'm going to do. I might do one of a lot of things. Now I'm saying, "You know, it's a nice day; I want to go and do that shopping," and not feeling at five o'clock, "Oh my God, I didn't do this, and didn't do that and didn't get the supper made yet and what's Roger going to say?" I just said, "I don't give a damn what he's going to say," and it's a completely new . . .

THERAPIST: Don't you also feel more justified in that attitude without drinking?

SUSAN: Yeah.

THERAPIST: Like you're more entitled when you're not secretly guilty about the drinking?

SUSAN: You're right . . . I came to that conclusion. [Susan had conducted an experiment yesterday, and decided not to drink anymore.]

In this transcript, Roger's overresponsibility both functionally ("maybe I'm not doing enough") and emotionally (preaching) sets the stage for Susan's continued irresponsibility. She can never be as good as he is nor can she live up to his expectations. Drinking serves to relieve the pressure she feels to be overresponsible with regard to focusing too much on him. Toward the end of the transcript, both move in the direction of self-focus.

In this example the therapist is also addressing what we refer to as the saint/sinner dynamic inherent in the complementarity of the alcoholic system. The therapist is conveying that there are alternatives to viewing the system in terms of good guys and bad guys and that everybody's behavior has effects that are not necessarily linked to intentions. The therapist continually shifts sides, rapidly joining first with one spouse, then the other. When working on this point, the therapist may find it helpful to use a good deal of humor and story telling to express his amazement and disbelief that some people could want to do so much for or focus so much on somebody else. Often, we tell clients stories about other clients who, for example, lay their husband's clothes out for them every morning or, worse still, do the same for their teenage children. Often, in the apparent ridiculousness of the behavior, the client recognizes her own overdoing. On occasion, much to our horror or the client's, the story may replicate the client's actual behavior at which point we are quick to shake our heads in wonderment and tell the client we just don't know how he does it—certainly *we* wouldn't be so capable.

When Overresponsibility Is Primarily Emotional

When working with spouses or parents, it is typically very easy to identify their areas of functional overresponsibility. Often, however, families or individuals come into treatment and it is less than clear that there is a principal overfunctioning person performing tasks inappropriately for another in the family.

In this situation, emotional overresponsibility is typically more at issue. It is also more difficult to identify and more difficult to interrupt. This type of overresponsibility is characterized by a need to protect the other's feelings, a tendency to rationalize or excuse the other's inappropriate behavior, fear of the other's response if one takes positions, or an inability to tolerate the other having a feeling different from one's own. The overresponsible person often feels that he knows what is best for the other, or communicates that the other is somehow not competent to handle her own feelings or her own problems. The overresponsible person tends to communicate a message that "I really can't expect this person to be responsible because she has this or that problem, failing, weakness, fear, inadequacy."

Often this form of emotional overresponsibility is expressed by spouses who claim that they can't leave a marriage to an actively drinking alcoholic because they feel so "sorry" for the spouse. The overfocus on the problems of the other, of course, represents an inadequate sense of responsibility for and an avoidance of one's own feelings and needs. Often we point out to clients that "feeling sorry" for a "bag lady" or a Bowery derelict doesn't help them to change their lives.

In some cases one sees in therapy, it is not realistic to coach an overfunctioner to stop doing if to stop doing will also endanger her own well-being or that of children. For instance, it is not realistic to tell a wife to stop working and stop paying the mortgage and utility bills for her unemployed husband. However, it is important for her to look at the ways that she communicates to him on an emotional level that she doesn't really expect him to function or that she assumes that he can't.

For example, one client who was paying all the bills for her unemployed alcoholic husband left money for him in an envelope on the hall table, rather than handing it to him. She wanted to protect his pride, but could not understand why he was not motivated to look for a job. It was very difficult for her to connect her protection of his pride with his lack of motivation.

In the situation where it is not realistic for a spouse or parent to stop functioning, it is helpful to coach the client consistently to take calm positions about what he expects. Eventually, the client has to be helped to exercise alternative options if the other partner in an interaction fails to respond. Reactive anger or hostility in response to the underresponsible person should be avoided, since it provides a form of emotional response that tends to perpetuate the dysfunctional interaction.

Emotional overresponsibility is typically very pronounced in parent-child interactions. Often, the parent is projecting his own feelings onto the child and attempting to control or correct the child in ways that will have the effect of correcting his own feelings about self. Overresponsibility for the child actually represents underresponsibility for one's own feelings and needs. The child, who may actively rebel or act out, becomes functionally underresponsible, but is on some level being asked to take emotional responsibility for the parent's feelings about self. The tremendous anger and hostility that may be generated in these relationships in the guise of "caring too much" is actually a function of blurred boundaries around issues of emotional responsibility.

For instance, in one family a mother, who was very focused on and did everything for her only son, began to comment on, criticize, and disapprove of every behavior he engaged in regarding his appearance, his friends, what he liked to draw, how he decorated his room, whether or not he smoked cigarettes, and so on as he developed further into adolescence. At the same time, she failed to provide clear limits and expectations in terms of how he was expected to behave. The father sided with his son, agreeing that the mother was too much "on him," and compensated by totally excusing all inappropriate behavior. The son proceeded to act out and to abuse drugs and alcohol.

The son violently objected to his parent's overresponsibility for him in areas where he rightly wanted and needed to make his own decisions, and responded with rebellious, irresponsible behavior. Meanwhile, the mother overfocused on the son to avoid painful feelings about some of her own problems with her own alcoholic father and with her husband. The husband overfocused on the son to avoid both difficulties with his wife and feelings of loss related to the death of his own father when he was a very young child. Neither parent was appropriately responsible for self, nor did they responsibly parent their son. Conversations with the son revealed an intense anxiety about his parents' relationship, particularly his father's isolation. He feared that he was his father's "only friend." His irresponsible behavior covered or relieved a tremendous sense of emotional overresponsibility for his parents' feelings.

After the more functional issues have been addressed by coaching, firm limit setting, and contracting with children, it is always helpful to ask the parents to discuss their own family and parental relationships. The goal is to increase the parents' self-focus emotionally and to help evolve alternate avenues of growth and need gratification for each parent so that the child is freed to learn more appropriate responses to her own feelings and needs.

Admittedly, it is very difficult not to move in to "do something" about a negative emotion in someone one is emotionally tied to. Alcoholics can be particularly inventive and creative in presenting their negative emotions in guilt-producing ways. It seems helpful to use extreme examples like those presented earlier with clients to indicate that it is difficult not to be "hooked" into taking responsibility for another's feelings, but that if one can avoid it, positive consequences will eventually result.

Alternatives to Over- and Underresponsibility: "Responsive to" Versus "Responsible for"

It is often the case that a person pulls for emotional overresponsibility (take care of me, protect me, solve my problem) in part because the other is not emotionally *responsive*. The underresponsible person's claims, demands, and expectations tend to become more extreme as the overresponsible person becomes less able simply to acknowledge and respond to the fact that the other has feelings. Circularly, the overresponsible person becomes less responsive out of fear that with all feelings of the other come expectations that something be done for or about them. The greatest stress that the overresponsible person can experience is to have to say no to the other's need or demand in her own self interest.

The task oriented posture of the co-alcoholic often represents a necessary deadening of feeling in response to the perceived inordinate demands of the alcoholic as well as the damaging effects of alcoholic behavior. Often lack of responsiveness also represents a misinterpretation of the Al-Anon principle, "detach with love." The co-alcoholic frequently uses this prescription as an excuse to cut off all response to the alcoholic. It seems to offer permission to say no or remain uninvolved with the alcoholic that the overresponsible dictates of his behavior would never allow.

It is important for families to understand the difference between emotional overresponsibility and responsiveness. They quite literally need to be taught that one can respond to another's feeling without having to do anything about it and that even if asked to, directly or indirectly, they have the right to say no. Often clients ask if responsibility for somebody else is ever justified. Often religious beliefs about caring for others seem to them to be contradicted by the concept of overresponsibility.

At the beginning of treatment, the therapist typically needs to push the system to its opposite extreme—the client is coached not to take responsibility for anyone else at all to the degree that this is realistic or possible in a given situation.

Eventually, however, as treatment proceeds, it becomes more clear to the client that one's responses to another may involve an element of choice. The client is encouraged to "do" or "care" for others under the following circumstances.

1. They experience caring for others as a choice. They will know that they are making a choice only if they don't feel angry and there is no hidden string or expectation attached.
2. Caring for or giving to does not infantilize or demean the other person.
3. Both people acknowledge the give-and-take nature of the interaction without having to pretend it isn't so.
4. If in a given situation one feels compelled to give or take responsibility by virtue of circumstance (caring for an aging parent, attending a child's school function) even though one would prefer not to, it is important to acknowledge to oneself that one doesn't want to, but will do it anyway and that one is ultimately responsible for this choice.

Taking Positions

The person coached to stop overdoing and overcaring quite literally feels at a loss for words, behavior, or any concrete framework for knowing who she is or how to behave in relationship to others. The therapeutic task is to encourage a focus on self—an opening up to new experiences of self and new understanding of feelings and needs not colored by old premises about how one must behave to be acceptable in the eyes of society or the significant others in one's life. Again, in Bowen terms, the ultimate goal of therapy is differentiation of self for all family members, and some degree of this differentiation must take place for sobriety to be achieved.

Often it quite literally does not occur to the overresponsible person that he is free *not* to do something that somebody else seems to want him to do or that, conversely, the other person is equally free from his expectations. More than one client has directly asked, "Well, if I can't control, nag, comment on, or take responsibility for anybody, then what can I do? If I can't "love" [focus on someone else], who am I?" Unfortunately, they truly don't know—the question is not a manipulative or dependent posturing.

Since therapeutically, the process of differentiation is an ongoing one that is never perfectly achieved, the therapist's task is to encourage the client from the beginning of treatment to take positions and make statements that represent self-focus rather than other-focus. These statements should represent to the other person in a given interaction the following:

What I will do, what I won't do
What I will tolerate, what I won't tolerate
What I want, what I don't want

Often, since the person initially really doesn't know what he or she wants or feels, it is much more constructive to help the client formulate statements about behavior.

As one person in the system begins to take self-focused positions, it is important to predict that the rest of the family will react with some version of "you're bad, crazy, selfish—you don't love or care about me." Initially, underresponsible behavior such as drinking may intensify as the family seeks to elicit the familiar patterns of complementary response.

It has seemed helpful to explain this concept to families in whatever way the therapist feels is relevant for a given family. Didactic explanations help to provide the client with a rationale for change, and an understanding of process helps to reorient the client's thinking about family experience. Didactic explanations also communicate that the therapist views the family as competent to understand process and change it.

In predicting that the system will initially react to a position by some version of "you're crazy, bad, selfish, and you don't love me," it is helpful to outline for the client two possible sequences that may occur. He is told that reactions are defined as "feeling" statements, positions are "I" statements. Person A is told to take a position. If Person B responds with a position, you can have a good clean fight. If, however, as is more likely, Person B responds with a reaction, Person A is at a choice point. If he can respond with a position, and hold to that position until Person B responds with a position, the interaction is productive and can be resolved. If, however, Person A responds to a reaction with a reaction, the interaction escalates into the kind of fight in which both people quickly lose track of the issues they were fighting about because the fight has now become a fight about reactions and not about the original position. It is helpful to explain that most statements have both an "I" statement and a "feeling" statement component, and to give clients practice in identifying and responding just to the "I" statement.

One example we use is:

PERSON A: "I have to go to Philadelphia to the doctor. Do you want to go with me?" [non-I statement designed to make person B responsible]

PERSON B: "Do you want me to go with you?" [clear question designed to get person A to take a position]

PERSON A: "Yes, I would like you to [clear I position], but I can get someone else to go [position] although I don't want to" [reaction].

PERSON B: Well, going to Philadelphia is not my favorite way to spend a Saturday [reaction], but I'll go [position].

PERSON A: "O.K., I'll get the tickets" [position that responds only to person B's position and does not comment on person B's reaction].

It is very easy for clients to identify where they would have gotten off track and become reactive in this example. Usually, it's at the point that Person B says that going to Philadelphia is not his favorite way to spend the day. The client usually feels she would have responded with "The hell with you, I'll go by myself then."

We point out that if people are going to be intimate they must allow one another to have feelings and reactions, express them, but also take positions. We state that if they can learn to allow the reactions, but respond to the positions, they will be able to avoid over responsibility. Getting pulled into the other person's reaction by one's own reactivity is a form of emotional overresponsibility.

Internal Overresponsibility in the Alcoholic

While it is primarily the overresponsibility of the co-alcoholic that is the dynamic which interactionally maintains the alcoholism, there is an internal overresponsibility in some alcoholics which is equally crucial to interrupt. The alcoholic's internal overresponsibility may occur in the presobriety phase or may emerge only after sobriety. For both men and women internal overresponsibility may be represented by an inability to disappoint or to fail to live up to emotional or functional expectations of self (I should feel, I should take care of, I should want, I should do, and so on). Drinking functions to relieve this emotional and functional overresponsibility.

Often, the alcoholic's overresponsibility, like that of the co-alcoholic, is related to a rigidified notion of appropriate sex role. For example, a woman alcoholic who suffers from internal overresponsibility may be unable to relax her expectation of self as a wife or mother except when she is drunk. A man may have such high expectations of himself as a provider that he compulsively overworks, and then can let down only by drinking. Overresponsibility in any form, either interactional or intrapsychic, will inevitably result in the underresponsibility of drinking behavior or in a failure responsibly to acknowledge realistic self-limitedness. The therapist must address the issue in the internal as well as the interactional dimension.

Special Considerations in Working with Over- and Underresponsibility

As people struggle with the assaults to pride, emptiness, guilt, and sometimes subsequent irresponsibility that follow relinquishing the overresponsible position, frequently they will expect the therapist to take over for them. Berenson (1979:233) talks about the isomorphy of the therapist system. It is very tempting for the therapist to replicate the overresponsible position of the co-alcoholic. For instance, Margaret's husband, Bill, had gone off to a motel after a fight. Presumably he was going to get drunk. Normally, she would have been frantic, but she was trying very hard not to "do anything" about the situation. Therefore, she placed an emergency call to the therapist to say, "Bill and I had a fight. He left. I'm pretty sure he's at the Howard Johnson's if you [the therapist] want to call him." (The therapist did not call him.)

Often, one is working with only part of the system. When one tells an overresponsible family member that he must stop doing what he is doing or the alcoholic will continue to drink, it is important not to communicate that he is responsible for her drinking, but that the role he plays makes it possible for her to continue to drink. Always stress the notion of reciprocity: The more *you* do, the less she has to do. The more you worry about her feelings, the less she has to take care of her own.

Track the sequence of events following prescriptions to give up overresponsible behavior very carefully. Do not necessarily take the client's word that she has stopped or started a certain behavior consistently or completely. If no change is occurring in the family or if there has been no reactivity or heightened crisis, there has usually been a failure to follow through accurately on a prescription. Track *behavior* very carefully.

Treating over- and underresponsibility in the family does not involve only stopping one form of behavior, it involves active encouragement of new behavior. Clients are encouraged to stop doing for the other and start doing something for themselves and they typically need help defining or identifying what this new behavior could be. If the underfunctioning person is present in the session, he should be coached regarding what represents responsible behavior in a given situation. Often, parents, for instance, are quite unaware that they are responsible for dealing with certain problems related to child rearing, such as setting limits or participating in certain school events with their child. The male may assume that the wife has sole responsibility for the children's care and maintenance. The thorny issue of sex-role related responsibilities will often rear its head here: Should men have to work all day and do housework too? Should women have to contribute to the financial support of the family? In our work we stress equality of responsibility and equality of power.

These values represent *our* political bias as feminists, but we equally believe that, as a clinical issue, more balanced power relationships represent a critical goal in the evolving structure of family life. We do not, however, impose our views on a family, particularly if a more traditional role complementarity is working effectively for that family. We typically discuss these values directly with clients when it seems clinically relevant, and attempt to facilitate discussion regarding how the family as a whole reacts to changing attitudes regarding male and female power. Ultimately, changes in power balances remain the couple's or family's decision.

Realistically, economic and social structures still do not provide a context in which the equality is possible or even desirable in all families. Men often do not want emotional responsibility and women often do not want financial responsibility. Men tend to want to retain the overt power, while women often prefer to remain in the overtly dependent role. While the therapist may encourage equality, its achievement will be more limited in some families than in others.

Finally, it is typical in this phase that marital relationships are characterized by serious sexual dysfunction. The male alcoholic may be intermittently or consistently impotent. He typically accuses his wife of being cold and unresponsive. She, in turn, feels repulsed by his drunken sexual advances, but also seriously questions her own sexual adequacy. Both may engage in sexual relationships outside the marriage.

Frequently, conflicts about sexuality predate the progression towards alcoholic drinking in a relationship. Often, the male experiences himself to be in the uncomfortable role of the emotional (sexual) pursuer who is repeatedly rejected or kept at a distance by a wife who experiences tension or conflict about sexuality. Often religious sanctions against sexuality, rigid prescriptions about birth control methods, and inconsistent or negative family of origin messages regarding sexuality based on ethnic and religious factors figure heavily in marital sexual dysfunction which prompts the need for self-correction with alcohol. Males and females both may drink to either enhance or diminish self-perceptions related to their sexual identities.

As much as it is necessary to be aware of these issues relative to sexuality and marital conflict in presobriety treatment, the focus of treatment must remain on behavioral issues related to shifting patterns of responsibility in the family. Once drinking enters its most addictive phases, it is not helpful to try to work on other marital issues, nor does it help directly to define as a goal, "closing the distance between two partners" so that "drinking is less necessary" (Bowen, 1978:268). While this approach may have some relevance when drinking is in its very early stages as indicated by less defensiveness, less denial, and less focus on drinking in the family in general, once truly addictive drinking behavior is in motion, no amount of work on the marital issues is likely to permanently interrupt the progression of the drinking. The drinking must be interrupted first. Issues of sexuality, communication, equalizing of power, feelings of inadequacy, cannot even be approached while the bitterness, resentment, and repulsion built up after long years of drunken behavior have occurred and are still activated and present in the face of continued drinking.

Summary—Treatment in Presobriety (Phase 1)

Treatment of alcohol problems in the presobriety phase is focused on three goals:

1. To anticipate and deal with denial
2. To help motivate the drinker to achieve abstinence in AA, or in a rehabilitation or detoxification program
3. To interrupt patterns of over- and underresponsibility

These goals help to destabilize a family system that has been organized around drinking behavior. The primary focus of this period of treatment is to stress appropriate self-responsibility for all family members in both the functional and emotional domains, since it is hypothesized that behavioral patterns in which individuals are either overresponsible for others or underresponsible for self tend to maintain the dysfunctional organization which helps sustain drinking behavior.

Intervening in Alcoholic Systems After Sobriety

Phase 2: Adjustment to Sobriety—Stabilizing the System

It is characteristic that in this phase the alcoholic and the family have acknowledged drinking as a primary focus of treatment. The alcoholic has agreed to the necessity to stop drinking and/or has agreed to attend Alcoholics Anonymous. This period usually encompasses the first six to twenty-four months after the initial ninety-day attendance at AA or the return from a rehabilitation program. Potential for and frequency of relapse is high in this phase. In cases where the alcoholic has stopped drinking, but does not attend AA, presobriety issues may still dominate the clinical picture.

Treatment Goals

1. Keep system as calm as possible—focus predominantly on stepping down conflict, stress.
2. Address individual issues of family members more than interactional ones.
3. Stress self-focus for all family members.
4. Anticipate and predict extreme reactions to sobriety on the part of the co-alcoholic.
5. Address fear of relapse.

6. Begin to teach new behavioral skills for coping with stress and conflict.
7. Make minor structural changes that will insure at least minimally adequate parenting.

The Newly Sober System—When the Bad Guy Is Suddenly the Saint

The newly sober family is in a state of crisis—the equilibrium evolved by the family during the course of chronic drinking is now thrown into pandemonium. Before real change can be effected to ensure maintained sobriety, the crisis must be weathered and a stable pattern of new behavior must be adopted by the family.

Achievement of sobriety represents a shift in the functional premises of the family which involves living at interactional extremes—either wet or dry, conflicted or dead, emotionally distant or emotionally reactive; one person overresponsible, the other underresponsible; one person in control, one person out of control; one person the good guy, one person the bad. Most important is that as the alcoholic becomes sober, other people in the family, most notably the co-alcoholic, lose a sense of their own importance. While the alcoholic's "bad" behavior or neediness had served as an indirect source of self-esteem, and a buttress to the pride system of the overresponsible person, the alcoholic now must be viewed as "good" for deciding to face and deal with his problem. What tends to emerge in place of the co-alcoholic's experience of righteous "goodness" is a barrage of feelings of bitterness, resentment, and a tendency to experience rage in the present for all the negative behavior that she has tolerated and coped with in the past. The alcoholic often gets sober only to find that those in his immediate environment are more directly or indirectly angry with him now than they were when he drank.

The predominant experience of the co-alcoholic during this stage is one of fear. Sobriety, even though desperately desired, represents a frightening change. New power issues will have to be faced and resolved. Questions of sexual and emotional intimacy must be addressed. Although previously all the co-alcoholic's fears and anxieties about self could be submerged in the interests of responding to the drinking and in being overly responsible for the drinker, the co-alcoholic is now faced squarely with the need to focus on self and deal with anxiety rather than dealing with the alcoholic. To make matters worse, AA members, friends, and family express praise and support for the alcoholic, while nobody mentions the ordeal of the spouse nor offers praise or support for the role he has played in "holding the family together." For the co-alcoholic, sobriety becomes an unjust demotion—a loss of all avenues of self-esteem and a loss of a tenuous sort of status. Whatever self-deceptions alcohol has functioned to mask or whatever behavior it has served to permit must now give way to a more real and responsible approach to the problematic issues affecting the family. Before this more responsible approach emerges however, loss of the need to overfunction for the alcoholic and experienced loss of the one-up position in the relationship may result in the co-alcoholic's shift to underresponsible behavior. In other words, he may respond to sobriety by alternatively assuming the symptomatic position.

The co-alcoholic is vulnerable to developing one of a range of symptoms at this point or of intensifying those that may have begun to emerge in the presobriety phase. Spouses who had taken prescription drugs for anxiety may begin to abuse them. Somatic symptoms may intensify or appear. An addictive disorder such as overeating, smoking too much, use of drugs other than alcohol, or alcohol itself, may emerge or intensify. The spouse may experience acute depression or anxiety or may decide at this point to end the marriage. If sexual infidelity has been part of the marital interaction during the drinking phase, it is common for the spouse to have an affair early in the sobriety phase. The drinker's "bad" or irresponsible behavior is assumed to justify the spouse's.

Children are equally likely to develop symptoms, particularly if one child in the family has tended to overfunction for the nondrinking spouse and now finds herself without a role in the face of the drinking parent's reentry into the role of parent and husband or wife. Having focused to a great degree on family issues, the child typically has few alternative sources of self-esteem and the loss of role represented by sobriety often results in suicidal behavior, acting out in school, or abuse of alcohol or other drugs. A child's problems may become a substitute focus for those of the drinking spouse so that family patterns only revert to their old balance with a new member playing the symptomatic part.

It is important for the clinician not to view the family's response to sobriety as a statement that somehow covertly the spouse or other family members are invested in keeping the alcoholic drunk. Shifting of the symptom to another family member is a homeostatic mechanism that represents the system's tendency to revert to its prior balance. The alcoholic, at least initially, may experience himself as successful at achieving sobriety with a resultant increase in self-esteem. But, in their attempts to correct for the assault to their individual and collective sense of themselves other family members may simply find new ways to play the same old role. One woman in treatment commented sadly after her husband stopped drinking, "Somehow I felt more important when he was drinking."

Clearly, then, the goal of this phase of treatment is to help the family anticipate and absorb the after shocks of sobriety in a way that is most likely to prevent symptomatology in other family members or relapse for the drinker.

Walking on Eggshells

In their concern that the alcoholic will drink again, family members in early sobriety tend to avoid all confrontation with the alcoholic. They avoid telling her about problems that arise in the normal course of events, and they tend to protect her from normal responsibilities. There is typically great concern about whether to attend social events where people will drink, or whether to serve or drink liquor in front of the alcoholic. These concerns are all manifestations of the overresponsibility dynamic, emerging in a different form for different reasons. The family should first be reassured that although relapse is possible and, in fact, likely, they are not responsible for it. It is the alcoholic's responsibility to decide whether or not she is comfortable in drinking situations. In the early phases of sobriety, spouses are encouraged to respect the alcoholic's decisions regarding drinking situations, even if it means that they not drink themselves while with the alcoholic, or that they attend social events alone. If the alcoholic asks directly that all liquor be removed from the house, for instance, this should be done. But, it is up to the alcoholic and not the spouse or children to raise the issue.

The other major tendency of the family is to expect that with sobriety will come normalcy. It is assumed that once the alcoholic stops drinking there will be no more fighting, no more abuse, no more irresponsibility. The family can be spared a good deal of anger and disappointment if they are forewarned that this will not occur. The physiological realities of alcoholism should be discussed so that the family clearly understands that alcohol has actually caused damage to brain cells and that the effects of drinking on the brain take months to reverse themselves. Certain patterns of thought or behavior that are characteristic of the alcoholic while drinking will probably recur under stress permanently. Finally, the newly sober alcoholic has not yet learned new behaviors for coping with feelings that were once masked or augmented by the drinking. Life for a while may not look a lot different after sobriety than it did before.

The AA/Al-Anon Dilemma

The ultimate recovery of the family is greatly enhanced and, it might be argued, almost entirely dependent on the family's commitment to Al-Anon along with the alcoholic's commitment to AA. Al-

Anon attendance, particularly for the spouse, will directly address many of the self-esteem issues that occur in the early sobriety phase and lessen the likelihood that other symptomatology or covert sabotage of sobriety will occur. Al-Anon provides a source of self-focus and support that is very important for the co-alcoholic because the alcoholic will tend to find most of his support at this time in AA.

It is typical at this point for the family to reorganize itself and its primary focus around AA/Al-Anon. The reorganization takes one of two forms. The first possibility is that both spouses attend and become involved with their separate meetings, develop separate support systems, and continue to operate at a fixed emotional distance from one another, much as they did when active drinking was the primary focus. The social contacts made in AA become the substitute for the old drinking friends, and the alcoholic becomes, more or less, a righteous and radical convert to AA thinking. She frequently reminds family and spouse that AA is a "selfish" program and is thus able to justify any and all time spent away from the family. The spouse in this configuration typically becomes very involved with Al-Anon where he may misinterpret the directive to "detach" from the alcoholic as permission to remain emotionally distant. Al-Anon may become a vehicle for his continued moral superiority. The actual organization, functional or emotional, of the family has in fact changed very little. The symptom has been eliminated, however, and as the effects of drinking recede, the family will become more open to changing the dynamics underlying the drinking and dealing with the emotional distance among family members.

In the second type of reorganization, the drinker becomes involved with AA, but the spouse refuses to attend Al-Anon. While in the first instance, the spouse was able to adopt Al-Anon as a support to her pride system, in this case no such support for the spouse's pride is accepted. It is typical for the spouse in this situation to become depressed, angry, and resentful or to complain about the amount of time the alcoholic spends at AA meetings. She may complain bitterly that the alcoholic is terribly bad-tempered and impossible to live with. Often she will explicitly verbalize a wish that the alcoholic were drinking since it is perceived that he was "easier to deal with" when drinking. Obviously, the likelihood that the alcoholic will drink again is high in this situation, since the spouse in this dyad continues to be relentless and highly inventive at finding issues and problems that the alcoholic can be blamed for.

In the first postsobriety situation, the prognosis for continued sobriety is fairly good even though the underlying dynamics of the relationship remain somewhat unchanged. Both spouses are moving toward self-focus and developing support networks outside the relationship. Both are to some degree taking the first steps towards responsibility for their own problems. This expansiveness will help significantly to undercut some of the hostility, resentment, and bitterness that are inherent in the alcoholic relationship. Stabilization around AA/Al-Anon is the optimum situation for the newly sober family in terms of the groundwork it helps to lay for further change in the family structure.

In some situations, the spouse's attendance at Al-Anon will have significantly predated the alcoholic's sobriety. If the spouse has tended to view Al-Anon as a vehicle for continuing to focus on the alcoholic rather than focusing on self, the reaction to sobriety may be as extreme initially as for the spouse who does not attend Al-Anon.

The Difficulties of Early Sobriety for the Alcoholic

The alcoholic in early sobriety must cling tenaciously to the external structure that AA provides because his internal sense of self is almost completely confused and distorted. As a result of the physiological effects of the disease, as well as the process of psychological numbing that drinking has set in motion, the alcoholic may have little ability initially to discriminate or express any range of emotions. The achievement of sobriety usually brings with it a momentary euphoria, described in AA as the "pink cloud." Once the alcoholic begins to make sober decisions, he usually notes that things in his life do begin to improve, he feels a great sense of accomplishment at having gotten sober, and for a while experiences a sense of pride and new-found well-being. Within three to six months, however, it is typical for depression to set in, and this period of feeling "bad" may last up to two or three years after sobriety. Again, these are general patterns and not necessarily true for all alcoholics, though some depression after sobriety for a period is almost universally experienced.

The range of emotion experienced in early sobriety tends then to be rather limited, with feeling "good" being at the one extreme and feeling "bad" being at the other. This is one reason why AA suggests that the alcoholic make no major life decisions or relationship commitments during the first year of sobriety. The suggestion is that the newly sober alcoholic is not prepared to adequately integrate a sober experience of self and must find a foothold in very simple behaviors such as attending meetings regularly before she has a clear enough grasp of what is true emotionally for herself to act on it. Frequently, the first feelings that do emerge as the alcoholic gets more sober are resentment, anger, and fear, and these are precisely the emotions most likely to precipitate a relapse. Thus, the alcoholic is told to work on resentments and to avoid situations that may arouse the desire to drink.

It is for these reasons that therapy for the alcoholic is often contraindicated in early sobriety. Therapy and the shifting of roles, alliances, and power hierarchies in marriages and families are processes that typically arouse—rather than allay—anxieties and resentments. If therapy is undertaken in the early phase of sobriety, it should be with the intention of helping the family to "settle down" into a comfortable, if temporary structure. Early sobriety is usually not the time to encourage intense confrontation of the alcoholic with the anger and resentments of other family members unless this confrontation takes place within the regular program of a rehabilitation center where the alcoholic can be helped to absorb the feedback productively. Work on very toxic issues in the marriage such as sexuality is not usually indicated unless the two spouses each express a strong motivation to do so. When marital partners do seek therapy during this time, because of a threatened separation or because of problems with a child in the family, the possibility of relapse should be discussed and a strong commitment to AA with therapy as an adjunct should be encouraged.

Some of the dimensions of early sobriety treatment are illustrated by a family who first sought therapy about six months after the husband stopped drinking. The precipitant for their entering treatment was the extramarital affair of the oldest, married son, Bob, which later resulted in a separation and divorce. Bob's mother, Dora, made the first contact with the therapist. Dora felt an intense concern about the effects of her husband's drinking on their children. Even though this child was twenty-seven years old, she felt he needed help to deal with his feelings about his father. She made an assumption that Bob's pending marital rift had to do with the alcoholism in the family and was literally "frantic" to do something about it. Bob had been allowed to come home to live temporarily and this gave her the leverage to insist that he see a counselor.

A sound framework for sobriety had been laid for the family in the rehabilitation program that the husband, Tom, had participated in. Dora attended Al-Anon, Tom had been exposed to AA, and all family members, including the older, married children, had attended family education groups and at least two sessions of family counseling. The children had all gone to Al-Anon meetings, some with more involvement than others. Tom had been forced to attend the rehab or lose his job. He acknowledged his problem and attended AA regularly, although not frequently, and he avoided seeking out a sponsor.

The therapist began by suggesting that Bob contact her directly. He did so, and was seen individually to discuss his conflict with his marriage. Family-of-origin work[1] figured heavily in therapeutic work with him and the effects of his role in relationship to his father's alcoholism were elicited in detail. As Bob began to resolve his marital difficulties for himself, the focus of Dora's anxiety shifted and she called for help for herself and her husband. She had found her own reaction to her son's problem to be so extreme that her life had been completely disrupted. She also experienced a great deal of anxiety about how the situation was affecting her own marriage which was in what felt like a very unstable state since her husband had stopped drinking.

Dora was a warm and exceedingly anxious woman who had all but exhausted herself working and taking care of the most minute details of the lives of her husband and six children, particularly her sons. She was given to making long discourses to all of them about how to behave and conduct themselves in life and she held "inspections" on Sunday mornings to check for appropriate dress as the teenage children filed out the door to go to church.

She and her husband came in for a first session. The therapist commented that the focus of concern for the two of them had shifted from alcohol to her son's divorce. The therapist then evolved a contract, with which they agreed, that she would work with them to help each of them focus on themselves and then on strengthening their marriage, which was undergoing a good deal of stress as a result of the shift to sobriety. Dora was almost relieved to be given permission not to focus on her son, and her husband told the therapist that he had been telling Dora that all along. Dora's anxiety, however, and her role as the over-responsible emotional caretaker in the family made self-focus very difficult. The therapist arranged the following treatment plan:

1. Dora was placed in an ongoing women's group which focused on issues of overresponsibility in relationships affected by alcoholism.
2. Dora and her husband were told that they would be seen intermittently, but infrequently, as issues in the marriage arose.
3. Tom was asked to help Dora with her anxiety by taking over the job of dealing with intrusions by the grown children who kept returning home with their problems.

Ongoing treatment involved the following specific interventions:

1. The oldest son's marital problems were defined as his own and, therefore, separate from the involvement of the two parents. One or two joint family sessions were held for the explicit purpose of defining boundaries and setting limits on the length of time the son would be allowed to stay in his parents' house.
2. The son's marital problems were defined as a substitute focus (or triangle) in the absence of alcohol in the parents' marriage. Dora and her husband began to realize that intimacy and closeness had been missing in their marriage as a result of the drinking.

They both agreed that the marriage, not the problems of the children, was their first priority.

3. In her women's group, Dora was to deal with her issues of over-responsibility. The basis for her overresponsible behavior was tracked back to her family of origin. She received support and encouragement from the group for any attempts to focus on her own needs rather than on those of her children, ex-daughter-in-law, or husband.

4. Dora's husband was encouraged to continue his participation in AA—suggestions by the therapist that he find a sponsor were initially disregarded.

5. Intermittent sessions were held with Dora and Tom in which Tom frequently avoided emotional confrontations, asserting that he was "comfortable" with his present adjustment and didn't see any need to go into things—he defined Dora as too emotional and excitable. The therapist did not push him on his avoidance, but worked initially with Dora's anxiety.

6. Therapy took place over the course of two or three years during which the son successfully managed his own divorce and remarriage, Dora became less overly responsible, and Tom began to be a more active participant in the marriage and in the family interaction in general. Both were able to define and participate in both personal and joint interests and activities, and to cope very effectively with the two younger male children who returned home with problems.

Stabilizing this family after sobriety meant helping to remove the triangled issues (first alcohol, subsequently Bob's marriage) from the marital context and to encourage self-focus for both spouses. As Dora lessened her overresponsibility, her husband gradually assumed more responsibility. For instance, as she gave up her role as middleman with the children, Tom began to develop a relationship with his children separately from Dora. Entire interactional sequences in the family began to change. In her groups Dora was helped with her feelings of loss as she began to realize the changes occurring in the nature of her relationship with her children. But, the group also pointed out that her willingness to change had moved her husband and the family toward greater emotional contact and health. Dora began to take pride in her ability to back off.

She was then able to deal with the marriage in a way that promoted slow but steady growth toward intimacy rather than disruptive bursts of emotional demands followed by distance which had tended to be her pattern. This pacing allowed the husband's adjustment to progress without threatening his sobriety. Many members of the family, including the ex-daughter-in-law, were seen individually at various points in time. As of their last session, Dora and her husband had taken up some new recreational activities together and were planning for their retirement. The husband took almost complete responsibility for dealing with his youngest son's latest crisis. Dora was free of the somatic symptoms that had plagued her each time she had contemplated doing anything by or for herself in the past. This was a case in which a series of interventions with individuals helped move the entire family to a healthier postsobriety integration.

It is important not to misinterpret the relative lack of focus on the alcoholic in this phase as a message that the spouse is more responsible for the marital problems or for changing them. The alcoholic is not viewed as incompetent to assume responsibility. The principle underlying treatment in this phase is that it is easier to ask the overresponsible person to stop doing too much than it is to tell an underresponsible person that she must start doing something.[2] This approach also acknowledges the realities of early sobriety in which the alcoholic has typically not stabilized enough physiologically or psychologically to acknowledge or deal directly with the immaturities of her thinking and behavior. It is assumed that change in the alcoholic at this point in time is accomplished more effectively through intervening with other parts of the system.

Important Clinical Issues in the Adjustment Phase

The reaction of the co-alcoholic to sobriety must be anticipated, predicted, and dealt with. It is important for the client to feel that the therapist understands the conflicting feelings associated with sobriety. The clinician should keep in mind the "bedrock of inadequacy" on which the co-alcoholic's sense of self is established and the fact that the co-alcoholic frequently has no sense of self other than that gained by doing for others. In the presobriety phase, the co-alcoholic's pride system can be engaged as leverage to move the alcoholic toward sobriety. In this phase, however, the assault to the co-alcoholic's pride is the most frequent source of conflict that may tip the drinker toward relapse. Group therapy is often more helpful than individual work at this point because, depending on the type of group, it may provide the support that the co-alcoholic needs to confront and change lowered feelings of self-worth. The client's anger, resentment, and sense of emptiness are often more effectively absorbed and responded to within a group than in either individual therapy or marital work. The group provides a setting in which the client's pride can be engaged in making productive changes rather than in tearing down self or the alcoholic. This period will often be characterized by feelings of intense depression or emptiness in the co-alcoholic. Resistance to change and the impulse to leave treatment will often be intense. The therapist must establish a solid rapport with the co-alcoholic before making major interventions.

A major focus of work in this phase continues to be the encouragement of self-focus and a backing off from the overresponsible role. Gains made in the presobriety phase on this issue need to be consolidated and sustained. In this phase, emotional overresponsibility tends to be more at issue than functional overdoing. The co-alcoholic is taught to take nonreactive positions and not to react to the alcoholic's reactions. The alcoholic is taught *how* to be appropriately emotionally responsible and responsive. Self-responsibility remains a consistent focus of treatment.

Finally, for the person recovering from alcoholism, there are sex-specific differences that should be taken into account. For males, achieving sobriety in AA rarely represents a major change in behavioral patterns in the sense that attending AA meetings doesn't usually affect their functional role in the family. It is typical for the male in a family to spend more time away from home and move more independently when and where he wants to. His spouse may complain about his AA attendance, but the effect of this behavior is really no different from when he spent time in bars away from the family. The family has typically already organized around his absence, so the life of the family tends to go on as usual.

Because the norm is that the female has responsibility for the emotional functions in the family, the male is typically less disturbed by guilt about the effects of his drinking on the family. He is more likely to feel guilt about his failure to be a good provider if he has become unemployed as a result of his drinking and he tends to focus more after sobriety on this aspect of his functioning than on the emotional damage his drinking has caused. The male may tend to overfunction at work or in a new job after sobriety and the pressures he imposes on himself can often threaten his new-found sobriety.

For the woman, AA attendance and the work of achieving sobriety have a much greater effect on the family and a much greater impact on self-esteem. The family has typically not reorganized around a woman's drinking so much as it has simply defined her as bad or crazy. Much of her drinking may have occurred at home, and she usually continued to function, if minimally, as housewife and mother. When the woman becomes sober, she must face at least two dilemmas: particularly if she works, how can she find the time and how can she disrupt the family by leaving frequently to attend meetings—and how does she deal with the resentment of her spouse and children at her absence? Secondly, how does she cope with the guilt surrounding her past failure to meet some of the physical and emotional needs of her family? To function poorly at being an emotional caretaker represents an absolute kind of failure to a woman and her postsobriety guilt tends to be more intense than her male counterpart's. She may respond to her guilt by reverting to an overresponsible role with her children. If this shift doesn't threaten her own sobriety, it may set the stage for alcohol abuse in one or more of her children. For the woman, the achievement of sobriety in itself challenges the fundamental premises of the relationship relative to sex roles. It acknowledges her status as a "drunk"—a role less acceptable for a woman than for a male because it is defined stereotypically as "male" behavior, and it requires a direct focus on self in terms of the time and work required to sustain sober behavior. In general, the family will typically react more negatively to a female's drinking behavior as well as to her attempts to be sober, simply because they represent a radical departure from the expected norms for female functioning.

Phase 3: Maintaining Sobriety—Rebalancing the System

In Phase 3, the alcoholic has been sober for at least six months but more ideally for one to two years. He may or may not have had periodic relapses to drinking. He expresses discomfort either with the marital relationship or with family problems involving the children. He may be experiencing acute depression or may be having difficulty maintaining sobriety despite contact with AA or other after-care treatment.

The family may continue to struggle with role adjustments more characteristic of Phase 2. A spouse may experience depression or marital dissatisfaction; children may have become symptomatic. While the family has made an initial adjustment to sobriety, it seems clear that relationships in the family remain unstable and dysfunctional and will set the stage for a return to drinking or other symptomotology if not addressed.

The therapist must assess whether the alcoholic has sufficient length and quality of sobriety to sustain the anxiety this phase of treatment may arouse. Some presobriety and early sobriety issues may need to be addressed in the preliminary stages of treatment.

Treatment Goals

1. Shift extremes of reciprocal role behavior from rigid complementarity to greater symmetry or more *overt* complementarity ("correct" complementarity for the specific relationship).
2. Help the couple/family to resolve issues of power and control.
3. Directly address the pride structures of both partners so that new

forms of role behavior are permitted without the need for alcohol.

4. Help the couple to achieve whatever level of closeness and intimacy is desirable for them.

In many families the gains achieved in the adjustment phase may provide a sufficiently stable and workable organization for the family to terminate treatment. But, it is more typically the case that once some stable sobriety has been achieved, it is necessary to help "rebalance" the family around more flexible emotional and functional patterns.

In presobriety it is characteristic of the alcoholic relationship that its balance has been achieved by one person behaving at an extreme that must be balanced by the other person behaving at the opposite extreme.

In some marriages, for example, the alcoholic looks like the more needy partner, and the co-alcoholic seems extremely self-sufficient. Getting drunk permits the alcoholic to be needy in a way that frames dependency as "independence" (you can't tell me not to drink), and it permits the self-sufficient partner to become emotionally involved either with angry reactivity, or in the "morning after" phase with offers to help. The alcohol permits the co-alcoholic a pride-saving reason to be emotionally available. Being needed, the co-alcoholic can drop her "self-sufficiency" and move toward the drinker. The apparent neediness of the alcoholic helps the person at the self-sufficient extreme to be emotional or dependent without having to acknowledge her own need. Her dependency is framed as "giving" or responsiveness. The two are mirror images of each other in terms of their ultimate dependency, but they reciprocally evolve a relationship in which the one's pride evolves into a self-sufficient, "in control," idealized image, while the other uses alcohol or out-of-control behavior to be dependent in a face-saving way. Alcohol functions to correct the self-experience of both, but slowly pushes the behavior of both to extremes such that it becomes necessary to use more and more of the alcohol to keep the experience of self consistent with the idealized image of self. Phase 3 of working with the alcoholic system is one that is predominantly focused on pride and all the resistances to rebalancing that two rigid pride systems can invent. The marriage or family after sobriety functions in a state in which pride is as intense as it was before sobriety without the mitigating influence of the alcohol on which to focus it.

The objective of therapy at this phase in sobriety is to get the marital partners into what might be referred to as "correct complementarity" or correct balance, or at the very least, a less extreme balance along the key dimensions of pride, responsibility, and sex roles. Where balance is preserved by extremes in the relationship, the goal would be that the partners openly acknowledge and accept this. Additionally, the therapeutic goal is to prevent the triangling of other issues or use of a child in the relationship to provide ballast in a struggle to achieve a balance that benefits one partner more than the other.

It is crucial to rebalance the system in relationship to the dysfunctional balance characteristic of the presobriety system. Consequently, an accurate assessment of what Berenson refers to as the "adaptive consequences" of drinking in the presobriety phase is essential, as is the understanding of the pride and sex role issues specific to the particular relationship.

Wet and Dry Extremes

Berenson (1976) developed the concept of "wet" and "dry" states which essentially refers to extremes of either in-control (dry) or out-of-control (wet) behavior characteristic of the alcoholic. Eventually, the marital interaction in an alcoholic system tends to become characterized by these same extremes of behavior. In other words, reciprocally, one partner is usually more in control when the other is out of control, or more overresponsible when the other is underresponsible. However, the general nature of the interactional balance in the relationship tends to oscillate back and forth between these two extremes as well—the interaction may be rigid, controlled, nonemotional, distant, or "dry" for periods, and may then become highly reactive, emotionally charged, out of control, or "wet" for other periods. The building intensity of the one state flips the interaction into the other state and vice versa. These oscillations tend to be more fixed and rigid as addiction to alcohol progresses. In earlier phases of drinking in some relationships we have noted a third phase of interaction which we have described as the "morning after" phase (see Chapter 3).

The "morning after" does not necessarily refer only to the actual day after a cycle of wet or drunk interaction, though it is typically set in motion by a "drunk." Rather, it refers to a period of calm and contact in the interaction characterized by an absence of reactivity to pride issues. After the "drunk," the alcoholic typically feels remorse, guilt, and physical depletion. Her defenses are "down" so to speak, and she experiences herself as having been "bad" for a very specific reason—she drank too much. This does not, in her mind, make her a bad or very dependent person, but rather gives her a very concrete reason to experience negative feelings about herself—she had too much to drink. Because she acknowledges her "badness" directly, and suffers so visibly, the spouse can relax his defensive, distant posture and move toward her emotionally. The good guy/bad guy configuration in the relationship is overtly acknowledged and the pride systems of both can relax for a time during which some physical and emotional contact may be permitted. Gradually, the defensive structure of the pride system builds up again in both partners and the relationship shifts back either into a dry phase, which slowly sets the stage for a shift to wet, or directly into a wet phase which may be extreme enough to set the stage for a shift directly into a dry phase with no intervening morning after. The "morning after" phase tends to occur less frequently as the serverity of drinking progresses in most couples—for others it becomes a standard, rigidified response pattern even when drinking is severe and even physical abuse is present. In situations where a male alcoholic abuses the spouse, for instance, it is typical for her to leave or distance temporarily, but compulsively return when he says he's sorry.

It is in the analysis of the wet, dry, and morning after phases that it is possible to elicit the ways in which alcohol has functioned to help the couple "save face" or rather to maintain their pride while still expressing the opposite extreme of their customary behavior. It is important to note that these oscillations typically continue to occur after sobriety without the alcohol as a precipitant. In the postsobriety phase the system continues to oscillate between extremes of behavior since these patterns have become a very sustained part of both the self and the interactional experience in the family.

The first intervention in this phase consists of asking each spouse to list behaviors, both for self and for the partner that characteristically take place during each phase. The therapist may suggest examples, such as, in which phase do/did you express anger, do you feel/act close, do you feel/act more in control, do you have sex, do you not have sex, do you accomplish more tasks, do you worry more? Some phase-related behaviors may be specific and distinct; more often they may tend to blur or overlap. Following is an example of one female co-alcoholic's list—it focuses only on wet and dry phases, since a morning after phase tended not to occur in this particular interaction.

Wet Phase (alcoholic drinking)	Dry Phase (alcoholic not drinking)
My anger is justified.	I feel resentment and anger all of the time, but I try to keep it under control.
I have more power or control over things—I know I have to be in charge.	
	I feel tense about his wanting sex or affection.
I can be more independent—I can do what I want.	I feel more trapped—I feel I have to get his permission for things.
I can make my own decisions.	
I don't have to question myself so much.	He always lets me know what a failure I am.

He doesn't try to tell me what to do with the kids.	There is just a lot of tension.
My fantasies about other men are justified.	He tries to take over things—I feel resentment that the kids cater to him during these times.
I get my own way more.	
Sometimes it feels good just to be able to explode and be angry.	

It is important to remember that the behaviors, feelings, and attitudes described are adaptive reaponses to drinking, not causes of drinking. Issues related to anger, control, lack of differentiation, and competitiveness may well have existed in this marriage from the beginning. They did not cause drinking behavior; rather, drinking became a mechanism for correcting for a discrepant experience of what the marriage "should" be as opposed to what these two partners may really have wanted or desired from the relationship. As the drinking progressed, it became functional in terms of permitting certain behaviors in a pride-saving way, and these behaviors in turn reinforced the drinking. For this woman, her spouse's drinking clearly functioned to provide a justification for anger that may have been unacceptable to acknowledge otherwise; it provided the illusion of independence or separateness, and it conferred a sense of power in the relationship that she could not claim openly.

For another couple, the morning after phase elicited more useful information. Both spouses realized during the course of exploring their adaptive reactions at different points in the oscillating response to drinking behavior that the "morning after" a "drunk" provided a time in which they could experience emotional and sexual intimacy. The husband could allow himself to act emotional, needy, and vulnerable in the guise of "making up." It was as if the drinking created a distance or gap in the relationship during which his "heart could grow fonder" and because of which he needed to make direct and heroic efforts to renew contact. The wife felt she could move toward her husband, relinquishing her anger and distance because "he is needy and being considerate, sorry, and nice." Thus, she could be close to her husband in a face-saving way that released her from her typical stance of overfunctioner or regulator of the moral and emotional environment. For this couple, anger, task focus, and alcohol regulated closeness and helped avoid feelings of dependency and vulnerability. The "morning after" became the only safe, face-saving period in which both could experience intimacy.

Analysis of this type of phase-related information should permit the therapist to identify key behaviors that alcohol permitted or allowed both individuals to engage in without offending their pride. In other words, the abuse of alcohol functioned to permit behaviors in both that the idealized image of self would not normally have allowed. These behaviors would otherwise have been experienced as intolerably incongruent with, or threatening to, the self-image. The goal of treatment in this phase is to help both partners accept the reality of their own needs and behavior and to free them to engage in or change that behavior without the need for alcohol in the system.

Interventions that Rebalance Behavioral Extremes

The pride issues that tend to emerge most consistently in the alcoholic couple and around which behaviors change from phase to phase are control, anger, needing/asking, making mistakes, taking power overtly, and sexuality. These are typically the issues around which the couple is out of balance so that, for instance, one is always making mistakes while the other is "perfect," one has all the overt power while the other has all the covert power, one always pursues sex while the other always rejects it. Both the co-alcoholic and the alcoholic typically take great pride in dry behaviors. These issues often reflect one's experience of self as being consistent with sex role expectations in that a male may experience himself as very "masculine" and a female very "feminine" in a more controlled phase.

The Control Assignment

The question of who controls whom in an alcoholic relationship is a moot one because alcohol controls both people. Overtly, however, the alcoholic may make tenacious demands or bids for control and the spouse may feel "controlled" by her bullying, aggressiveness, guilt-inducing behavior, or other subtle or not so subtle forms of intimidation. The co-alcoholic spouse may feel equally "controlled" by a lack of emotional responsiveness or a concerted refusal to deal with issues or problems. The alcoholic may tend to control in the dry phase to the degree that she is out of control in the wet phase. And in the wet phase, the co-alcoholic may be tightly controlled or indirectly controlling. Frequently, the alcoholic will accuse the co-alcoholic not only of being controlling, but of being controlled. On the surface, a balance typically evolves in which the alcoholic becomes more and more out of control while the co-alcoholic becomes more in control.

These dynamics take place at times in any marriage, but they take place in extreme form in the alcoholic marriage. In postsobriety treatment, control issues need to be made explicit and the couple has to be helped to a more moderate balance in terms of deciding who controls what or whom.

One intervention that is particularly effective in the process of making control issues explicit involves prescribing control—in other words, controlled control. The assignment tends to make the pride issues or anxiety issues underlying controlling behavior accessible to therapeutic work and often makes the "secondary gains" of "being controlled" clear to the couple. The assignment is highly diagnostic and may often prove to be a powerful enough intervention in and of itself to shift the balance of controlling behavior in the relationship.

General instructions given to the couple are as follows:

> Each of you is to take an equal chunk of time. It may be three hours or an entire day of the weekend. For example, one of you take three hours on Saturday, one of you on Sunday. On one day one of you is to be in total control. The other day the other. When it is your day to be in control, you are to take complete charge. You are to issue orders. For example, you are not to ask, "Would you like to go to the Chinese restaurant?" You are to say, "We are going to the Chinese restaurant. I want you to be ready by seven." You may tell the other person what to wear, order food for them, tell him how to behave. Off limits are orders to have sex or to do anything physically hurtful. The other person is to comply, although he is permitted to grumble or be nasty about it. But, he is to do it. On the other day, you reverse the procedure. Each of you is to keep a log of your reactions during both assignments. You are not to share these with each other prior to the session.

No two couples complete this assignment in the same way. Some have great fun with it, others carry it out with grim determination. Some resist it and refuse to do it at all, others comply only minimally. Often, an instant control battle emerges over who will take what chunk of time. The therapist should make it clear that this is a very serious assignment and should track the actual orders and manner in which each spouse has taken control very carefully. Some couples take charge with vindictive delight, others feel hesitant and uncomfortable with being directly controlling. Some spouses clearly try to avoid responsibility for their orders, or they attempt to protect their image of themselves as "not wanting to control another person." They tend to phrase their "orders" in a "Would you mind doing this" manner, seeking approval for the order from the spouse.

Often a more overresponsible spouse finds that she enjoys being controlled and not having to make decisions. Men, in particular, often enjoy the opportunity to be passive since their pride is protected by the structured nature of the assignment. Women often enjoy the opportunity to be overtly controlling without guilt. It is important to discuss reactions to being controlled.

If it becomes clear that control issues are so dominating the relationship, the therapist may inform the couple that he will no longer focus on the content of their interactions, but rather on the overriding issue—who has a right to define the rules of the relationship.

The therapist may develop other techniques for making control issues explicit. Once the couple has recognized the issue in their relationship, the use of reframing helps to depersonalize controlling behavior. For example, one might say to the client; "Every time you see your wife as needing to be in control from now on, I want you to recognize that she is asking you for your protection, that she is frightened of something. Ask her what she is frightened of."

It frequently happens that when the alcoholic sobers up and gets in control, the spouse will develop an eating problem, start drinking too much, or in some other way go out of control. Apart, then, from looking at and correcting the imbalances in the degree to which spouses control each other, it is equally important to correct the degree to which they have self-control. The controlled person needs to be helped to be less in control. The out-of-control person needs to be able to take greater responsibility for self.

People in alcoholic families often suffer from what one alcoholism counselor describes as a "pleasure deficit"—they often have difficulty "letting go," and without the use of substances they cannot "have fun" or be less than compulsively perfect and controlled in most of their behavior. It is helpful to introduce an element of playfulness and fun into therapy. One technique that is useful in either marital or group treatment is to prescribe that the controlled person metaphorically lose control or "not be perfect." Examples might be to require that they come to a session dressed sloppily or in uncoordinated colors, serve a frozen dinner incompletely thawed, or have a temper tantrum. In therapy, group members are frequently asked to come to group in a costume that represents another aspect of their personality. Not surprisingly, one very controlled person complied with the assignment, but appeared as a "perfect" clown with an elaborately designed costume and two perfectly symmetrical red spots on her face.

The person who is out of control is asked to increase his or her level of responsibility by taking charge of areas that he or she doesn't typically take charge of. Issues of control of self versus control of others are always defined and dealt with directly in this phase in contrast with Phase 1 or 2 of treatment in which control issues are more productively reframed or approached from the perspective of the responsibility dimension. This shift is based on the assumption that the pride system evolved around issues of control for both partners must be confronted at this point and that a period of stable sobriety will make that more possible.

Taking Power Overtly

The power issue is closely related to the issue of control, but with some differences. Power is a term that carries more gender-linked connotations, and it relates more to the underlying premises of the relationship about who should have more power than it does to the interactional sequences that are characterized by covert or overt attempts to control self or others. Power basically refers to the politics of the relationship—who gains self or gives it up at whose expense. Power in a relationship tends to be defined by the dictates of the larger social and ethnic context and/or the patterns of the larger family system. Alcohol frequently functions to balance what are perceived to be inappropriate power patterns in a relationship. A traditionally socialized woman, for instance, who may not find it inconsistent with her femininity to be called controlling or manipulative, would be horrified at any suggestion that she wanted power for herself. Yet, frequently, when asked about behaviors permitted by alcohol during the wet phase, women will respond, "Alcohol made me feel powerful," or "His drinking gave me more power and control."

Likewise, a traditionally socialized male might take pride in being perceived as wanting and taking power, but would resent any suggestion that he was manipulative or controlling. Drinking for the male might represent an indirect way of giving up power.

It is traditionally assumed that men should have more power in a relationship than their wives and it is rarely questioned whether or not males really want it. Clearly, men would be reluctant to give up the advantages of power, but frequently they experience the pressures and responsibilities of power as forms of tyranny in themselves. Intensive work with men in a group context often allows them to admit that they would sometimes prefer to be in the dependent, more nurturing role typically assigned to women. However, social pressures related to their work environment and the perceived expectations of women, as well as other men, make it difficult for them to acknowledge these impulses within the context of a relationship.

The abuse of power in alcoholic relationships is often extreme. The degree to which either spouse attempts to assert extremes of power-seeking behavior which intimidate, dominate, manipulate, or control the other is usually related to a more fundamental experience of threat or powerlessness. Inappropriate assertions of power and control are often directed at children and tend to have lasting and damaging effects on parent-child relationships.

Strategic therapists have developed many refined paradoxical techniques for dealing with more covert manifestations of one-up/one-down interactional power imbalances. But, frequently, in alcoholic families the evidence of abusive power relationships is so overt and manifest in sessions that we have found it most efficient and effective to deal with the issues of "who should have power over whom" very directly and explicitly. Two situations occur frequently in our sessions relative to power. The first is that spouses rarely define or think about their interaction in terms of attempts to have power over one another and when this situation is suggested by the therapist, they are very quick to deny that this is their motivation. Since most people do not think of themselves as the kind of person who would attempt to have power over another person, they will quickly respond to the therapist's suggestions about how to achieve their goals more diplomatically, and their energies shift to behaviors in which they experience power as the capacity to prove that they do not want to be powerful.

This kind of cognitive and behavioral shift must be accompanied by a thorough exploration of underlying feelings of being out of control, threatened, frightened, and angry. The couple must be helped to define what rules regarding power they want in their relationship.

A second frequently occurring situation is that people assume that having power over their children is their right and responsibility as a parent, even if it is abusive. In this case, it is useful to teach basic parenting skills and to discuss intergenerational patterns of power that influence how the person experienced her role in her family of origin.

In general, it is important to relate discussions about rebalancing power to the larger social context, since most assumptions about power in families are directly influenced by cultural sex-role stereotypes.

Specific changes may be suggested to change power balances. For instance, a woman may be told to open her own checking or savings account or to take more responsibility for financial planning in the family. The male may be asked to take more control over parenting and decisions regarding children. Any shifts that couples have already effected in the distribution of power are sanctioned. Often couples who have made such changes begin to experience themselves as isolated from friends, neighbors, or family who continue to function more traditionally. One woman who had a highly competitive and demanding job in a growing corporation constantly faced envious teasing from her co-workers about her husband whose less high-powered job allowed him to assume more of the traditionally female responsibilities. He rearranged his schedule frequently to care for their young daughter and became the primary nurturer when his wife went on business trips. He supported and encouraged her growth in the company and felt untroubled by her higher salary. The woman's professional colleagues, most of whom were unmarried, kept insisting that she "made him up"—no such man could really exist. In fact, he did exist, but their relationship obviously represented a type of "deviance" from traditional expectations and tended to set the woman apart as "different" in her work context. The good-natured teasing seemed to represent a collective discomfort with such a radical departure from traditional power balances.

It is increasingly true that women are becoming more aware of their desire for power and it is also true that they would not always care to have the responsibility that goes with it. In marriages where women do work, it is often still assumed that the male has the primary financial responsibility for the family and that the woman is working because she wants to and, therefore, has the choice not to. The therapist should take the strong position that people can't have it both ways—if they want the power they must accept the attendant responsibilities. For certain couples, some consciousness-raising is accomplished by assigning or recommending the reading of such texts as *The Cinderella Complex* (Dowling, 1981) or *The Hazards of Being Male* (Goldberg, 1976).

Another potential and often very fruitful intervention is to suggest that the couple totally shift responsibilities for two weeks, particularly if the wife works, and note reactions. Inconvenience should not be accepted as an excuse for not attempting this exercise. Beyond its potential for promoting gender empathy, this assignment often results in a realization of both a competence for and an enjoyment of the other spouse's traditional gender role.

The bottom line in working with power issues in Phase 3 is that power be overtly owned and acknowledged mutually. Some couples are neither willing nor able to make gender role related shifts in their interactional patterns, but sobriety stands a much better chance of being sustained if both spouses can agree on the issue of who has power in what area over whom. Covert or indirect bids for power which typically manifest themselves in highly confused reactive or vindictive "schizophrenogenic" communicational patterns will almost always result in a return to drinking behavior.

Power and Limitation

Kurtz's concept of "essential limitation," discussed in Chapter 3, underlies all discussion of power issues as they relate to the alcoholic and the system in which he operates. Often, as Kurtz points out, the alcoholic experiences power as the power of no limitations. A better word for it might be grandiosity—the power that is "out of control" through the mistaken belief in "unlimited control." As indicated in Figure 3–2, p. 46, both the alcoholic and others in the alcoholic system seem to reach a point at which they begin to lose the recognition of their own limitations, begin to ascribe "good luck" to something under their control, begin to feel that they can climb all mountains, conquer all obstacles. They essentially forget that they are limited.

The person who suffers from these ideas of his own power may or may not try to assert that power over other people. But there are other ways in which forgetting one's limitations is damaging. A person who does not consider himself limited is vulnerable to becoming a "workaholic" who ignores his body's need for rest and in myriad ways attempts the impossible, perhaps achieving it for a period of time. But even the attempt, let alone the achievement, will inevitably lead to a return to the state of powerlessness. Unfortunately, this return is not usually so simple as the individual's recognition that he is, in fact, limited. Rather, it takes getting drunk, or having a rage, or developing physical symptoms to convince the person that he is not all-powerful.

The first step of the AA program is an intended correction for what Bateson would call an incorrect epistemology. The first step of AA refers to powerlessness over alcohol and the first step of the Al-Anon program refers to powerlessness over the alcoholic. The AA step states: "We admitted we were powerless over alcohol—that our lives had become unmanageable." In therapy, it is helpful to build and expand the notion of powerlessness to include many other areas of the client's life. The important concept is that control over one's life is truly an illusion. This is not to suggest that one shouldn't attempt to control or take responsibility for what one can. The AA Serenity Prayer makes this point succinctly:

> God grant me the serenity to accept the things I cannot change, the courage to change the things I can, and the wisdom to know the difference.

Commonly this prayer is interpreted in AA to mean that one has to accept other people and circumstances, but one can change oneself. It is hoped that as an alcoholic progresses in sobriety, she will also progress in "wisdom" and will bring more areas under the rubric of "things she can change." In the beginnings of sobriety, however, she is strongly and well-advised not to try to change much except her own attitude.

Most clients relate rather easily to the concepts detailed in Figure 3–2. They can be asked to devise methods for keeping themselves and their behavior in the "middle" or "not God" range, avoiding both grandiosity (a sense of unlimited power) and self-loathing (a sense of total powerlessness). Often, if they are in AA or Al-Anon, it is helpful to examine how they work the program, since the program stresses precisely these issues.

Many clients have direct and tragic experience of the illusion of control in their lives. One group member spent much of her energy trying to control her seventeen-year-old alcoholic son. The son unpredictably, and without her doing, "found Jesus" and through religion got sober. That same summer her daughter, twenty-two, enormously talented and never a problem, was brutally raped and murdered by an unknown assailant.

Clients need help in identifying the areas where they are most likely to become "out of control" because they erroneously assume they have unlimited control. In one situation, a client had managed to get the control and power balances in his marriage well in hand. The therapist was surprised when he started to drink again. As he described his situation it became clear that he had transferred his belief in being able to control everything from his marriage to his work, and had been totally incapable of setting limits for himself. The drunk or relapse made the limits necessary. The alcohol had functioned in this case to help correct the erroneous self-perception of having unlimited control, or conversely of being completely controlled by the demands of work.

The client was, consequently, given a therapy appointment in the middle of the day, despite his protests that he couldn't take time off from work. This "gimmick" helped him to set priorities, examine his expectations of himself, and to take responsibility for arranging his time in a more realistic way.

As a part of therapy in this phase, clients need to develop an awareness of their personal limitations and to assess realistically the limits imposed in general by life circumstances, their lifestyle choice, and ultimately, by the reality of death.

Needing/Asking

Dependency has long been viewed as a central psychodynamic factor in the abuse of alcohol. Often, it does not appear to be the case that alcoholics are inherently more dependent or unable to cope with their lives than other people, but rather that they have greater difficulty acknowledging and accepting their dependency needs. They tend to be engaged in a continual struggle to deny the ways in which they truly are dependent while demanding help or attention in areas in which they would find themselves to be perfectly competent to function without help.

Often, relationships in alcoholic systems are characterized by an absence of directness about what one spouse or family member wants from another. To ask is tantamount to admitting one's dependency and both the alcoholic and the co-alcoholic have difficulty with this "admission."

The co-alcoholic typically finds his or her own dependency masked by the more overt dependency of the alcoholic. In other words, he or she avoids feeling needy by being needed. In the alcoholic, dependency is couched in the form of demands. While the co-alcoholic has great difficulty asking for anything, sometimes because her needs have gone ignored for so long, the alcoholic acts entitled or gets drunk to pull for attention, but is fiercely resentful of any suggestion that he is dependent or needy. The alcoholic typically resents what appears to be the co-alcoholic's self-sufficiency and will frequently make attempts to get the co-alcoholic to admit need or to become emotionally reactive or out of control.

The following transcript is a segment of a therapy session with Patrick and Sheila, who are living separately at this point, but are in therapy to try to work on their marriage. Patrick is a recovering alcoholic who has been having periodic "slips."

PATRICK: We had another thing the other night at the train station.

THERAPIST: What was the thing?

PATRICK: I happened to be coming in from Washington and got off the train the same time my son was coming from college and I was in the smoking car and he was in the nonsmoking, and we met at the train station.

THERAPIST: Right.

PATRICK: Sheila was picking him up.

THERAPIST: Uh huh.

PATRICK: When she saw me there, she riled. What was I, a piece of garbage? I should take a cab or something? You were coming to pick him up. That just bugged the hell out of you that I was there. I should have turned around and said, "Well, you guys go, I'll walk," or some nonsense.

THERAPIST: I'm confused. You're not living with her anymore. What was your expectation, that she would give you a ride?

PATRICK: Yeah [*high-pitched voice*]. Cause I'm there.

THERAPIST: Why should she?

PATRICK: I'm talking to my son and she's coming to pick him up [*raised voice*].

THERAPIST: So?

PATRICK: So [*loudly*]?

THERAPIST: Why should she give you a ride home? She's not living with you.

PATRICK: She's my wife [*emphasis*]. That's my son. We're attending therapy together. Why the hell couldn't she give me a ride home?

THERAPIST: Did you ask her?

PATRICK: I ask her [*incredulous*]?

THERAPIST: Ask.

PATRICK: [*loudly astounded*] Ask? Ask for a ride home?

THERAPIST: Yes, humble yourself.

PATRICK: [*laughter*] I said, can you open the door of the car?

THERAPIST: You know what I'm saying, don't you, Sheila?

SHEILA: That's what I was mad at. He took advantage every single time.

THERAPIST: Humble yourself. Ask.

PATRICK: [*high-pitched voice*] Ask what? I mean I, I, I . . .

THERAPIST: Ask Sheila.

PATRICK: Would you give me a ride home? In the car that I'm paying for, and you're here and I'm here?

THERAPIST: Right, that's right.
PATRICK: I don't buy that. I can't buy that.
THERAPIST: I know.

As Patrick puts it, Sheila gets "riled" when he wants a ride. Her pride is invested in being giving so she gets angry when she is confronted with a situation in which she has to say "no," because that makes her look like a bad person.

Patrick, on the other hand, is outraged at the suggestion that he should have to ask for the ride. The idea of asking is humiliating to him because it represents an admission that he does not have the power in the relationship. He continually asserts that power in the face of increasing evidence that he has lost that power with his wife. His reminders to her that it is "his car" that he "paid for" are again assertions of power coming from a man who feels truly powerless.

In the alcoholic interaction, pride prevents people from communicating directly because they have to hide the true nature of the communication from themselves and from the other person. If Patrick were to "ask" Sheila directly for something he would be admitting that in this instance he needed something from her, that she was "one-up" in the relationship. This admission would assault his pride in being the more powerful partner.

Anger and Dependency

Much of the anger, rage, and abuse that is predominant in an alcoholic relationship results from the uncomfortable experience of oneself as dependent, and therefore powerless or out of control. Expressions of rage, bullying, intimidation, or acting out help the client to avoid the intolerable experience of asking for what one wants. More to the point, the self-experience represented by asking is intolerable—that is, that of being weak, limited, and "one-down" to the person one is asking of. This rage at being dependent is aptly illustrated in the following short segment of transcript of a recovering alcoholic who was asked to visit his mother's grave and to pour a bottle of vodka on it because he was having trouble staying sober. His flair for the dramatic prompted him to record his reaction:

SPENCER: So, you bitch, so you controlled my life. You made me into a little robot and I became a robot. Only I've fucked you up since. I've become a boozer, an alcoholic, and I'm going to pour the goddamn vodka right down your fucking throat, right now. [*He proceeded to empty two bottles of vodka on her grave.*]

The therapist's hypothesis was that Spencer's anger had been repressed as part of his unresolved mourning for his mother, and that repressed anger was the most frequent psychological trigger for his drinking episodes. Her intent in coaching this visit to the cemetery (Betty and Norman Paul, 1975) was to encourage the mourning process to emerge and thus to allow Spencer greater access to the anger. Following the cemetery visits, he was increasingly able to recognize how his anger was often directed at his wife and he sometimes could avert a drinking episode.

Another male alcoholic sought treatment with concerns over his sexuality. He was an ex-marine who bragged in the first session about wanting to cry for his mother, but not doing it, when he was shot in the leg during his stay in Viet Nam.

It is crucially important to sustained sobriety that partners in a relationship be helped to achieve a more functional balance around issues of dependency. A basic premise for treatment is to assume that all people are interdependent, and that interconnectedness is a more accurate epistemological framework than absolute self-reliance or absolute independence. The steps to rebalancing along this axis of the relationship may include the following:

1. Breaking down isolation from extended family and other potential support systems—encouraging active involvement with AA or Al-Anon.
2. Intensive work on recognition of feelings and development of alternate ways to express anger. One can ask or identify needs only on the basis of accurate data about self in the feeling dimension.
3. Work with the alcoholic to be more independent and to admit dependency where indicated without defensiveness. Work with the co-alcoholic to act less rigidly self-sufficient and to acknowledge dependency.
4. Rebalancing the interaction by coaching the co-alcoholic to ask the alcoholic to meet his needs. The alcoholic's defensiveness will be greatly tempered by this "equalization" of acknowledged neediness.

In initial work with one couple, the wife was told that whenever her husband was having a rage, it probably meant that he was feeling needy. She was coached to approach him by saying, "I love you—what's really bothering you?" She was very vocal in her resistance to this suggestion because she felt a need to assert her moral "rightness" and to control the interaction. When she was faced with the choice either to resolve the interaction or to "be right" in an out-of-control, negative way, however, she complied with great success. Her pride was invested in seeing herself as someone who would work to resolve the relationship. This intervention, of course, forced her to meet his dependency need without his having to ask. Later the therapist worked with the husband to be more direct about his needs. Both parts of this particular interaction needed to change, however, and the greater motivational leverage initially was with the co-alcoholic. Eventually she also was coached to "be needy" and ask her husband to take care of her in some way.

Frequently, the dependency issues of both spouses can be addressed by prescribing a weekend totally alone for each. It is surprising to discover how few people have ever spent this much time completely away from other people or from their spouse. People tend to emerge from such an experience with a renewed sense of their own inner resources and competence and, paradoxically, this allows them to be more accepting of their dependency. One client, a successful doctor, was delighted to learn for the first time, for instance, that he really could light the gas stove by himself.

Right Makes Might—The Need for Self-Justification

The drinking alcoholic typically tends to externalize responsibility for her own negative behavior onto the co-alcoholic, or in lieu of that option, onto any one of a number of people, events, or circumstances in an attempt to avoid responsibility for her own feelings, needs, and behavior. Because the co-alcoholic tends to internalize blame and responsibility for everybody else's needs, he is typically highly reactive to the alcoholic's accusations. In other words, on one level the co-alcoholic believes that he must be doing something wrong, but because it is intolerable actually to acknowledge that, he fights, justifies, and defends his position, and develops a rigid posture of "rightness" or self-justification.

These dynamics continue in more subtle form after sobriety. They are more threatening to the stability of the marriage after sobriety precisely because there is no longer alcohol in the picture to help absorb the blows to pride. The co-alcoholic can no longer point the finger at the "bad" alcoholic, at least not for his drinking. And the alcoholic can no longer use alcohol to either deaden his feelings or to provide punishment for his sense of guilt.

Frequently, in this phase of sobriety, the co-alcoholic tries with an almost desperate intensity to continue to prove that the alcoholic is the "bad" one. While the alcoholic may try her best to address some of the damage caused by the drinking or to take responsibility where she previously did not, the co-alcoholic is often relentless either in denying change or finding something else wrong. The co-alcoholic is particularly vulnerable at this point to any suggestion that he makes mistakes or has negative input into the interactional dynamics. In therapy, the co-alcoholic will try to find an ally in the therapist and will typically be very reactive to any perception that the therapist is "siding with" or "coddling" the alcoholic.

One client whose husband had been sober for two years had an ongoing struggle with him over whether or not she was "justified" in wanting to spend an "evening out with the girls" at a bar. The husband objected strenuously to her choice of activity. She justified her choice based on her enjoyment of dancing, something the husband refused to do. She also countered that he had spent inordinate amounts of time in bars and she didn't understand why there should be a double standard. She wasn't interested in meeting other men, so that his anxiety on that score, according to her, was unfounded and there was no reason for her to give up doing something she enjoyed. The argument was chronic in the relationship and threatened to push the couple toward a separation. The wife's major concern in therapy was to find reinforcement for her belief that she was right or *justified* in her desire to do something for herself. Any exploration of the possibility that she might not be "justified" only stepped up her defense of her position, the same interaction that occurred with her husband. The client was also unable to recognize the way in which her choice of activity represented a "you can't tell me what to do" statement quite similar to the effect of her husband's drinking behavior presobriety. As is very typical, the reciprocity in the relationship had reversed itself so that she had become the acting-out, underresponsible one while he now became righteous and morally superior.

The therapist finally defined the problem as one that had to do with her intense need to be "right" rather than simply responsible for her behavior and its effects on the relationship. Once the client could accept that behaviors and feelings weren't right or wrong, but rather that they either helped or hindered a relationship between two people, she felt more willing to negotiate a compromise with her husband. She began to realize that much of her reactivity to his "put-downs" was related to her need to be viewed as right, good, pure of motive. As she accepted the possibility that his view of her as right or wrong didn't necessarily make her right or wrong, it became possible for her to listen to his feelings and concerns without allowing them to represent such an intense affront to her pride.

Both partners in a relationship need to work on their tendency to self-justify at this phase in treatment. But in addition, because the alcoholic's "bad" behavior and mistakes have been so glaring in contrast to the "good" behavior of the co-alcoholic, it is helpful in rebalancing the relationship to encourage the co-alcoholic to make mistakes. This represents a direct, yet paradoxical, challenge to the pride of the co-alcoholic because it forces him to be wrong, but within a context of being "right" for complying with the assignment. The purpose of the technique is to encourage more flexibility and to begin to detoxify some of the pride issues.

Some clients work at this assignment quite half-heartedly while others, in their zeal to be "perfect" clients, outdo themselves:

Jill had twice married alcoholics and twice divorced them. She was married for the third time to another co-alcoholic, a man who had divorced his alcoholic wife. She was experiencing the usual battles with the stepchildren and making the usual mistakes about believing the myth that the remarried family can be just like any other family. Her husband, long used to having the control of the co-alcoholic in his own first marriage, was equally unable to relinquish it. Someone had to give. Jill was asked to go home and make a mistake and allow herself to be caught by her husband and stepchildren. Her first response was to say, "I can't think of any mistake I could make." This is a typical response and clearly indicates how strong the pride system is. She was encouraged to use her creativity, praised for her intelligence, and told that the therapist was sure that she could come up with something. When she came in, she gave the following report. "I served raw shrimp for dinner. I'm used to Japanese food and can eat shrimp raw. But, my husband made several comments such as "Do you always cook them this way?" and "Is this a new recipe? I don't believe I've ever had them like this." His pride in never criticizing Jill stopped him from directly saying, "I think you forgot to cook the shrimp." The children, however, were quite amused and made comments about how the dinner was going to swim off the table. Finally, Jill, in mock horror, said, "Oh my God, I forgot to cook the shrimp. How stupid of me."

Jill never told her family that the mistake was deliberate. The experience of being caught in a mistake that made her look foolish was emotionally corrective in that she realized that she didn't need to function perfectly in order to maintain a sense of her own integrity and that other people didn't immediately take vindictive delight in her mistake.

Both alcoholics and co-alcoholics are frequently coached simply to agree when a spouse is very invested in proving them wrong or bad. This technique helps break the symmetrical interaction that typically occurs in the relationship and provides an opportunity for more productive patterns of interaction to emerge.

Finally, when one spouse continues to be invested in seeing the other as bad or is unable to let go of an issue unless the other admits he's wrong and is suitably punished, it is often helpful simply to confront the client with a choice: "Which do you want more—for her to be adequately punished for his behavior or to have the marriage work out? You can't have both." This choice needs to be stated in different ways and repeated frequently, always in concert with family-of-origin work on issues related to anger, trust, and fear. Frequently, when the person who "thirsts for justice" stops insisting that the alcoholic be punished, she experiences intensely painful memories of having been very unjustly accused or punished herself for being unable or unwilling to respond to the inappropriate demands of a (sometimes) alcoholic parent (see Chapter 10).

Sexuality in the Alcoholic Relationship

Some couples in alcoholic systems have maintained an active and satisfying sex life throughout the drinking phase, but this is not the norm. More typically, sex has been absent from the relationship for a considerable period of time and frequently a poor sex life is viewed as one of the factors precipitating the drinking. The wife in a relationship with a male alcoholic is often accused of being "frigid" or inadequate to meet her husband's needs. She, on the other hand, will often accuse him of being uninterested in sex, or of "treating her like an object." Both partners tend to express dissatisfaction with the other's sexual performance. Sometimes alcohol permits more relaxed expression of sexuality in a marriage for both male and female drinkers. Ultimately, however, the consequences of increased alcohol consumption tend to deaden all desire for sex and to increase the physical and emotional distance in the marriage.

The first step in treating sexual dysfunction in an alcoholic relationship is to normalize it by pointing out that most couples have some sexual difficulties and that alcohol has some very specific physiological effects on sexual functioning. Frequently, men experience impotence either prior to or after sobriety.

Ethnic and religious conditioning regarding sex are both important factors to discuss. The sexual self-experience of each spouse is highly dependent on the messages each received as a result of living in a particular family and the cultural and religious values that family communicated. Frequently, if two people from very diverse backgrounds in terms of the messages communicated about sex are involved in a relationship, they give one another feedback that may contradict or challenge deeply held convictions about sex. This gives rise to fear and a sense of inadequacy in particularly vulnerable areas of self-experience.

The use of alcohol in itself tends to distort one's experience of sexuality. Often, people who had a fairly clear sense of their sexuality before drinking alcoholically find themselves in sobriety to be totally confused about their sexual needs. The process of disintegration of the relationship precipitated by drinking renders the couple's sex life a battleground and sexuality tends to become more associated with pain than with pleasure. Individuals often need to reexplore their own attitudes and feelings about their sexuality before any interactional work can be suggested.

Finally, it is often the case that sexual issues in an alcoholic relationship express deep conflicts related, again, to sex role issues. Frequently, the male in the relationship (whether alcoholic or co-alcoholic) prefers the more passive role sexually, or he prefers a more emotional approach to sex. He may be more fastidious about sex, or have a greater discomfort about sexuality than his wife. The wife, on the other hand, may enjoy sex for the sake of sex, not needing the emotional closeness that is typically a more female request. Alcohol has often helped to blur or avoid these differences from traditional gender conditioning and has thus helped to salvage the pride of both partners.

Anne and Larry came into therapy after Anne had been sober for approximately six years. The presenting problem was their youngest son's irresponsibility and incipient drug abuse. Once the adolescent boy's problem was resolved, which was achieved over the course of several months by helping Anne and Larry to relinquish their over-responsibility, the focus of treatment shifted to the marriage.

Anne was very active in AA. Larry was overinvolved in his corporation and even when away from work, like so many co-alcoholics, focused almost compulsively on tasks around the house. Their sexual relationship was minimal and, interestingly, Anne rather than Larry, was the more dissatisfied. They had essentially maintained a fixed emotional distance. With the resolution of the youngest son's problem and his removal from the triangle, achieving some intimacy in the marriage received more priority.

In one session, the therapist showed Anne and Larry several pictures of couples making love and asked them each to select a picture which appealed to them. Anne chose one that showed a woman resting, presumably after orgasm, and commented on the wonderful release of physical tension the picture signified. Larry was quite reactive to her selection. To him, making love was an emotional, not a physical act. To Anne it was more physical. A further exploration of their attitudes confirmed that Anne's attitude was the more stereotypically male one whereas Larry's was stereotypically female. Permission to express attitudes that were not congruent with their sex role socialization was crucial in helping this couple begin to resolve their difficulties.

It is crucial to explore these attitudes about sexuality and to normalize more "female" preferences in the male and more "male" preferences in the female. The bottom line in dealing with sexual issues as they relate to alcoholism is to deal with guilt—the experience of self as being not right, not adequate, or not "normal" within the context of socially defined roles about who a person is, how he should act, and what he should feel. Once these issues are addressed, the therapy of sexual dysfunction is accomplished consistently with techniques outlined by Helen Singer Kaplan (1974) and other practitioners specializing in the treatment of sexual dysfunction.

Alcohol and Incest

Boundaries around sexuality often become highly diffuse in an alcoholic system as the drinker goes to greater and greater lengths to correct a sense of his or her sexual or personal inadequacy. While many alcoholics, male or female, may resort to affairs outside the marriage, incestuous relationships with children in the family tend to provide a sexual outlet without imposing the pressures of needing to feel adequate to meet adult sexual demands. Males, in particular, tend to engage in incestuous interactions because (1) they tend to feel less responsible for the parental or nurturing function with a child; (2) they are more invested in feeling powerful in the realm of their sexuality; (3) their dependency is less socially sanctioned in adulthood, and, consequently, rage toward the female for not "mothering" them is intense. An incestuous relationship is one way of "getting back at" an unresponsive and therefore "more powerful" wife. Finally, alcohol breaks down boundaries and provides inaccurate feedback to the self about the self. When one is drinking, any behavior can be rationalized.

In some families, incest is more covert than overt. Fathers may develop flirtatious, overly close relationships with daughters; mothers may do the same with sons. Boundaries defining who may have what kind of physical contact with whom are often absent in the family and either parent may be overly affectionate, overly physical, intrude on the child's privacy, or not maintain sufficient physical privacy him- or herself. Such a covert incestuous relationship with a child often represents an attempt to anger the distant spouse or to create jealousy. Such triangling of a child into the marital relationship always represents the spouse's attempt to gain power in the face of the experience that the other spouse has more power by virtue of being emotionally and physically unavailable and unresponsive.

Overt incest always represents a crisis in a family and must be stopped by whatever means necessary when presented as an issue in the course of treatment. In general, boundaries in the family need to be more clearly defined, and issues of power versus intimacy in the marriage need to be addressed.

Reestablishing Intimacy

Finally, to make a broad generalization, it is typically the case that even after sobriety alcoholic couples may never desire or achieve a significant degree of emotional or physical intimacy. The therapist must be cautious about imposing his or her own values regarding how much intimacy in a family or relationship is either desirable or possible. Frequently, people in alcoholic systems fear intimacy intensely. It is common that their own family backgrounds include situations in which they experienced either an overly close relationship with a same or opposite sex parent in which self-boundaries were never adequately experienced, or, conversely, they experienced a highly distant or conflicted relationship in which the reality of emotional neglect or abuse left them unable to trust sufficiently to allow emotional closeness.

While this is not to say that greater intimacy cannot be achieved for couples who desire it, it is a statement of caution regarding therapeutic expectations.

Our belief is that work at rebalancing the structure of the relationship as outlined in this chapter sets the stage for more open and clear communication about rules and expectations in the relationship. These techniques must be used in conjunction with work on family-of-origin patterns if the greater differentiation required for more sustained intimacy is to be achieved. Finally, true intimacy suggests shared behavior at many different levels in a relationship so that, again, couples and families frequently need very direct coaching aimed at teaching them how to share activities such as recreational time, for instance. It is important to encourage self-directed activity that can then be shared with a partner. This encouragement of self-focus represents effective work on intimacy since an enhanced sense of self will typically free the individual to communicate and share more openly and with less fear.

Once alcohol has been eliminated from the family environment and once many of the issues specific to alcoholic interaction have been addressed, work at establishing greater intimacy can proceed in the same way that it might for any couple in treatment with similar difficulties.

Achieving Correct Complementarity

To repeat our general assumptions, in order to maintain sobriety, couples in this phase must be helped to achieve a more correctly complementary balance in the areas where their behavior occurs at reciprocal extremes.

Techniques suggested in this chapter, along with the arsenal of tools already developed by both alcoholism counselors and family therapists, are directed at helping the couple to achieve this balance both intrapsychically and interactionally. A relationship that continues to be balanced around either complementary extremes or symmetrical struggle where true equality is neither tolerated nor perceived as possible is one in which either drinking will recur or symptoms will emerge in other family members.

"Correct complementarity" refers to a relationship in which rules are overt, acknowledged, and agreed to by both parties, and in which dependency is mutual, acknowledged, and responded to by both partners. Role reciprocity in the relationship is flexible and balanced in the interests of both individuals given specific needs and specific sets of circumstances.

Summary—Treatment Phases 2 and 3

Treatment of alcohol problems in postsobriety, Phase 2, is focused on the following goals:

1. Work to stabilize the system.
2. Address individual issues of family members more than interactional ones—stress self-focus.
3. Anticipate and predict reactions to sobriety related to loss of role, fear of relapse.
4. Begin to teach new behavioral skills for coping with stress and conflict.
5. Make minor structural changes that will ensure at least minimally adequate parenting.

The emphasis in Phase 2 treatment is to help the family react to the "crisis of sobriety." Therapy is directed at stabilizing the family as it seeks to acquire and adjust to new roles while blocking its tendency to return to dysfunctional patterns that may cause relapse or promote a shift of focus to another symptom in the family.

Goals for Phase 3 treatment include the following:

1. Help the marital partners and family members to achieve a balance in reciprocal role behavior that is less extreme and more flexible.
2. Resolve issues of power and control.
3. Address the pride issues and presobriety adaptive behaviors of family members so that new patterns of interaction and self experience can occur without the need for alcohol.

4. Help the couple or family to achieve whatever level of intimacy is desirable for them.

The focus of Phase 3 treatment is maintenance of sobriety in the family and long-term prevention of alcoholism in other family members. Treatment is based on the assumption that role behavior in the presobriety phase evolved into rigid, complementary and symmetrical extremes that maintained the need for alcohol to correct discrepant experiences of self. Treatment in this phase is directed at helping the family to find a corrective or more "true" balance in its interaction that eliminates the need to bolster false self-images with the use of alcohol.

CHAPTER 8

Pride and Paradox
Dealing with Resistance to Change

IN WORKING with alcoholic systems, many clinicians and researchers, including Sharon Wegscheider (1981), Claudia Black (1981), and Janet Woititz (1983), have identified general characteristics or personality traits common to people in alcoholic systems. The self-experience and behavior of individuals in response to alcohol abuse within a system tend to assume somewhat predictable and generalizable patterns. Roles and behavior become fixed and tend to be repetitively consistent even if alcohol is not part of the current reality of the client.

A major emphasis in our work has been an attempt to identify the characteristic emotional, behavioral, and interactional patterns of alcohol-involved people—in short, the factors that form the basic building blocks of the pride structure. Life in an alcoholic system may be experienced as so chaotic and unpredictable that the behaviors and self-experience people evolve become more rigidly entrenched in defense of a very deeply experienced and reality-based sense of vulnerability and threat. Roles that people assume are survival roles, and pride is a tool of survival in the face of overwhelming feelings of helplessness and loss of control. Change involves helping clients to replace pride, rigidity, and dysfunctional roles with a more realistic assessment of their own capabilities and with the ability to discriminate real threat in the environment from feared threat.

The clinician must have a thorough understanding of the pride structure of each client before he can either use it or dismantle it in the interests of change. While an assessment of pride dynamics and characteristics is an ongoing part of our work, we have been able to make the following *broad* generalizations with regard to the characteristic patterns of women and men in specific categories of alcohol involvement and their most typical reactions to treatment.

While all clients present problems and characteristics unique to themselves, these descriptions are presented to suggest the more typical patterns, roles, and self-experience that seem to emerge in response to alcoholic interaction in a family. These descriptive passages are not meant to imply a linear, cause-effect analysis of individual role behaviors, but in the interests of conciseness they may be presented in more or less linear terms. It is important to bear in mind that behavior and self-experience evolve in response to the entire range of interactional feedback that occurs in a system and that the characteristic behaviors outlined here both affect and are affected by the total systemic dynamic.

Female Roles and Pride

The Alcoholic Woman

The woman who becomes alcoholic may have experienced one of two possible roles in her family of origin. Either she was an overresponsible daughter who assumed an emotional and functional caretaking role with parent or siblings, or she operated in a highly underresponsible fashion while one or both parents overfunctioned for her.

For the woman who was overresponsible either emotionally or functionally or both, alcohol usually functioned to permit a release from overfocus on others. Alcohol may have become a mechanism for self-gratification—an attempt to meet personal needs that were never adequately responded to by parents. The woman in this position may have used alcohol to permit underresponsible behavior, to express anger and rebellion, and to provide an outlet for sexuality in the face of intense fears of intimacy. Her typical self-experience is one of emptiness, valuelessness, and anger. She may experience herself as unimportant except in the service of other people's needs and she often experiences intense conflict between needs for approval that result in overly compliant behavior and a desire to express anger and overt rebellion. Frequently, her overfocus on others has created a binding type of dependency in which she may function very competently, yet feel unable to separate herself from her family because she has so poorly established a sense of herself. In most cases, she is an oldest daughter, has usually felt the need to form an intense alliance with one parent against the other (often the alcoholic in the system), and may often have had male siblings who were considered to be more important while expected to be less responsible then the females in the family.

During recovery, this type of client reverts back to her overresponsible mode of functioning. She feels intense guilt and shame about her drinking and may attempt to make up for it by becoming a "perfect" AA member, wife, or mother. She often begins to overfunction again for her children and may unwittingly set the stage for their alcoholism.

In treatment, in contrast to the co-alcoholic who may take false "pride" in her ability to be rigidly in control, the recovering alcoholic woman in this category has already experienced a loss of competence through her drinking. She is usually able to laugh at herself, admit weakness, and is less resistant to work on her overresponsibility than the co-alcoholic. She has less to lose. She usually responds well to attempts to help her to be appropriately angry. She is most emphatically a woman in search of self and finds suggestions and interventions designed to teach alternative role behaviors helpful. She needs a great deal of support and reality-based intervention to help reverse her low and sometimes nonexistent opinion of herself.

The second category of potential family-of-origin patterns affecting the alcoholic woman involves overfunctioning parents who may have been both functionally and emotionally overresponsible for their daughter so that her alcoholic drinking became an expression of continued underresponsibility and underdeveloped coping skills in either the functional or emotional dimension. The parents alternatively may have overfunctioned for their daughter because she was female, but demanded emotional focus on their own emotional or social needs and expectations. (It is important to note here that in all categories these family-of-origin patterns may have involved extended family members and other dysfunctional patterns of triangulation or generational boundary violations—for instance, the grandmother or aunt who overindulges the child against the wishes of the parent.)

This type of client was singled out and defined as "special," often by her father. She may be an only daughter, a youngest daughter, or an only child. If her parents were overresponsible in both dimensions, she experiences herself as incompetent to deal responsibly with her life. She is angry that in adult life she is not viewed as special and is expected to function for herself. She views herself as entitled to caretaking and special consideration in all aspects of her life on the one hand, while on some deeper level she feels "false" or fraudulent and unconvinced that the attention that was lavished on her reflected her own value as a person. Frequently, the latter assessment is accurate since the parents' behavior usually reflected their need to enhance their own feelings about self. The child's real needs may have been neglected. Drinking now provides her with an outlet for her rage, an experience of pseudo-independence, an alternative to responsible behavior, and an equalizing solution to anxiety raised by the conflicting messages about self communicated by her parents' overresponsibility.

On a more fundamental level, drinking may have helped avoid questions about her status and role as a female, since issues of dependency versus autonomy could never adequately be resolved while her family continued to maintain her in a dependent role.

Alcoholic women who function at an extreme of underresponsibility or who tend to be functionally underresponsible in their family of origin tend to express overt anger while drinking and tend to feel deprived, exploited, and betrayed by others in the early phases of sobriety. In general, in treatment they are more defiance-based than their overresponsible counterparts. In early sobriety they tend to be predominantly underresponsible emotionally rather than reverting to overresponsible behavior, and they continue to look to others to meet their needs, frequently feeling angry and vindictive when others don't respond. If they are mothers, they often resent the demands of their children and tend to be less than adequately responsible emotionally in the parental role. They often have divorced or separated from their husbands and find their relationships with men highly conflicted. A theme of wanting, demanding, or expecting something from others dominates their emotional life and their pride issues revolve around their sense of being "right" in their assessment of the failings and shortcomings of others. This "rightness," of course, serves to protect the underlying sense of fraudulence or "wrongness" that they experience about themselves. In treatment, they tend to be distrustful of the therapist or group, and often express anger covertly by missing appointments. They tend to be demanding and seemingly needy of time and attention and are frequently in a state of chronic crisis in their emotional relationships with spouse, children, employers. Often they directly or indirectly plead for help with a problem and then refuse to take the suggestion of the therapist or group members. They are intent on proving that no one can really help them and set themselves up to be rejected at the same time that they verbalize feelings that they are unliked by or are somehow inferior to others.

Whether the treatment structure is the family, individual sessions, or a group, the task is calmly and consistently to expect the client to take responsible positions regarding her own feelings and needs. Pride reactions can be circumvented with humor, by agreeing with the client that she can't trust anybody and nobody likes her, and predicting that she will ask for "answers" about what she should do only to resist doing it. Frequently, it is helpful to tell the client, "I will give you the 'answer' only if you promise before you hear it to do exactly what I tell you." This technique is useful in making the paradox overt—the client will rarely promise to do what is suggested so she rarely gets answers. This kind of work must be undertaken with care and with the therapist's thorough understanding of the pride paradox the client presents.

If the therapist responds directly with help, concern, or answers, the client is faced with direct feedback that others experience her as needy and helpless—this offends her pride because she finds this image of herself to be intolerable. Consequently, she either leaves treatment or in some way finds fault with the "help" she has been given and thus creates excuses for not following through with it. The more she begins to experience herself as vulnerable or needy in a real way, the more she must fight this experience. The grandiose, demanding part of her personality experiences responsiveness or help as a trigger for feelings of worthlessness and inadequacy.

The case of one client in group treatment illustrates this dynamic.

Monica was the only child of an alcoholic father. Her mother, also alcoholic and probably mentally ill, deserted her and after a period of being cared for by extended family, Monica was brought to live with her father and his new wife.

Monica adored her father, but could never win his approval. Both father and stepmother were unresponsive to her emotionally, but totally overresponsible for her functionally. She became an angry, rebellious adolescent who began acting out sexually at a young age.

In college, she met a man who represented stability and married him. For a time, he acted as her control and was overresponsible in the relationship. She gradually began to drink alcoholically and eventually entered Alcoholics Anonymous.

After five years of sobriety, Monica entered therapy. She was suicidally depressed, and was sexually acting out, although sober. Her husband was totally unaware of her feelings or her sexual encounters. She had been emotionally overresponsible for him throughout the marriage.

Monica was put into group therapy where she played the role of the "bad child" of the group. Most people found her very endearing. She left her husband and engaged in a series of sexual affairs. With one man who was married, she began using cocaine. In response to a contract with the group, she stopped cocaine use, but the relationship was still very destructive for her. Following her father's death from alcoholism, she clung even more to this man.

In the group, she continued to discuss her unhappiness with the relationship. Group members kept giving her advice to help break the intensely destructive tie with her lover. Ultimately, Monica came to group one night stating that she was again suicidal and expressing a desperation for help and a willingness to take any advice. The group took her exceedingly seriously and the therapist offered to arrange for hospitalization. Two sessions later, Monica left the group outraged that people should have perceived her as so "sick."

In treatment, it is important to be conscious of this pattern and to help the client clarify her expectations. Frequently, what she really seeks is nurturing, attention, or approval, not help, or at least not help that forces her to experience herself as dependent. The therapist can circumvent this dilemma by making the paradoxical comment that, "I know you want help with this problem, but I also know that if you get help, you may feel worse and even angry at having been helped. I will tell you what I think would be helpful, but I'm not sure you should take the advice because it will make you feel worse." It is not helpful to avoid responding to a direct request for help with this type of client, because responsibility for her failure to change can then be directed at the therapist or group.

Daughters and Spouses of Alcoholics

Women in the roles of daughter and spouse of the alcoholic often present the same type of pride paradox as alcoholic women, but in a slightly different form. Nonalcoholic daughters and spouses of alcoholics will be discussed concurrently because frequently women occupy both roles at once.

Co-alcoholic spouses are often oldest daughters, or oldest children of alcoholic males. The daughter of the alcoholic usually experiences an intense need for approval. She has often been triangled into the dysfunctional marital interaction of the parents as caretaker of the mother or the father or both, and her only sense of self or self-worth lies in the approval she receives or the sense of competence she acquires by parenting her parent. Her sense of self is derived from an experience of gratifying the other rather than an experience of her own needs, wants, and interests. This type of woman has typically been a "reactor" in Black's terms, and is extremely sensitive to the extremes of emotion versus lack of emotion characteristic of the oscillation of the family system. She tends to carry this experience with her into her own relationships. Frequently, she will define herself as being an "all or nothing" person—she is either extremely reserved with people and mistrustful of them, or she "throws herself" into emotional involvements, trusting blindly, often only to be very hurt when her trust is betrayed even by some minor event. She is often attracted to the emotional intensity of the alcoholic because it is familiar. Also, because her own range of emotional expression has been so severely limited by her other-focused role, the emotionality of the alcoholic is experienced as "a lost part" of herself. Her self-experience is characterized by intense ambivalence and an unquestioned assumption that her own feelings and needs are unimportant or less important than those of other people.

At one end of the pride spectrum, the daughter of the alcoholic often evolves an intense need to feel "special" or an actual experience of being "different" from others—more isolated and less able to be part of a group. Her sense of alienation may be intensified by the emergence of a strong but unacknowledged competitiveness, a need to experience herself as more "perfect" or "better" than others. On the other end of the spectrum, she has low feelings of self-worth which are rarely assuaged to any degree by real accomplishments, and any feedback that she *is* special to someone, or special in her accomplishments, is vigorously resisted. She frequently feels responsible for the problems in her family or her marriage. She often questions her adequacy sexually or as a woman in general.

Because the daughter of the alcoholic has learned to parent her parents, she will often repeat this role with her spouse or children, setting in motion the extreme complementarity of over- and under-responsibility that sets the stage for further alcoholism.

The daughter/spouse co-alcoholic presents her own set of paradoxical pride injunctions. Typically, she feels that she *must* be in control because others in her life have been inadequate. Women in such roles become social workers, psychiatrists, nurses, or enter other helping professions. This client has a sense that she is the only one who can *do things right*—this assessment may be reality-based, though colored in adulthood by the distortions of childhood perception. The fact that she has rarely had her own needs met makes her feel somewhat morally superior. She turns her very real deprivation into a sense of pride in her own strength. She is almost incapable of asking or allowing herself to feel needy, and yet she has tremendous underlying rage at never having been given to. She takes pride in being a "good" functioner, alternately experiencing herself as a victim who has never been given to.

The daughter's sense of moral superiority is born of a reality-based sense of injustice. Often, she was erroneously accused and unjustly treated as a child. Promises made were never kept. She gave of herself but no rewards were forthcoming; no matter what she said or did, she was told by the alcoholic or others in the system that she was wrong. Often, if she failed to overfunction, she was rejected.

If she marries an alcoholic, it is typical that she first perceives his attention as representing the love and affection she has so desperately wanted. Eventually, however, she comes to perceive that same emotionality as self-involvement and selfishness. The co-alcoholic thus has a continued excuse to experience righteous anger at her deprivation, and she steps up her attempts to control her situation in the face of her experience that she is faced with the "same old situation"—an incompetent, inadequate, self-involved person to whom she must cater.

The pride paradox for the co-alcoholic generally takes the following form:

The client has the grandiose experience that the other can never respond adequately to her feelings and needs. The other is always a failure, less competent, less giving. This "pride" response allows the co-alcoholic to live in the tension between wanting or needing too much and receiving too little. Her underlying feelings are ones of being valueless because she is not given to.

When, however, the therapist, group members, or others in the environment respond with emotional support, caring, and genuine involvement, the client's tendency will be to cut off, attack, find fault, or threaten to leave treatment. Realizing that others are responding to her true needs and true dependency, her pride becomes a defense against an intolerable feeling of vulnerability, loss of control, or a feared experience of a fathomless, infantile neediness that cannot be assuaged. To receive appropriate, realistic response from others would deprive the client of the anger and emotional distance that have been used as a successful defense. It would also require her to assume appropriate responsibility for her own feelings and needs.

The client in this role in therapy is frequently the most frustrating and contradictory to deal with. She will take no responsibility for asking for what she wants, and then will explode with anger, directly or indirectly, weeks later because no one has attended to her needs. She will often complain about feeling that her problems are uninteresting or not relevant. Her life, in contrast to that of the recovering alcoholic woman, is almost static in its lack of overt crisis or conflict—on the surface she is highly stable but chronically unhappy, with a constricted range of emotional expression. Consequently, when she does become very emotional or appear to be very needy, the therapist or group may tend to overrespond, feeling that this vulnerability was what the client has needed to express all along. Frustratingly, the client will typically return the following week with her problems all solved, deciding she is ready to leave treatment, having read a book that solved everything for her, or having found another therapist. At the very least, the brief glimpse of the true person may be gone and the old defenses will be firmly in place again.

The therapist must be ready to predict this event and must always respond to the underlying fear, trust, and pride issues involved for the client. Often, the client's foray into highly emotional territory is a "test" to determine whether therapist and group are really strong enough to deal with the co-alcoholic's true feelings. Paradoxically, it is often helpful for the therapist or group to express anger at the client at this point in a controlled and caring way because for the co-alcoholic anger sometimes represents strength, and it tends to instill trust that the therapist really "cares."

Anger makes the client feel less vulnerable. Ultimately, she needs help in developing trust, in taking responsibility for her own feelings of neediness, and in recognizing that she can focus on personal needs and sometimes have them met without becoming hopelessly vulnerable and exploited, or rejected by others for having needs.

Although we have discussed daughters and spouses together, it has been our experience that daughters are at the more extreme end of the continuum of rigid pride characteristics that we have described. A spouse who was not a daughter of an alcoholic usually has more prior experience of healthy relationship. Although the alcoholism has damaged her, she has usually experienced some healthy interaction that will represent a firmer foundation for recovery. A daughter who becomes a spouse has had a more intense experience of dysfunction in her relationships. She may seek an outlet for her anger in her alcoholic spouse, who becomes an acceptable target for rage. A daughter who does not relate to an alcoholic as an adult is the most trapped by childhood experience and her anger is often vindictively turned against herself and expresses itself in interaction with others primarily in an extreme degree of mistrust and emotional distance. Often, the woman alcoholic who is involved with AA recovers more fully than the co-alcoholic who never experiences the corrective emotional context of a supportive group such as Al-Anon.

Mothers of Alcoholics

Finally, the mother of the alcoholic incorporates characteristics of both a daughter and a spouse. The primary pride issue for the co-alcoholic who is a mother has to do with the societal image of caretaker bestowed on this role. Any and all caretaking behavior on her part can be rationalized under the umbrella of being a good mother and, consequently, it is an extremely difficult task to coach the co-alcoholic mother to stop being overly responsible for a child because of a paradoxical fear: although she operates on the conviction that because she is overly responsible she is a good—even perfect—mother, she is driven to be an overresponsible mother by her fear that she may really be a failure, an inadequate mother.

The mother of an alcoholic will typically go to any lengths to protect her child from the consequences of his own behavior. Emotional overresponsibility tends to be more at issue than functional, but some mothers also direct the activities of their children, operating as "mission control" for every aspect of the child's life—what he wears, eats, takes to school, doesn't take to school, who he talks to, doesn't talk to, what he says, feels, thinks, buys, and so on. She conveys the attitude that "mother knows best" and is either concerned that the child be "perfect" as a validation of her own adequacy as a mother, or she becomes over-protective to "make up for" the abuses of an alcoholic spouse. She perceives herself as giving rather than controlling. While she may feel resentment at the demands of her role, this anger is rarely expressed directly and may take the form of guilt-tripping her children. She is usually quite deprived and constricted emotionally, and may single out one son or daughter to be her emotional ally. In general, she is unable to be truly responsive to her children.

Such a mother's denial of the damage her over responsibility may cause for her children is second only to the denial of the alcoholic that he is out of control of his drinking. The mother's denial is based on a complex set of premises about what it means to be a mother in our society—premises dictating that caregiving is the only appropriate female behavior. Selflessness, other-focus, and the care and nurturing of husband and children have acquired the mythical power of a sacred value to many women, and the concept of allowing the child to suffer in the face of the consequences of his own behavior is unthinkable.

Finally, breaking the overfocus of the mother on the child represents a loss of perhaps the only emotionally gratifying relationship the mother may experience. The relationship with a child may be one that provides her with a consistent, familiar experience of self, of competence, and of emotional closeness. Even if the relationship is characterized by hostility, ambivalent anger at the demands of the mothering role, and anxiety that the child may not always be entirely controllable, so long as the relationship remains intact, the mother retains a sense of appropriate role identification. She may use the "bad" behavior of the child to protect her from her own anger and vulnerability in the same way that the alcoholic's "bad" behavior functions to salvage her pride.

The mother of the alcoholic in treatment must always be approached within a framework of developing alternate strategies to help her child. Her pride in her mothering initially must be used positively and she must be helped to reconsider her premises about the most loving thing she can do for her son or daughter at the present time. It is frequently a good idea to take a one-down position with a mother, acknowledging her caring and concern and defining her as the expert on her child. The therapist may compare her own role as therapist to the parents' and suggest how difficult it often is to know the right thing to do for a child. The therapist can then suggest some strategies that she knows have worked even though they may sound harsh or punitive. It is important to appeal to the parent's willingness to do whatever is necessary to help the child. The mother will need a great deal of support and encouragement to "let go," and an alternate area of focus must be suggested during this time. The clinician's work with the mother of the alcoholic is greatly aided if the client attends Al-Anon or some other group such as Tough Love or Families Anonymous, since these groups all provide the same framework and permission for letting go and forcing the child to assume responsibility for self. Loss issues in the mother's family of origin should always be explored, as intense overfocus on a child is frequently a response to unresolved grief in the mother's own experience.

Male Roles and Pride

The Male Alcoholic

Like the female alcoholic, the male may have been overresponsible prior to his drinking, but this is less frequent than with the female. He may have felt emotionally overresponsible for one or both parents, but more typically he was overresponsible in the work domain since male socialization reinforces instrumental responsibility for the male. Often he was an underfunctioner in terms of home responsibilities. He may have had a mother who was very overresponsible for him or, alternatively, he may have been very dominated by older sisters. He frequently fears being a "sissy," a "baby," effeminate, or homosexual, and he may insist that he is independent at the same time that he feels dependency on and rage towards his mother or towards his father for not being "more of a man." Frequently, if his father was alcoholic, he experiences an intense sense of overprotectiveness for his mother and may often have had to intercede when his father abused his mother.

The male alcoholic tends to be highly fearful of new situations. He expects his wife to maintain the illusion that he "is in charge" but expects the same dependent emotional tie with her that he had with his mother. At the same time, he retreats from this emotional tie with a woman and finds in drinking an outlet that allows him to be "one of the boys."

He is often adored by his children and is characteristically perceived as "more fun" than his wife. In fact, he often acts like one of the kids and is frequently perceived as being "charming" and childlike. He may be more emotionally expressive than his wife or other males, but tends to need alcohol to allow him to be expressive.

Once he achieves sobriety, the male often demands an immediate return to his role as head of household. He may develop very rigid expectations of his children and expects his wife to carry out his dictates for them. He demands and expects that family members immediately begin to trust him again. In sobriety, passivity may become a problem because he experiences such an intense need for approval. He has difficulty being assertive and his experience of dependency on a female may perpetuate feelings of anger and possessiveness that severely limit his capacity for intimacy. He may feel threatened at any self-focused behavior on the part of his wife or children. He tends to intimidate his wife in an attempt to retain control and save face with himself. If he is an alcoholic who has been an emotional overfunctioner prior to becoming sober, he experiences feelings of depression and inadequacy, but rarely as intensely as his female counterpart.

The pride dilemma of the male alcoholic is to struggle with intense needs for emotional dependency while being unable to allow himself to be viewed as weak. He must manage to be taken care of while continuing to experience himself as in control.

While this dilemma is similar to that experienced by female alcoholics or co-alcoholics, there is a crucial difference. Traditional sex role socialization typically dictates that men *are* taken care of emotionally and physically while women do the caretaking. Because the male experiences himself as entitled to caretaking, he need not define this status overtly as dependency. He does not resist receiving the caretaking he asks for, he only resists a definition of it as rendering him one-down.

The female must deny her need for emotional help precisely because she learns that she is not entitled to it.

Sons and Male Spouses of Alcoholics

Sons of alcoholics share many of the characteristics of daughters of alcoholics. Their particular response to alcoholism in the family system is colored by sex role pressures and expectations, but in general their roles are determined, like their sisters', by sibling position in the family and by reciprocal interactional responses in the responsibility dimension. Oldest sons, only sons, or those born at a point in the family life cycle where drinking is a significant focus of family interaction may become highly overresponsible in the emotional dimension. They are at risk either for flipping to the opposite extreme and drinking as a way of coping with or reacting to their intensely rigid expectations of self and their unmet dependency needs, or they may continue to function in the overresponsible role. Frequently, sons of alcoholics marry alcoholic women or women who become alcoholic. A son may tend to be overresponsible both functionally and emotionally, and often has rigid expectations of himself, high moral standards, and takes pride in being right, good, and unselfish. Like his female counterpart, he is mistrustful in relationships. When he does become involved, he may tend to overidealize his partner and overfocus on her to the exclusion of all other relationships in his life. He typically has tremendous unmet dependency needs and, particularly if his mother was the alcoholic, he may suffer from chronic depression.

The overresponsible male is more likely to leave an alcoholic wife than the female is likely to leave an alcoholic husband. But if he stays in the marriage his attitude towards his wife becomes one of protection colored by contempt. He frequently attempts to play the role of both mother and father to his children. He tends not to be very expressive emotionally nor very aware of his feelings. He often feels like a failure and wonders why he can't fix the marriage.

While the overresponsible male child of an alcoholic frequently becomes alcoholic himself as a response to his overresponsibility, the underresponsible son of an alcoholic—often a youngest or middle son, sometimes an only son—may drink either out of overt rebellion and rage at his unmet dependency needs, or rage at an overly demanding, inconsistent, or abusive parental figure. To generalize broadly, it appears to be more the case that sons of alcoholic fathers become underresponsible and alcoholic while sons of alcoholic mothers become overresponsible, both functionally and emotionally, and marry alcoholics.

The pride dilemma of the nonalcoholic son in an alcoholic system is that he has a tremendous need to see himself as good, reasonable, and hard-working at the same time that he conveys and experiences contempt and rage. The harder he tries to achieve and to be morally "correct," the more contempt and rage he feels for others. The more rage he feels, the more intensely he needs to be "good." His pride is highly invested in denying his rage. He may either impose his rigid standards on his wife and children, at times abusively, conveying that they can never really meet his expectations, or he may resort to alcoholic drinking which may function to help either suppress or express his anger. Like his female counterpart, he has an intense need to be in control at all times, and he has an intense need for others to view him as "good."

The son of the alcoholic needs to be helped to acknowledge his feelings and needs, to accept his dependency, and—much like the co-alcoholic female—to be encouraged to relax his intensely rigid moral and functional standards. He can be encouraged to be "bad" using the same clinical techniques that have been described in Chapter 7 in Phase 3 treatment.

Fathers of Alcoholics

Fathers tend to have two potential responses to alcoholism in their children, depending on their own role in the context of over- and underresponsibility, and depending on the dynamics of the marital relationship. They may either minimize the problem or overreact to it. If he is alcoholic himself, the father often overidentifies with the child and minimizes the seriousness of the problem. Frequently, he views the wife as too controlling and subtly, or not so subtly, sabotages his wife's attempts at discipline or limit setting. He may be easily manipulated by his alcoholic daughter. With his son he tends to react as if "boys will be boys."

If his alcoholism is in the recovery stage, or if he tends to be a more rigidly overresponsible type of alcoholic, he may overreact and become punitive with his children or involve himself in an intense control battle with them. This battle usually displaces the control issues that exist between him and his wife.

If the father tends to be overresponsible as opposed to indulgent, he may have a more difficult time relinquishing his overfocus on a child than even the overfunctioning mother. However, the roots of his overinvolvement with the child tend to differ from a mother's, which are more prescribed by sex role socialization. Often, the overinvolved father is the child of an alcoholic himself or has an unresolved grief reaction to the loss of his own parent. Male socialization tends to mitigate against the acknowledgment of grief; consequently, the father tends to replace his loss through an overly intense attachment to his child. Certainly a lack of intimacy in the marital relationship may result in a father's overfocus on a child, but loss tends to be a more predominant issue when this type of interaction occurs.

In one case in which the father, Jack, sought help for his twenty-year-old son's drinking, the overinvolvement was exceptional. Bobby, his adopted son, had been diagnosed by a doctor as alcoholic but the doctor attributed the alcoholism to vitamin deficiencies. Jack accepted this misexplanation. It allowed him to rationalize Bobby's behavior and continue his overfocus by monitoring Bobby's vitamin intake. He had been alcoholic himself, but had stopped drinking, without treatment, five years earlier. Chronology in the family development was as follows: Jack's mother died, he had cancer from which he miraculously recovered, and Bobby became an intensified focus of concern.

In therapy, every time the therapist mentioned Jack's father or mother, Jack filled up with tears. He was unable, however, to see a connection between the loss of his parents, the removal of alcohol as a release, and his overly intense focus on Bobby. He checked Bobby's vitamin levels to see whether Bobby was likely to drink, read everything possible on alcoholism, paid several thousand dollars that Bobby owed for an alcohol-related accident, and told Bobby that he could repay it but described it as a $300 debt. When he did begin to "back off," he could do so only if he thought the therapist would take his place and demanded that the therapist "find the right person" to take Bobby to AA.

Although Jack made some small progress in backing off, the unresolved grief that he could not acknowledge continued to result in an intense focus on his children.

Some General Observations About Pride

In our clinical experience, and again as a broad generalization, women in alcoholic systems tend to evolve more rigid pride structures than men because they consistently experience greater vulnerability and lower self-worth. This factor seems directly attributable to differing patterns of entitlement, status, and power defined by traditional sex role socialization. In terms of treatment, this distinction tends to heighten women's resistance to role changes and to necessitate interventions that circumvent pride responses.

Some general characteristics apply to both males and females in treatment:

1. A tendency to blame problems on other people or circumstances rather than taking responsibility for self
2. Difficulty with expressing or acknowledging anger
3. Difficulty asking directly for needs to be met
4. An intense need to feel in control
5. Intense feelings of loneliness, inadequacy, and fear
6. Unrealistic expectations of self and others

In treatment situations, whenever a client indicates resistance to a role shift, it can be assumed that he takes pride in the behavior he is being asked to relinquish. Stiffening facial expressions, smiles, or hostile jokes often mask an angry response to a pride-offending intervention.

Dealing with pride in the treatment of alcoholic family members can be a complex and long-term process. A thorough understanding of the dynamics of self and interactional experience in response to alcoholism will result in more effective, accurate intervention.

CHAPTER 9

A Model for Group Treatment of Alcoholic Family Members

THE PRIDE ISSUES that tend to block change in alcoholic families can become the therapist's stumbling block in directing effective treatment. Particularly in the early stages of presobriety treatment, any attempts to address role behavior that is embedded in a pride-based sense of self will ultimately arouse the client's defensiveness and may result in an abrupt termination of treatment. Frequently, the context of individual interaction with a client, or treatment with the family as a whole, does not allow the therapist sufficient leverage to challenge pride issues without setting in motion a countervailing response from one or more family members that results in a breakdown of the treatment relationship.

Since appropriate intervention with the alcoholic often requires allowing feedback from the outside environment to slowly chip away at and erode the pride that prevents him from seeking help for his drinking, it becomes crucial to work with other members of the system on their resistance to change in their own roles so that the feedback to the alcoholic becomes more congruent, reality based, and less embedded in the dysfunctional reciprocity of interaction that has evolved in the family over time.

In trying different approaches to this problem we have found group work with individual family members to be a particularly effective method for addressing pride issues and teaching alternative role behaviors that can be taken back to the family context by the client without arousing a defensive response that threatens their continued motivation to remain in treatment.

Self-awareness in a group context tends to evolve as a result of identification with other group members rather than through initial direct confrontation with the therapist. Clients easily see in others what they have difficulty accepting in themselves. Consequently, the tendency for a symmetrical struggle to occur between therapist and client is lessened by group dynamics, and the client does not have to face other family members with her pride exposed. Because her aid is enlisted in helping others, the client retains a sense of power and experiences herself as less one-down in the group context than in either individual or family sessions. The group essentially provides a context in which the interactional dynamics make it safer for pride issues to be exposed and dealt with. We have found in general that clients in groups have made more progress more quickly in terms of actual change in both self-experience and behavior, and that their changes were often radical enough to result in the sobriety of the alcoholic or prevention of symptoms in other family members without the family or the spouse having been in treatment directly. Much as AA becomes a fixed reference point for a new experience of self for the alcoholic, the group tends to function as a fixed reference point for a changing view of self in the co-alcoholic.

Always the basic assumption of group treatment is a systemic one: by treating one member of the family, we are treating the entire family's interaction. Treatment in the group is based on a clear understanding of the dominant issues and dynamics that are characteristic for all alcoholic family members as well as a clear understanding of the particular individual's family.

The goals of group treatment can be summarized as follows:

1. To foster a direct, experiential understanding of role reciprocity in the dimension of over- and underresponsibility and to foster behavioral change to reverse that reciprocity in each client's family
2. To address the pride issues or self-experiences that maintain a rigid inflexibility of role behavior
3. To encourage maximum responsibility for self in both the emotional and functional dimensions
4. To promote greater emotional and behavioral flexibility
5. To encourage development of social skills and interpersonal resources
6. To teach concepts of family interaction and to promote an understanding for each member of the adaptive functions of alcoholism in his or her family

Group Structure

Groups are composed of six to nine men or women. Our initial experience over five years of work has been with women, but the model seems equally applicable to men, and a men's group is running in slightly modified form as of this writing. A coed group may be an eventual experiment, but groups are now homogeneous in terms of sex. Other factors such as age, ethnic background, socioeconomic background, and other demographics are heterogeneous.

A crucial aspect of group composition is that the following family roles be represented in the group:

1. Recovering alcoholic
2. Daughter/son of an alcoholic
3. Spouse of an alcoholic
4. Mother/father of an alcoholic

The rationale for this composition evolves from the primary goals of the group: to provide members with a different perspective and experience of the reciprocity of role behavior that maintains dysfunction in the area of over- and underresponsibility. In this way, the spouse of an alcoholic, for instance, may come to understand the experience of the alcoholic and equally to see how his overresponsibility maintained alcoholic behavior. The mother of an alcoholic similarly may come to understand how her overresponsibility contributes to the underresponsibility of the alcoholic child. The alcoholic may come to understand how her underresponsibility pulled for more of the same overresponsible behavior from a parent or spouse. Seeing these roles played out in people who are not immediate family members provides an experience of role reciprocity without arousing pride as intensely as work in the immediate family tends to. Eventually, a process we refer to as "mirroring" occurs in which both alcoholics and nonalcoholics recognize that they each have similar feelings, needs, and self-experiences and that their differences lie in the behavior with which they coped with those feelings. This tends to address the good guy/bad guy or saint/sinner dynamic which is at the heart of pride as well as the symmetrical struggles in alcoholic interaction. Group members begin to enact some of the same reciprocity within the group that occurs in the family—consequently, the presence of a balance between alcoholics and co-alcoholics is crucial to the group process. Frequently, one group member fits more than one category—that is, he may be alcoholic himself, as well as the child, spouse, or parent of an alcoholic. This overlap of roles is not problematic—the only issue of crucial concern is that at least two recovering alcoholics be members of the group at any given time.

On occasion, an actively drinking alcoholic has been allowed to participate in a group. This provides a further dimension to the group interaction, and often the group is confronted with the dilemma of how best to respond to an alcoholic who fails to meet her contract with the group by, for instance, continuing to drink, or not attending Alcoholics Anonymous meetings. The problems posed by the presence of an actively drinking group member give other members firsthand experience at learning new role behaviors, setting limits, and dealing with anger, resentment, and feelings of superiority. However, in our experience, this process tends to be more beneficial for the group than for the alcoholic and should rarely be undertaken unless the group has worked together on a long-term basis and the new drinking member has made initial commitments to attend AA and to stop drinking. Groups tend to be most effective for alcoholics who have at least one year's sobriety in AA. Other points of group structure involve the following:

1. Groups are usually most effective when open-ended rather than time limited, though some brief groups have been run on a twelve-week contract. An average length of time for group participation is two years on a weekly basis. Clients determine their own length of participation in a group. They are expected to give the group three weeks' notice of their intention to leave the group.

2. Clients may have done individual, family, or marital work before entering group, or may occasionally have family or marital sessions as an adjunct when changes in the family precipitate stressful or crisis situations. Individual sessions with clients are rarely indicated during the course of group treatment unless the problem directly involves interaction with another family member as opposed to interactional problems or feelings generated within the group and related to group process. When any group member is seen outside of group, a contract is that the therapist may communicate the contents of that session to the group if the information is relevant to group process. This helps to avoid the tendency of the client to deal with uncomfortable group interactions by triangling or allying with the therapist in family or marital sessions. The group is considered the primary treatment modality and any other sessions as adjunct work.

3. Group members are encouraged to relate to one another outside of group. This is meant to address the typical isolation of the alcoholic family member, to encourage a sense of equality in group relationships and interactions, and to encourage group members to develop relational skills. It is more the exception than the rule that subgroups develop unless specific group members have known one another previous to joining the group. When a subgroup does develop it provides very

valuable material for the group to process in that members are encouraged to express feelings of being left out or excluded, and to make direct statements about what they want from others in the group. Members make a contract with one another and the therapists that any group business that is discussed during social time together will be brought back and discussed during group time. Periodically, the therapists will raise this issue directly, particularly if tension within the group provides a clue that triangling interactions may be occurring outside the group time. These process issues provide group members with very valuable experience and are always related back to interactional processes within their families in which it is typical for triangulation, indirectness, or inappropriate alliance building to be creating significant dysfunction.

4. The group is co-led and it is highly desirable for the leaders themselves to have direct personal experience with and training about alcoholism or, at the very least, with the reciprocity of under- and over-responsible roles. To avoid power hierarchies in which the therapists are viewed as somehow "better" or more powerful than the clients, therapist self-disclosure is very important. The therapist must always be willing, within appropriate boundaries, to clarify her own position on issues, to share relevant personal experience, and to make interventions in the form of "suggestions." The therapist's role is one of teacher and facilitator rather than one of "expert." Since a primary goal of the group is to promote self-responsibility, clients are encouraged to help one another reach solutions rather than to depend on the all-knowing therapists. The therapist's job is to communicate information about family and alcoholic interaction, to clarify interactional processess occurring within the group and within each client's family, and to direct group interaction productively. The group should be consulted and agree on all decisions regarding addition of new members or any changes in process or structure. The therapists do take responsibility for being directive, making all covert issues overt, and for consistently framing all issues within the context of reciprocal over- and underresponsibility and the pride involved in maintaining those roles. The therapist models negotiation and problem-solving skills by interacting openly and directly with the individual group members on any interpersonal issue that may arise directly between them.

5. An hour and a half to an hour and three-quarters appears to be an optimal time frame for group meetings. A norm is established that each group member is responsible for asking for group time if he needs it or wants it. This requirement alone produces significant process material around which clients learn to take positions, be more direct and responsible for self, and become aware of the ways in which their over- or underresponsibility prevents them from interrupting, taking time for self when others seem to need it more, or calling another group member

or the therapist on her tendency to dominate group time. Feelings of anger at being deprived or not cared for, and tendencies to be self-effacing or to give up one's own needs in the other's interest are frequently elicited as a result of this rule and are quite productive and instructive to group members. It is typical that the alcoholics in a group will act needy and demanding and tend to dominate the time, while the co-alcoholics sit quietly and smolder with resentment. This type of interaction is framed as the co-alcoholic's envy that their pride won't allow them to be as direct and up front about what they want as the alcoholics are. It can be pointed out that both have the same need for attention and response, but that each thinks about and handles these "wants" differently. The co-alcoholic thinks of himself as "good" for not asking, but is then angry at not getting his needs met. This anger is directed at the alcoholic who tends to go to the opposite extreme and demands that all of her needs be met all of the time. The lesson of the group is that each needs to move behaviorally more toward the middle.

Group Process

Groups are content-focused with a shift to discussion of group process whenever the interactional dynamics in the group begin to mirror the patterns that predictably appear in an alcoholic family. For instance, in discussing her alcoholic husband, a co-alcoholic may express considerable resentment or a sense of judgment or superiority about alcoholics. A recovered alcoholic in the group may react with anger, hurt, or may express distrust that the group is a safe environment if others feel such hostility toward alcoholics. At such times, it is important to shift from a focus on content (the one client's discussion of her husband) to intervention with the process occurring between the two group members. Not only is this type of process issue ultimately important for the entire group, which ideally is divided equally between alcoholics and non-alcoholics, but it is also, of course, a critical kind of interaction that occurs within any alcoholic system. The therapist at this point needs to facilitate a discussion between the specific group members involved and the group as a whole that is oriented toward exploring the experience of being in the role of alcoholic as contrasted and compared to the experience of being the co-alcoholic. The goal is to foster mutual understanding, a sense of the similarity of underlying needs and feelings, and a sense of joining or mutual collaboration in a fight against alcoholism rather than a fight between alcoholic and nonalcoholic.

The Stages of Group Life

Groups are begun by having all members introduce themselves and describe their relationship or experience with alcoholism. The therapists themselves participate in these introductions and in fact should begin them to help establish a tone of openness and equality. Once the group rules have been explained and agreed to, each member is asked to discuss his goals and expectations of the group in the context of the present situation existing in his family.

Each time a new member joins the group, these introductions and statements of goals are repeated briefly. Older group members are asked to describe what progress they feel they've made in the group—new members are thus encouraged to see hope in their situation while older members have a chance to provide one another with feedback about changes accomplished.

Each group session is structured by the content individual members bring to discuss during that meeting. The therapist talks directly with the group member speaking and also encourages other members to offer feedback and comments. It is typical for the therapists to work directly with one group member on family issues while others in the group listen or comment on their own experiences. Because group process and structure are based on Bowen techniques and because the goals of the group involve helping individuals to change their family roles, group interaction may differ significantly from those of other group therapies where change in interpersonal interaction within the group is the therapeutic goal. Not all group members will participate at each meeting.

Using the material that group members present, the therapist attempts to accomplish several tasks in a sequential order as the group progresses. Each new member who joins the group must accomplish these tasks at some point even though the rest of the group may be functioning at a different level and may assist the therapist in teaching new concepts to newer members.

The sequence of "tasks" to be accomplished by the therapists with group members is as follows:

1. Teach the concepts of over- and underresponsibility as they relate to both function and feeling specifically within the context of one's family interactions.
2. Help each client assess her role in her nuclear family and family of origin, focusing particular attention on intergenerational patterns of over- and underresponsibility. Help each client to develop a family genogram which she presents to the group.
3. Foster group identification by encouraging discussion of the many ways in which social norms encourage overresponsibility in the male/female role.
4. Relabel "control" or enabling behavior as forms of overresponsibility and encourage an awareness of the typical sense of fatigue that often accompanies response to the demands of this role.

5. Discuss all interactions either within families or within groups in terms of the concepts of complementarity and reciprocity. Help group members to define their complementary role in all interactions—i.e., if A does more, B does less; if A talks a lot, B will appear to be quiet; if A pursues, B will distance, but if B pursues, A will distance.

6. Teach other systems concepts such as triangling, boundaries, and the concept of symmetrical struggling. Discuss the reciprocal roles of pursuer and distancer and the notion of "distance regulators" in relationships. Provide a framework for discussing interactions in terms of power and dependency.

7. Help the client to relinquish the overresponsible role and begin to focus on self by coaching specific moves in the context of the family material the client presents.

8. Predict the ensuing emptiness as well as the response of the system as the client begins to give up overresponsible functioning. Let group members "hit bottom" and encourage them to sit with their despair and depression rather than run from it.

9. Teach group members how to take direct "I" positions without being reactive to the reactions they experience from others.

10. As the group members begin to experience their own resistance and to identify others' resistance to relinquishing overresponsibility, encourage a discussion of the anxiety underlying their need to maintain the sense of control that their role provides. Discuss the ways in which the anxieties and lowered self-esteem fostered in any alcoholic system give rise to a sense of pride and moral superiority in experiencing oneself as competent, "good," right, and in charge. Point out the reciprocity this sets in motion between the alcoholic and the co-alcoholic: the more right, competent, and "perfect" the co-alcoholic becomes, the more "bad," irresponsible, and incompetent the alcoholic becomes. The more out of control, chatotic, and unpredictable the alcoholic acts, the more in control, rigid, and "right" the co-alcoholic feels.

11. Encourage group members to give feedback and confront one another on their resistance to change, but express doubt that change would really be appropriate for the client at that point in time. Do not become overly invested in the client's changing and restrain the group from doing so once it has voiced its opinions.

12. Coach motivated members to pursue extensive family-of-origin work. Use transferential dynamics provoked between group members to heighten awareness of individual roles and family patterns.

The group will proceed through these tasks in its early phases and double back through each of them at various points depending on changes in group composition and events in the families of members. It is important to go back to earlier tasks (focus on over- and underresponsibility and genogram work) periodically with both individuals and the group collectively to refocus the group's attention on its original goals.

As an ongoing group proceeds over time, members become more trusting, more open, more responsible for taking what they need from the group and more direct in confronting one another. New members become more easily absorbed and accepted. Older members may decide to leave as they become comfortable with or eager to cope with their family situations without the direct support of the group. Often, group members develop an ongoing network of relationships that outlives the group meetings.

Specific Group Techniques

Frequently, experiential exercises facilitate awareness in the group and help to address, in a more immediate and nonverbal way, the dynamics that tend to perpetuate dysfunctional behavior. The following exercises are specifically designed to address issues of pride and overresponsibility. They are meant to accomplish a number of other purposes beyond heightening awareness of dysfunctional dynamics.

Ultimately, it is important to establish an approach to the seriousness of the problems that arise in the group that incorporates a sense of humor and a spirit of play. Both elements tend to relax the rigidity and tension experienced by any member of an alcoholic system and to undercut anxious self-absorbtion. Group members learn new behaviors, they develop a sense of perspective, and most importantly, they experience themselves differently in interaction with other people. Thus it is hoped they will carry a greater sense of liveliness, spontaneity, and openness to new experience back to their families.

Family Sculpting

Family sculpting (Papp, 1976) is a technique that is particularly useful in highlighting the family-of-origin issues and roles that preceded the current life situations of group members. It is a highly vivid, dramatic technique that cuts through intellectualization and helps to elicit the emotional responses that usually perpetuate dysfunction. The "sculptor" selects other group members to play his family members and will typically choose people who are "in character" to represent the various roles in the family. An alcoholic member may be chosen to represent an alcoholic father, for instance, or a highly overfunctioning mother of an alcoholic may represent either the sculptor himself or the nonalcoholic spouse. Since each of the family-of-origin roles is actually represented by a member of the group, not only the sculptor, but other group members as well are treated to vivid experiences of their own feelings and the reactions of others to them in their roles in the sculpted family. Awareness of complementarity in the family is usually heightened— "she was always holding him up and so I always held her up"—as are feelings of isolation, rejection, or role confusion. What may previously have been only discussed in the group is now experienced, and group members become acutely aware of the difficulties and dangers inherent in being too embedded in any one of the possible dysfunctional roles in the family. Sculpting the family as one would like to see it helps concretize goals and evolve a sense of what different role one could play in one's present family. Therapists may sculpt their own families if they feel this self-disclosure will promote a climate of trust and mutuality in the group.

Masquerades

Periodically, especially at Halloween or during holidays, group members are asked to come to group in costume. The particular assignment can be varied and can be defined as "come as some aspect of yourself that you haven't revealed to the group," "come as your ideal or fantasy self," "come as somebody else you would like to be," or "come as some aspect of yourself you feel bad about." Group members are typically more than willing to put energy into this assignment and frequently those who tend to be perfectionists take great pride in coming perfectly costumed. Those who fail to come in costume may be asked to talk about how they might have come dressed. Others then talk about the character they have chosen to come as and why. For example one group member, an alcoholic with great unexpressed rage, came as a terrorist with a stocking pulled over his face. The daughter of two alcoholic parents, also a rape victim, came in an evening gown as her sexual, glamorous, nonrigid self. One daughter of an alcoholic came as a bag lady—the pathetic, unkempt, underresponsible person she both feared and wished at times to become.

There are many variations to the masquerade assignment. Group members may be asked to bring in a meaningful piece of poetry or a meaningful quotation to read to the group. They may be asked to bring in a sample of some piece of their own creative work and to talk about how they experience themselves differently when they work at such projects. One woman who had difficulty being self-confident and who loved theatre was asked to read a scene from a play to the group.

The goal of these assignments is to help group members experience and tap repressed parts of themselves. Frequently, in alcoholic relationships it seems to be the case that one partner acts out, expresses, or limits the impulses of the other for him or her—in other words, the marriage is balanced by the reciprocity implicit in the one expressing a behavior or feeling of the other that the other cannot express. For instance, the overresponsible, controlled co-alcoholic typically behaves in a way that sets limits or balances behavior of the underresponsible, out-of-control alcoholic. These roles render the co-alcoholic unable to express the chaotic, uncontrolled, more emotional aspects of himself, while the alcoholic is deprived of the experience of her own competence, power, and strength. Group members are helped to behave in less extreme ways by beginning to experience and express other parts of themselves in structured and playful ways.

Team Competition

Again, given the composition of the groups which include both nonalcoholics and alcoholics, original family dynamics tend to be recreated. In the first several months, most groups experience a subtle hostility and mistrust between people in reciprocal roles. When this hostility or mistrust begins to emerge in an interaction between two or more group members, the therapists move to heighten or amplify the conflict, competitiveness, or mistrust. Each takes a position on one side of the issue, divides the group into two teams, and stages a mock battle over the issue. For instance, a group member may complain about her alcoholic husband's messiness and inability to pick up in a room properly. She essentially conveys a sense that her neatness is of a higher moral order than his messiness—that she is more "right" than he. Whenever a group member conveys this sense that her value, belief, or behavior is more "right" than her partner's the stage is set for a battle. The therapist may choose to intervene or simply to note the process.

To stage a battle, therapist A may respond to the group member's comments: "Well, frankly, I'm an alcoholic myself," or "I'm very messy myself, and I believe that messy people are happier."

This is therapist B's cue to join the fray by "fighting" with therapist A: "Now wait a minute, how can you say that—it's clear that neatness is a sign of a more organized mind—it represents a mature way of coping with life. Besides, I prefer my neat office to your messy one . . . "

The group is then asked to identify which of them are on therapist A's team and which are on B's team, and the two therapists continue to battle, asking for reinforcements from their respective teams by encouraging everyone to discuss their reactions to neatness, messiness, to neat and messy people. The therapists set the tone by being either relatively

serious or some degree of outrageous in their behavior with one another, depending on the seriousness of the issue. The point is to use
humor to amplify and make explicit a very real mistrust, competitiveness, and hostility, to normalize the conflict, and convey permission to talk about it. Group members can be egged on to express their
hostility or anger, although in early phases of the group many will be
too "nice" to do so. It is important to balance humor and seriousness in
early phases of the group so that members aren't overly threatened by
an eruption of conflict. The therapists may limit the "fight" to themselves initially or ask only the more verbal clients to join the battle.

The battle is brought to a close by the therapists posing some version of the question, "Well, how are we going to resolve this?" The
question is thrown open to group members who by now have begun to
be aware of the concepts of difference and neutrality—that neither side
is likely to relinquish its position if the other fights it and that defining
issues or behavior as right or wrong is unproductive. The therapists may
model a negotiated solution, agreed to disagree, or simply let the group
struggle with a resolution as they begin to relate the symmetrical nature
of the interaction to the interactions they experience in their families.

Many different issues may be battled over in this manner—the
value of responsibility vs. doing your own thing, the advantages of
being alcoholic vs. the role of martyr, how good it feels to be bad vs.
behaving in a rational and logical way, the advantages of being a man
vs. the advantages of being a woman. Group members can always be
depended on to raise an issue which can be fought out because these
types of struggles inform their daily lives and most group members will
have positioned themselves at one extreme of behavior in relationship to
them. The therapist can capitalize on group content by using the group
structure in this intervention to ennact symmetrical battles and to help
the group evolve new responses to them. Ultimately, group members
may shift from blaming or judgmental, other-focused behavior to responsibility for their own chosen behavior, as well as evolving greater
behavioral flexibility. This technique also normalizes anger and conflict
and models more appropriate ways to resolve them.

Other Uses of the Team Concept

The team concept may be used in other forms to heighten
awareness of overresponsible functioning. While the therapist may devise any similar type of game to focus on the same issue, one example of
a game exercise that brings overresponsibility into sharp relief is the
following:

The group is divided into two teams. The therapist should choose
teams so that the more overresponsible members of the group are bal-

anced equally on either team. One person from each team should be chosen or volunteer to be an observer or recorder of team process.

The two teams are told that they are about to participate in a competitive exercise to determine how well they can accomplish a task cooperatively. The task is to sort a deck of cards sequentially by suit. The first team to accomplish the task will be judged more effective at cooperative functioning. No other directions are given and no further questions are to be answered by the therapist.

Meanwhile, in isolation, the observers are given instructions *separately* from their team. Essentially, they are instructed to observe who assumes what role in the process—who takes charge, controls or directs the process, who tends to sit back and participate less. They are to note how ambiguous issues are resolved and which group member manages to assert his or her opinions as to the "right" way to accomplish the task. The first team to finish the sorting "wins."

Predictably, certain group members will take charge and assume the major responsibility for accomplishing the task. Frequently, these members can be observed to wait to see what other members are doing, and to move in when it becomes clear that the rest of the team cannot resolve "how to do it."

In discussion of the exercise, the observers should first report their impressions to the group. Group members are then asked to report their feelings and reactions to the role that they assumed as well as their experience of team members. The "leaders" often report an intense desire to win and a feeling that they had to take charge because of their anxiety that no one else would get the task accomplished. Less active members often indicate that they feel upset with themselves for not being more persistent, but feel intimidated or feel a need to defer to the more dominant members. Some report feeling relieved at being able to sit back and let others take over.

The exercise provides group members with firsthand experience of the feelings and behavior associated with over- and underresponsible roles. It provides members with an immediate experience of complementary interactions with one another, resulting in new information and new perceptions that may or may not be consistent with the self report or the experience of the group member in verbal interchange. The competitive nature of the exercise provides an arena for raising issues of power, control, and the need to win or be "right" in a very nontoxic way.

Other Intervention Techniques

The ongoing work of the group is to coach individual group members to change role behavior within their nuclear or extended families. Frequently, in order to help group members to accomplish role changes, strategic kinds of techniques can be used to advantage, particularly when pride issues and resistance are emerging to prevent change. Paradox or restraint from change is useful when the client persists in bringing the same problem to the group week after week, asking for the suggestions and then not carrying through. At this point, the therapist may either suggest that perhaps the group has been incorrect in its perception of the situation (taking a one-down position), or he may convey to the group members some version of the statement that change would clearly be very dangerous right now, and nothing should be done. Or the therapist may express a mild skepticism about the readiness or willingness of the client to change and suggest that the group move on to other issues. Essentially, the use of paradox is a method for harnessing the pride and overresponsibility of the client in the interests of change rather than stasis. The group provides a context in which clients can compete to be "good" at being less overresponsible—in other words, to be good at being bad.

Prescribing Reversals[1]

A concept crucial to changing the dysfunctional complementarity of role behavior is, again, the idea of being good at being bad. Since all overresponsible people tend to view self-focus as "bad," therapists need consistently to convey that the group norm is to be "bad" and to coach bad behavior whenever possible. One technique is to give assignments in which overly perfectionistic clients are helped to make mistakes deliberately. In one group, a very perfectionistic client was the focus of a good deal of covert and not so covert resentment. The client happened to take particular pride in her culinary ability. It so happened that the holidays were approaching and the group planned a small party for the last session before the break. The therapists met privately with the client and suggested that the group very much needed someone to model some "bad" behavior. She was asked to make one of her special cakes for the group party and to make it perfect in every way except that she should use white pepper in the recipe instead of sugar. When the group began to react she was to express horror and act terribly remorseful about her mistake. She was never to tell the group the true story. The "perfect pepper cake" assignment, as it was dubbed, allowed the very perfect client to make a mistake in a face-saving way, and it allowed the group to respond magnanimously to someone who was previously resented for her air of superiority. The assignment helped to trigger a shift in the complementarity of roles within the group and both the client and the group were able to begin to relate differently to one another.

Finally, clients are coached in interaction with family members always to agree with any accusation that they are bad or wrong. While the normal tendency, particularly in alcoholic interaction, is to engage in symmetrical struggles perpetuated by defensive sequences in which the client continually attempts to justify himself to spouse or children, agreement with the accuser or the attacker helps to stop escalating sequences until issues can be resolved in a less reactive setting. For instance, a woman might be told to agree with her husband if he calls her cold and unresponsive or to tell him that it's just that she seems cold because he's so warm. When children argue, disagree with limits, or attempt to engage the parent in struggles about why they must adhere to limits, the client is told to respond, "Because I'm a mean mother," or some similar version of "I'm just bad." This technique disrupts the dysfunctional interactional sequence and helps the client to be in touch with his need to be in the right, good, and just position in all interactions. It conveys to children that the parent is not covertly asking for their approval. Once this type of interaction has been disrupted, clients can be coached to try more productive methods of resolving conflict.

Outcomes of Group Experience

Group members seem to follow a fairly systematic route on their journey to responsibility for self. First, they experience the tremendous relief that comes from identification with others, particularly as roles such as "daughter of" that have not been formally defined or explored in previous treatment approaches are explored. The term overresponsibility reframes the issue of enabling or control in a manner that does not offend the pride system, but rather defines it as "too much of a good thing." There is a sharing of the burden that overresponsibility creates and the fatigue that all suffer from. Members develop an acute awareness of their typically morally superior stance toward the alcoholic. They begin to laugh at their own rigidity and perfectionism. Members develop a comfortable style of poking fun at and confronting one another. There is extensive use of humor to lighten very serious interactions and situations. There is a sharing of particular immediate crises and all members help with problem solving. Then as members begin, one by one, to explore ways of relinquishing their overresponsibility, depression, hopelessness, and a resurfacing of all the pride issues come into focus. As the roles change, the families of group members begin to react to pull the system back toward the old equilibrium and group members need support to hold to their new positions. Ultimately, members come out of the depression and begin to define the kind of lives they would like for themselves and are supported in defining concrete goals and moving toward them.

Most group members tend to make significant changes in the nature of their interactions with either nuclear or extended family members. It is rare that marital problems are not resolved either in the direction of divorce or in more stable realtionships in postsobriety. It is frequently the case that the group is so effective in disrupting the individual member's part of the dysfunctional interaction maintaining drinking in the family that the drinker more rapidly "hits bottom" and enters treatment. Group members themselves become significantly more self-focused and may begin to deal constructively with issues of sexual dysfunction, prior incest experiences, vocational goal setting, and parenting problems. Frequently, group members begin to work on their own addictive problems such as overeating or excessive use of pills or cigarettes.

It is important to acknowledge that groups do not help all clients, or rather that the therapists are at times not skillful enough to use the group context productively for all clients. Again, the recognition of limitation is an important element in the therapist's work. Failures in group frequently result from the therapist's and group's collusion in acting overresponsibly, or of trying too hard, with a particularly difficult client. The good-guy/bay-guy complementarity characteristic of the alcoholic family begins to occur between therapist/group and the particular client who resists change more adamantly the more the therapist and group become invested in her changing.

Because the group environment promotes greater intimacy and involvement with clients, the therapist needs to guard against both her own tendency, as well as the group's, to become overresponsible for and overinvested in the other person's change. Part of the skill required in conducting such a group is the ability to recognize the emergence of patterns that repeat the experience group members have had in their alcoholic families, to acknowledge them, and to help evolve alternative patterns of interaction. This assumes a high degree of self-awareness on the clinician's part as well as a willingness to admit error to clients and to shift tactics when interactions become dysfunctional. The use of a co-therapy relationship is highly desirable precisely to provide this process of checks and balances.

Group Transcripts

The following transcripts represent segments of treatment sessions with an ongoing women's group comprised of daughters, mothers, spouses of alcoholics, and recovering alcoholics. The transcripts provide a flavor of the interaction that occurs in group as well as issues that are typically raised. While much of the description of group intervention in this chapter outlines group process, the transcripts illustrate the type of content that is most typically focused on.

Transcript 1

The first transcript involves work with a woman who is the daughter of an alcoholic father as well as a recovering alcoholic herself. In this segment, she is being coached to shift and resolve issues in her relationship with her father since his death of alcoholic cirrhosis is imminent.

NOTE: T1, T2 indicate the therapist speaking; the client is indicated by name; other group members are noted by P (for person) 1, 2, 3, etc.

T1: What happens now with your father?

MARY: Well, I saw him tonight. I cannot deal with him. I mean, I caught myself going into the same old act. I called him on the phone and said, "I'm coming up there to bring you something," and I was just waiting for him to say something nasty to me [*laughter*]. I forced myself into this whole thing, and I asked myself, what am I doing?

T2: You're still going after the approval.

MARY: Exactly, or trying to guess what's going to make him mad. I guess something always makes him mad, you know. I buy a new car, and he makes a comment that it's not a stick shift. God save the world because she's not driving a stick anymore.

T1: Do you ever get mad back at him?

MARY: No. I just don't have the ability to.

T2: That'd stop him . . .

MARY: I don't have the ability to say, fuck you.

T1: Well, not even saying, fuck you, but, listen, I really don't want to hear your anger anymore.

[The therapist here is encouraging the client to shift her part of the interaction in which she allows her father to intimidate and put her in a one-down position. We consider it important to acknowledge that alcoholic behavior is, in fact, abusive behavior, and that it does generate anger, hurt, and a sense of worthlessness or powerlessness. It is also important for the client to be aware of how her own responses perpetuate the negative interaction.]

MARY: It's really too bad. I just, he can turn me into a mess [*still sees herself as a victim*].

P2: That's why he keeps doing it. [*Other group members are aware of the reciprocity.*]

MARY: But, he's a basket case. I mean, he is just buying time, he's on the way down. He was very, very sick and he should not drink. And he's been right back to the same old behavior, and I saw him tonight. I think it's only a matter of time before either he's going to die, or he might live, but, he's very much like your father [*to P3*]. He holds a job, and he does all this, and who the hell knows how, but he's starting to slip. I mean, he even can't make it to work on Mondays anymore, and that kind of stuff. And I'm trying to figure it out, because there's nothing I can do about it. I mean, he knows I'm in the program [*AA*].

T2: There's something you could do about you to resolve it to some degree while he's still alive. And you may not be able to do it in person, but why don't you write him a letter, and just tell him how badly you've wanted his approval. Just write him a letter and make sure it arrives on Tuesday, not on the weekend, or Monday when he's too hung over to read it.

MARY: See, I guess part of my problem is that any relationship at all with him is better than none for me. And I'm afraid to rock the boat. But, also part of the problem is, too, I realize that I'm dealing with an alcoholic.

T2: But, I'm not talking about your doing it to change him.

MARY: Um hmm.

T2: What's going to rock the boat so much that you won't have a relationship?

MARY: I have such a relationship now, you know [*sarcastic*].

T1: Well, what'll rock the boat is your attempt to be real.

P2 Well, and also if you find out that you've created a relationship in your head, then you'll have to face an area that I faced, depression, when you find that there's really no relationship there.

MARY: Yeah. I don't think that he and I have a relationship, really.

P3: So, what is to lose?

MARY: Well, I can't explain it. I can't put my finger on it. It's almost like taking care of a dog that's hit by a car kind of thing.

P4: You feel sorry for it.

MARY: I really do.

[A common theme: I can't be angry or take a position because the alcoholic is so pathetic and pitiful. The client disowns her own anger. Realizing that the client is not ready to deal directly with her father, the therapist shifts tactics. Letter writing is a useful tool to begin shifting dynamics among family members and a technique we use frequently with group members to begin family work. The therapist continues to coach Mary to write a letter to her father.]

The group supports the therapist's attempts to help Mary shift her role in relationship to her father and conveys the message that she is responsible for her part of the interaction with him. The emotional tone of the group during this interchange is intense, but supportive and respectful of Mary's pain. Group members learn to let one another sit with their pain and to heighten it in the effort to free one another to interact differently. Part of the goal of this work is to help Mary "hit bottom"—to experience the despair involved in acknowledging what is *not* available to her in her relationship with her father, to grieve that reality, and to move to acceptance and an active involvement in establishing a tie with him in more productive ways. Mary's inability to acknowledge the depth of her anger towards her father, as well as her ambivalence towards him, is typical of the daughters of alcoholics that we work with.

Transcript 2

In the following transcript, Laura is the spouse of an alcoholic. The marriage is her second to an alcoholic. The therapist opens the session with a reference to guilt because the group is at the stage in which they have begun to make the first steps towards reversing their overresponsibility, and the emotional reactions to these changes have been a focus for a few sessions. Different group members are at different stages in this process, but they share a common framework and a common language for their work together. First the therapists, and now the group members themselves, have been relentless in focusing on and confronting issues of overresponsibility.

T1: Did anyone else think about guilt this week?

LAURA: Yeah. Probably because I'm going to Florida the extra week ahead of time. I've been figuring out ways to really feel guilty. My daughter is taking a test for Spanish that will either qualify her or not qualify her to spend a month in Europe this summer, and I'm not going to be here to take her up to the test, so Jack is going to take her. I'm not going to be around when she takes her driving test, so Jack is going to have to take her.

T1: How old is this daughter? [*The therapist is very aware of the daughter's age—the question is a challenge.*]

LAURA: She's just seventeen—just turned seventeen.

T2: She could never get herself any of these places?

LAURA: Not until she can drive.

P5: She doesn't have friends?

LAURA: Well, nobody else was going up to take this test.

P6: What about a bus?

LAURA: What bus?

P5: Does the train go there?

LAURA: No. Nothing goes there.

[*The group is confronting Laura on her overresponsibility and her inability to let her daughter solve this problem for herself.*]

LAURA: But Jack's going to help her do it. And I'm getting, I thought I was getting, two different messages from him, and then it suddenly occurred to me just as I was driving down tonight, that Jack is sort of looking forward to being totally responsible for her. And I'm projecting on to him the fact that he's going to resent it and I'm going to pay for it later. There's no indication that I'm going to pay for it later.

T1: It's your fear that he might not be comfortable or he might not do it right?

LAURA: Maybe a little, but I think it's just that I think it's my responsibility to do it.

P6: I was always afraid that my kids wouldn't like me if my husband did things for them. I always wanted to be the one to do it for them. I didn't want to share being nice.

LAURA: It feels lousy not to do it though, you know?

P5: That's what I'm experiencing now. I stopped doing for everybody, and in the beginning it was really high, and now I don't see anybody else taking over and I think, shit! Even in going about doing my own thing, I all of a sudden feel so depressed because there's nothing. Like what's the payoff with this? And it feels really lousy.

P7: Yeah. And the clutter is still piled high in the corner, and no one else really cares. I'm serious.

P5: Now that I'm not doing things they say, "Hey, what's with mom? She's really flipping out!" [laughter] It's a lousy feeling. I feel really terrible about it.

LAURA: Yeah. The kids are saying, "Oh, O.K." but, there's the question, the attitude, this is weird—she's weird.

T1: Where are the guilt cards?
 [laughter]

P7: I don't know that we don't do some of this in order to get a response out of people.

T2: Absolutely. But right now you seem to be asking why is it that I don't get some response, some kind of feedback like, "No! Don't go to Florida. We can't do without you."

LAURA: Right. Maybe that's it. I'm afraid that they can function without me.

P5: Then where will we be? Then what's going to happen?

T1: And what [P5] is talking about is the fact that in having given up that responsibility, she has lost her role and nobody is rushing in to give her a new one or to take over for her. . . .

 [later]

LAURA: As far as the house goes, I find myself caught in feeling crummy. It's *my* role. I think maybe what I'm worried about is what they think about me. That because I'm not doing these things, they're being critical. And that bothers me, because I want their approval. [*A perfect illustration of the symmetrical nature of overresponsibility—the mother overfunctions physically and emotionally for her children, but expects them to take care of her feelings about herself.*]

P5: You want to be able to back off and still feel that they care about you.

LAURA: Yeah.

P7: You want to be cared about for you.

LAURA: Right.

P7: Not for what you can do for them.

LAURA: Um hmm. Sure.

T1: You know, *we* really appreciate the fact that you're taking control of your life, and being a real person, but no kid's gonna do it.
 [laughter]

P7: They don't even understand.

P5: It's normal.

P4: I guess you have to get that kind of approval from other people.

P7: Kids are never going to give you approval for *not* doing things for them.

T2: Husbands aren't likely to either.

P5: So where do you look to, where do you get whatever it is we're looking for? The feeling that you're a terrific person yourself?

T2: Oh, if you're like me, you can get a little here, a little there, anywhere they'll give it to you.
[laughter]
[The therapist uses humor to lighten and normalize the very real pain and emptiness group members experience about losing their roles.]

LAURA: It never seems quite as good if you have to ask them.
[laughter]

T2: Mind reading. This is what she wants.

T1: As a suggestion, maybe you could ask the group to tell you what you want to hear. What is it you want to hear?
[Note that the therapist does not suggest that the client is dependent for needing to have other people "give" her this sense of herself, but rather suggests how to ask for and get it directly.]

P5: I don't know. I don't know. There's a pay-off when you're running around doing everything for everybody. They appreciate you or at least you invent it all.
[laughter]

The group realizes that overfunctioning has given people a false sense of self—and that it has helped to avoid a direct confrontation with each one's own needs and feelings. They begin to experience the emptiness of this role. At this point in the group process, major, accelerated changes in behavior will begin to occur and the therapist must be careful to caution clients against changing too much. Reactions in the families of each client will sometimes be extreme and need to be predicted.

Transcript 3

This last transcript describes the experience of a mother whose drug and alcohol addicted young adult daughter has been hospitalized repeatedly for drug overdoses. Mildred has received support from the group to limit her overinvolvement as the daughter lapses more and more into dysfunction. Mildred is herself a recovering alcoholic whose husband also drinks. Their marriage is strained and, because he is not their father, the husband has minimal involvement with Mildred's children.

At the beginning of the transcript, Mildred is talking about being called to her daughter's apartment and watching her through a keyhole because the daughter is too drunk to let her in. She finally calls the police to have her taken to the hospital.

MILDRED: When I got to her apartment, I could see her through the keyhole. She wasn't able to come to the door. She was crawling on her hands and knees. There was nothing in the apartment to eat and I knew that because her money went for booze. [Mildred left and her daughter was taken to the hospital, but was not admitted because she refused to sign herself in. The next night, Mildred *took her.*] On Tuesday night, she was real bad and she was monitored for a while. The admission on Wednesday, when I took her, messed up the whole day so to speak. She wasn't as bad and she refused to go in again because she didn't want [*Dr. X*] to treat her, which I thought was a very positive thought. I shouldn't say it. He's a professional in his own way, but he contributes to the problem by giving her more pills. So she didn't want him.

T1: Um hmm.

MILDRED: But they took the medicine away from her anyway, and then we just dropped her off home again and waited. And sat back.

T1: Um hmm.

P3: However did you get through it? What did you tell yourself to get through it?

MILDRED: I said a little prayer—I asked God to help me. I think it carried me for a couple days. It was rough. It was really bad this time. I kept busy. And I said whatever is to be will be and I was ready to accept whatever would be. Now I see she's O.K. Oh, I did go down to the apartment once, and I was nervous. Pete wouldn't go in the door at all. And I heard her cussing, and I said this is not for me.

T1: And you changed your mind.

MILDRED: I changed my mind and went back home. I heard her yelling at the door. And then I just stayed back and I waited. Finally, after a few days, she met my husband and said she was ready to go to a meeting [*AA*]. And she went Saturday night. We went, we both went with her, but it was very, very uncomfortable to do this. I don't know why I'm uncomfortable about that, but I am very uncomfortable. [*Mildred feared becoming overinvolved with trying to do something for her daughter again*] And she went, I guess, I presume she went Sunday night. She kept the appointment at the alcoholism unit with the counselor that she had agreed to see when we were in the hospital Wednesday. But, I tell you I was all in. So, Thursday I went and had a checkup for myself because I know I've been under a lot of stress, and I expected my blood pressure would be up, and it was perfect, so the doctor says, "You're functioning well under stress." You know he was joking about it. It couldn't have been a joke because I want to live, and if she wants to go that way, what else can I say?

T2: Well, congratulations. [*The entire group is moved by Mildred's struggle not to take responsibility for her daughter's life.*]

MILDRED: Thank you.

T1: I uh . . .

MILDRED: It's tough to stay away when somebody has no food, and you know they're pulling out all the stops and you're the mother and you don't go there. You know what I mean?

T2: Sure. A woman in the other group the other night, we were trying to confront her to cut her son loose, and she finally, she just couldn't hear it, and she was in awful, awful pain. It happens in that group there aren't as many mothers, which I think makes it tougher for her, and we talked about amputation. If somebody gave her advice to amputate her arm, she said, she might refuse that advice, because she wouldn't want to amputate her arm. And I guess what I heard her saying by that was that we were telling her to amputate her arm—that it felt that painful to her to cut her son loose.

MILDRED: Even when it might save her life.

T1: Right. And not to do that amputation sometimes is just helping somebody else go under. Sometimes we just have to stand by and watch people kill themselves, literally.

P3: Absolutely. . . .

MILDRED: I'm fairly open-minded. I've been a lot of different places. If anyone things I'm doing wrong, I'd like to know, because I feel that's where the help is.

P4: I don't feel you've done anything wrong.

MILDRED: I've detached just as much as I possibly can. When she went to the hospital Monday night, she called four times first and she was crying, and each time she cried and begged, "Mom, please don't leave me alone," and all that shit, you know, I don't pay attention to that.

Ultimately, Mildred's daughter died of alcoholism at age twenty-seven during a one-night relapse after a prolonged period of sobriety. At the wake, Mildred said she felt her daughter had at least had that period of sobriety because she had "backed off."

10

The Role of Children in Family Treatment

THE PARTICIPATION of children in the treatment of alcohol problems varies depending on the nature of the presenting problem identified by the family member who appears for treatment, the ages of the children in the family, and the phase of treatment indicated by the presence or absence of sobriety. Treatment approaches differ, for instance, when the alcoholic is identified as the problem and children are not symptomatic as opposed to the situation in which the child is symptomatic and identified by the family as the problem while the alcoholism of one or both parents is not.

Children are unquestionably always affected by the presence of alcoholism in a family, and in turn, they also affect the systemic dynamics that maintain a drinking environment. Currently, there is a growing awareness reflected in the literature and in the arena of self-help and treatment groups that children who live in alcoholic families have unique sets of problems defined by the varying roles they assume in relationship to the behavior of alcoholic parents. The presence of alcohol in a system distorts and disrupts the functional and emotional ability of a family to evolve appropriate rules, roles, and hierarchies, to sustain effective, realistic, self-validating feedback and communication, and to successfully accomplish normal developmental tasks.

In the midst of this disordered environment, children experience chaotic communication; inconsistent, abusive, or neglectful parenting; a lack of nurturing; and a sense of continual, ominous threat posed by either rigidly suppressed or violently explosive anger. Often, the only channel open to permit communication is crisis, and the roles all family members adopt are survival roles. Children living in such an environment evolve a distinct sense that something is "wrong" with them, and that they are somehow mysteriously responsible for the disorder and unhappiness that they experience. Because they often suffer from severe neglect and absence of nurturing, they experience chronic feelings of sadness and depression that may continue into their adult years despite therapy or the presence of nurturing relationships in their adult environment. As Claudia Black (1982) has pointed out in her book *It Will Never Happen To Me*, the learned response to living in such an emotional environment is "don't talk, don't trust, don't feel." The adult who emerges from a childhood based on such a survival ethic is one who feels continually unsafe and unsure of himself and other people and who really does not know how to cope with many of the emotional and functional demands of adult life. Much of his emotional energy will be directed at continuing to survive as he cautiously treads his way through an unfamiliar and potentially dangerous adult world where he feels as unsure of other people as he does of himself. The defensive personality and pride structures that evolve in an attempt to stay safe and keep life in order for the child of the alcoholic only serve to further deprive him of nurturing and healing interaction that would help to repair a damaged sense of self.

Roles Children Play

Sharon Wegscheider (1981) and Claudia Black (1982) have been responsible for providing descriptive models that identify potential role responses of children in alcoholic systems. According to Wegscheider, children will adopt one of the following predictable roles: the hero, the scapegoat, the lost child, or the mascot. She believes that depending on her particular role, each child behaves in specific ways, plays a specific function in the family interaction, and develops particular strengths and weaknesses that influence her potential for adult functioning. The hero, typically an oldest child, tends to be a compliant overfunctioner who in later life experiences chronic feelings of guilt and inadequacy. She frequently functions as a surrogate parent and is intensely involved in the parental triangle, usually being helpful to the co-alcoholic parent in that parent's struggle to deal with the alcoholism of the other.

The scapegoat typically functions to deflect the attention of the family away from the critical issues involving the alcoholism and marital conflict. Because the hero is so intensely involved with the parental subsystem, the scapegoat withdraws from it and his bad behavior becomes a foil to the hero's good behavior. While the hero enjoys the rewards of being special to his parents, the scapegoat acts out to get attention. He is as irresponsible as the hero is overresponsible.

The lost child simply adapts to a chaotic situation by "staying out of everyone's way." He is a "loner" who helps the family by making no demands. Receiving no attention, nurturing, or support when it might be available, the lost child experiences himself as quite worthless and confused. His seeming independence and self-reliance masks an intense fear of depending on others even in the face of his own limited resources for coping with the real world.

The "mascot" provides comic relief for the family—she learns very early to be a part of the family by entertaining or distracting it. Her ability to hold her audience gives the mascot some sense of control in what is otherwise a very chaotic, confusing, frightening world. Because she tends to act childishly to maintain her role, she develops few serviceable or mature coping skills and is often seriously limited by immature behaviors and attitudes.

Black's role models are broader in category, but they underline some of the same emotional patterns and outcomes for the individual child and for the family. Black's "responsible" role corresponds in certain aspects to Wegscheider's "hero." This child, according to Black, becomes an overfunctioner, often assuming parental responsibility at a very early age. The child's behavior is compliance-based and consciously or unconsciously directed at providing a sense of structure and order for the family. Consequently, the responsible child develops good organizational skills for which he is rewarded in both the home and the school setting. He becomes highly self-reliant because it is evident that the adults in the environment are neither functionally reliable nor emotionally responsive. As adults, children in the responsible role tend to be very dependable but somewhat constricted emotionally and socially. They approach most life situations by attempting to organize and control and are often severely limited in their ability to relax, have fun, or to take life less than seriously.

The "adjuster" role describes the child who, in the face of constant crisis, contradiction, and inconsistency, simply passively accepts all situations with some degree of detachment. This child rarely takes any leadership role and is usually in a middle or younger sibling position so that she follows the responsible child's lead in most cases. Her passive acceptance of all family and interactional circumstances results in an attitude of extreme underresponsibility. The adjuster never truly develops a sense of self and typically fails to actualize her intellectual or emotional potential.

Finally, the "placater" is the emotional overfunctioner in the family. He typically reacts more directly to the emotional dimension of the family interaction and tends to try to "take care of" everyone's feelings. Black describes this child as the one who will always say, "I'm sorry" in the attempt to make all situations better. He is often described as "more sensitive" than the other children and his parents typically take pride in his unselfish, compassionate behavior. This role may correspond to Wegscheider's "mascot" as well as to the scapegoat role. While Black tends to define the placater as a compliant, nonacting-out child, it seems that the acting-out child in a family may also be responding to the emotional tensions he experiences in the home and providing relief and distraction for himself and others by causing problems.

The role definitions provide a useful typology for understanding the self-experience of the child in the alcoholic family and they provide markers for the therapist's "mapping" of the family structure. They are useful tools for helping to explain the behavior of family members to themselves and for conveying a sense that the therapist understands the particular dynamics that surround alcohol abuse. Such role definitions tend to positively connote behavior and to relieve some of the sense of confusion that families experience about the interaction they engage in with one another.

Clearly, no child's behavior fits any one role with precise accuracy and it is also the case that a child's role may shift over time depending on the progression of the alcoholism and depending on events (shifting triangles, coalitions, life cycle events) occurring in the family that may demand different responses from different members. There may tend to be an overlap in roles depending on the size of the family. Older siblings may leave the family, relinquishing their roles to younger members. The gender of the child may determine to what degree he or she assumes a particular role. Frequently, a child who for one reason or another abandons the hero or responsible role becomes a scapegoat or a lost child. Some "responsible" or heroic types frequently also play the placater role and assume emotional as well as functional responsibility. Role configurations will also be affected by sex role expectations and by particular ethnic considerations.

Wegscheider's and Black's work is significant in the context of this discussion on two major points. The roles that they outline tend to underscore the emergence of complementary extremes in the family— the roles fall into one or the other of the categories of over- and underresponsibility in either the functional or the emotional dimension. The hero or responsible one may tend to be overresponsible in the functional dimension, but underresponsible in the emotional dimension. The "placater" and "mascot" may tend to be overresponsible in the emotional dimension, but underresponsible in the functional dimension. Scapegoats, lost children, and adjusters probably fall into the category of underresponsible in both dimensions. When one available role is already taken in a family, depending on birth order, sibling position, and patterns of triangulation in the family, a child typically responds by assuming another, complementary role.

Secondly, this evolution of extreme complementarity of roles points to the underlying distortion of self-experience in the family. People do not experience themselves as distinct and valued human beings, but rather as functions, as cogs in a wheel, whose only sense of self emerges in response to the demands, inadequacies, and inconsistent behavior of someone else. While this process of identity formation also occurs in normal families, in the alcoholic family self-definition emerges primarily in response to the need to avert crisis and to eliminate continual confusion about what is realistically true and "normal" about one's experience in the face of constantly intensifying oscillations of mood, behavior, and role functioning. Consequently, children evolve a self-definition that is either fluid and indistinct or rigid and, consequently, highly defended and tenuous.

As a result, the normal developmental sequences that occur in the life of any child are disrupted and intensified in their complexity (Burtle, 1979a). Normal life cycle stages and events are accomplished poorly, if at all, and the process of separation or differentiation of self from such a family is made more difficult by virtue of the fact that one has no distinct sense of self with which to separate. The legacy of addiction begins to perpetuate itself in future generations of the family.

The Child in Treatment: The Process of Shifting Roles

The purpose of this discussion is to identify the major issues that the therapist must address with children in family treatment and to outline interactional processes that typically occur between parents and children when alcoholism is present in the family environment. The concept of role functioning is a useful focus for discussing the goals of family treatment as they relate to children. Just as, in general, treatment principles with alcoholic families depend on an assessment of the continuum of behavior in the family from presobriety, through adjustment, to postsobriety functioning, the roles of children in the family shift and must be addressed accordingly.

Issues in Presobriety Treatment

In presobriety treatment, the therapist typically encounters children who operate in some version of the roles outlined by Wegscheider and Black. Latency age children in the family will frequently appear either old and mature beyond their years or markedly immature. Adolescents tend to be either very family-focused and withdrawn from a great deal of social interaction with peers, focused intensively on a particular hobby or sport, or totally peer-focused in an attempt to remove themselves from the family conflicts. Frequently, a "good" child will be balanced by a "bad," acting-out child. Children in presobriety stages typically experience intense loyalty conflicts. There may be covert or very overt bids on the part of one or both parents to side with them in their handling of the conflict caused by drinking. Predictably, one or more of the children will become the parental surrogate either in terms of taking over parental responsibilities of one or both alcoholic parents or providing emotional support to the other children and being a "spouse" to the nondrinking parent. Frequently, the child who sides with or "helps" one parent experiences intense rejection from the other.

For their part, the parents typically are:

1. Unable to nurture appropriately
2. Unable to set limits without being angry
3. Inconsistent in their expectations of the child
4. Driven by a need to have the child's approval—in effect, to have the child "parent" them

The style of parenting tends to shift with the oscillation between wet and dry states in the family. During "wet" phases, parenting may be abdicated entirely. Children may be neglected, left to their own devices, not disciplined, allowed to stay up late or to stay out. Essentially, the alcoholic may leave them to do what they want. During these phases, the alcoholic has typically joined the sibling subsystem and has assumed the role of another child in the family. The spouse may be so focused on the alcoholic that he or she pulls the children into parental roles or becomes completely unresponsive to them. The alcoholic may be violently abusive to the children.

One fifteen-year old girl in treatment, from a family in which both parents drank, described scenes that would occur when a crisis arose in the family, such as the injury of a sibling. Her father's response was to become abusive to the mother, while the mother's response was to become out of control and to beg her (the daughter—at age eight, nine or ten) to "do something" The daughter described how she would immediately become very calm and just "handle things."

In dry or more sober phases, parenting may become more perfectionistic and rigid, or the child may experience conflicting messages. If, in the wet state, the alcoholic has abdicated parenting, in the dry state he may attempt to reassert his authority in a very heavy-handed manner. Often, the spouse's tendency is to undermine the alcoholic and become overindulgent in an attempt to compensate for the abusiveness or cruelty of the alcoholic. If the alcoholic has been abusive, he may in the dry or "morning after" phase be very remorseful, come home bearing gifts, or be overindulgent.

The two parents may alternate competitively, with one being indulgent if the other is rigid, and vice versa. Both tend to base their behavior toward the child on their underlying sense of guilt about their inadequate parenting so that rigidity and harshness are also coupled with "giving in" or attempts to buy the child's affection or respect. The child who eventually acts out or becomes underresponsible tends to play heavily on this guilt because the parent communicates subtly a message that the child is not really responsible for her own behavior.

It is important to note that the overfunctioning spouse of the alcoholic, who seems to be "holding the family together," is frequently not responding any more successfully to the emotional needs of the children than is the alcoholic. He is typically as self-involved as the alcoholic, at least in his attempts to cope with increasing dysfunction. It is safe to assume that in an alcoholic family, all children are parentified in the sense that the children's feelings are all referred back to the parent's sense of adequacy and dealt with only in light of the parent's self-involvement. The parent's sense of adequacy is threatened if the child expresses *any* feelings, particularly negative ones. Effectively, all children in an alcoholic system are robbed of their childhood in the sense that they rarely have the opportunity to express or experience feelings in an environment of safety and trust. All feelings are responded to as reflections on someone else, if they are responded to at all. Fundamentally, then, the roles children assume presobriety involve either (1) being allowed to be childish, but neglected, (2) rewarded for becoming a caretaker or surrogate parent, or (3) offered the privilege of becoming a surrogate spouse. Frequently, the parents have no clear experience of themselves as responsible for parenting, nor do they have any clear sense that a parenting role requires them to treat children as other than peers or surrogate parents. Appropriate role hierarchies may be completely nonexistent in the family so that children do not experience themselves to be children and, consequently, they miss important developmental stages necessary to the formation of a clear sense of self in adulthood.

Goals for Presobriety Treatment

While children may not be included in every treatment session in the presobriety phase, they should be invited to participate some of the time. While it is true that the role configurations that children evolve help to maintain the drinking environment in the same way that the adult roles do, the direct attempt to disrupt survival roles in children, particularly younger ones, in the presobriety phase, is a less desirable treatment goal than addressing the parental behavior and interaction. Frequently, the involvement of the children in discussing the family problem—and their relief that the problem is now being addressed— will in itself lessen the emotional stress on the child and permit some change in role behavior.

The exception to this general rule is the situation in which an over-functioning or acting-out adolescent clearly presents as the "truth teller" in the family and is the person most motiviated to have the family acknowledge drinking behavior. In this case, the therapist needs to develop a strong alliance with the child in an attempt to use his over-responsibility in the positive interests of forcing the parent or parents to stop drinking. It must be made clear to the child in this role that he is to be asked to function in this capacity only temporarily and that as things in the family improve, he will be able to give up responsibility for taking care of everyone. Some substitute structure for being "special" must be provided for the child at the point that he is no longer expected to overfunction.

In the Smith family, several months of treatment with Joan and Peter had not resulted in any firm commitment on Joan's part to attend Al-Anon, although she had attended several Alcoholics Anonymous meetings and had moderated her own drinking. It was not clear that her own drinking was yet alcoholic, but it was clear that she was Peter's drinking companion, and that her drinking was at least potentially problematic. The change in her drinking pattern stressed Peter, but not sufficiently for him to go to AA. Joan was involved in more of the therapy sessions than Peter, who had begun to make excuses for not attending once Joan went to AA.

The therapist then held a family session with Joan, her college-age daughter Barbara, college-age son Peter, the oldest, and her adolescent daughter, Ann. Peter, Sr., was invited, but did not attend the session. The therapist thought that the session was fairly unremarkable. Peter, Jr., did talk about remembering his father being drunk from the time he was five, but he seemed to have achieved some peace in his relationship with his father. When asked whether he could go home and talk to his father about his drinking, Peter clearly wanted to let sleeping dogs lie. Barbara, the oldest daughter, was angry at Peter, Jr., and confronted him on wanting to get out of the family. Ann, the youngest, expressed relief at her mother's control of her own drinking and some hope-lessness about her father ever achieving sobriety. Joan listened, occa-sionally jumping in to give the kids permission to talk. It was clear that the kids had talked very little to each other about the problem, and not at all to outsiders. The therapist explained that they showed a very typical kind of family loyalty but that it was misdirected. A breaking down of the isolation, and a more candid airing of the problem could be helpful to their father and to everybody. Peter, Jr., explored his own drinking patterns some, and it was clear that he was a typical conscientious oldest, who had some trouble relaxing without alcohol.

Three weeks later, in the first subsequent therapy session, Joan and Peter, Sr., came in together again. Ann had gone home and confronted Peter, Sr., about his drinking, and had confronted her mother about her mother's resistance to Al-Anon. Joan was going regularly to Al-Anon. Barbara and Peter, Jr., were going to go to Adult Children of Alcoholics; Peter, Sr., was going regularly to AA. Peter, Sr., also reported that Ann had shown him an essay she had written for school on the topic, "My Most Significant Moment." Her essay began, "My most significant moment was the day that my father called Alcoholics Anonymous."

It frequently happens, as it did with this family, that children can be used as leverage to force the parents into sobriety or action related to sobriety. The therapist must make these types of interventions carefully, never stressing the already overresponsible child beyond reasonable limits. In this family, the therapist could not have calculated to what degree the child had power to influence her parents—the child herself will typically provide whatever information the therapist needs to make an accurate judgment about how much effective use he can make of the child's present role in the family dynamics.

Young children should always be interviewed presobriety to assess the specific role structure of the family and to determine, if they are symptomatic (i.e., depressed, acting out), how that symptom may function to mask parental drinking behavior. Goals for involvement of children in presobriety treatment include the following:

1. Educate children about drinking and convey understanding about life in an alcoholic family: relieve the child of a sense of guilt or responsibility.
2. Provide a safe environment in which feelings about drinking and the alcoholic parent can be discussed.
3. Assess the degree of neglect or emotional and physical deprivation occurring in the family.
4. Address any symptomatic behavior in the children themselves.
5. Establish what style of parenting is occurring in the family.
6. Map triangles, coalitions, and boundary positions.
7. Rule out potential unrevealed incest or abuse.
8. Attempt to restore or establish appropriate parenting to whatever degree is possible.
9. Take measures to counter the parents' tendency to scapegoat or attack the children for acknowledging drinking.

It is difficult, of course, to strengthen the parental subsystem when one or both of the parents is not functioning competently or when they deny either their own drinking or the failure to parent adequately. David Treadway's "bending the bow" technique[1] is useful in this situation. This approach involves assuming competence on the part of the nonfunctioning parent and when he fails to follow through on agreed-upon parenting responsibilities, using this failure to confront him about drinking.

If the alcoholic is not participating in treatment and the spouse tends either to deny the problem or to resist doing anything about it, the therapist may allow the obvious unhappiness and deprivation of the children to "guilt-trip" the spouse into taking action with the alcoholic for the sake of the children.

In one case, Claudia, a young woman in her thirties, sought therapy with our agency because she had finally specifically defined the family problem as alcoholism. She had been in therapy for two years with another therapist, had attended the outpatient family program of the local Alcohol Recovery Unit, and had attended a few Al-Anon meetings. She continued, however, to deny that her husband Charlie's drinking was progressing, that he needed to stop drinking, and that she needed to make changes in her own overresponsible behavior. For instance, when she took her thirteen-year-old son, Billy, to an Alateen meeting and Charlie got angry, she stopped taking Billy to meetings.

In the first session, the therapist talked with her about the importance of not denying how much the alcohol had affected her children. She said, "That is what got me here basically." She reported that she had had a call from school. Her thirteen-year-old son, Billy, was talking about suicide again. Earlier talk regarding suicide by this same son had led her to insist on a therapy session with the husband, but little had come of it. She said, "What I got from what she [the teacher] said is not that he feels responsible for his father and me, but he's a big brother and he's worried about his little sister and he's worried about his little brother—and he doesn't want us to split. He told the teacher, his father was drinking again."

One session was held with Claudia and Charlie. Although the therapist focused on drinking in the session, she focused more on the disruption of appropriate parenting that the drinking was causing. Treatment stopped shortly afterwards, terminated by the therapist who did not feel the family would make further progress until Claudia and Charlie were willing to do more about the drinking. Two follow-up calls from Claudia, one a few weeks after therapy stopped and another six months later, indicated that Charlie was strictly controlling his drinking and that his parenting had changed dramatically. Claudia had stopped some of her overresponsible functioning. The kids were doing well.

The therapist felt that eventually the alcoholism would probably progress and this family would be back in treatment, but the youngsters had been helped by the intervention, and when the drinking does become more severe, Claudia will be likely to seek help again, and perhaps then will be ready to take the next step.

When the child is the identified patient in presobriety treatment and the parents deny the alcoholism in the parent, the therapist is confronted with two choices. The first is to maintain the child-centered focus and work with the symptom. Depending on its severity and the severity of drinking, it may or may not respond to treatment. If it does, the therapist may indicate some fear that the symptom will recur unless drinking is addressed. If it does not respond to treatment, the therapist can then directly raise the issue of drinking as an obstacle to the problem's solution.

Given the severe consequences to children of alcohol abuse, it is often difficult for the therapist to sustain treatment without pointing directly to alcoholism as the potenial source of the problem. However, whether the child is the identified problem or the issue presents itself as a marital problem, presobriety treatment is, again, always the treatment of denial. It rests within the therapist's judgment whether a direct confrontative approach or a more patient, paradoxical style will best address the particular defense structure of the family.

The second possible approach is to define the problem as alcoholism early in treatment. At this point, it is helpful to have a strong alliance with the spouse or with another motivated member of the family since the alcoholic will typically leave treatment. In this situation, one focuses on the doubly difficult task of addressing the child's symptom while attempting to move the system toward sobriety (see Chapter 7).

Postsobriety Treatment: Dealing with the Child's Loss of Role

During the phase of active alcoholic drinking, children assume roles that, though inappropriate, have provided some safety, security, and sense of self-definition. Once sobriety has been achieved in the family, these roles are always eventually disrupted and shifted. In fact, they may have shifted frequently during the progression of the alcoholism over the course of the family's development. Postsobriety work with children involves two major goals: addressing the loss and restructuring of roles, and coaching the parents to repair the inadequate nurturing that occurred during the drinking phase to whatever degree they are capable.

Despite the anxiety and chaos of presobriety interaction in a family, children derive certain benefits from the roles that they assume. The overfunctioner may experience a sense of mastery, power, and specialness. An acting-out child may similarly feel quite powerful and experience an intense emotional bond with one or the other parent. "Lost" children or less highly functioning members of the family escape even appropriate parental expectations and are allowed to retreat from responsibility or from any of the mutual demands of normal family interaction.

As the alcoholic parent becomes healthier, she may begin to attempt to assume a more appropriate parental role, though this may not be successfully accomplished in the early stages of sobriety. The emotional relationship between the two parents may improve. Or, conversely, the spouse of the alcoholic may become depressed in the face of the shift to sobriety, and emotionally abandon what was previously an intense relationship with one or more of the children.

The typical reactions of all children in the family involve anger and a sense of betrayal or abandonment. Life in the family may have been difficult before sobriety, but the postsobriety family in general is faced with a necessary confrontation with reality involving role changes that may feel as disruptive as drinking behavior.

Without intervention, new roles assumed by children may take on as many inappropriate forms as presobriety behavior. The overfunctioning parental or spouse surrogate may become intensely competitive with the sober parent. A lost child may become an acting-out child in the face of newly experienced parental demands which are usually enforced with rigidity and hostility. The family may find new scapegoats to replace the "bad" alcoholic. In general, children after sobriety are expected to go back into the role of child divested of their power, but with no real gain in terms of nurturing or attention from the parent to replace it. In most cases, children are given the message that they are now powerless and one-down to the parent, but the expectations of their behavior continue to involve their acting like adults or being responsible for the parent's sense of adequacy. The child is now faced with the dilemma of experiencing the burdens of adult responsibility with none of the prerogatives of power. Frequently, any sense of having a special emotional bond with one or both parents is lost.

The blurring of boundaries and functions between parental, spouse, and sibling subsystems in alcoholic families is intense. Adults tend to depend on children in the family to meet their emotional needs, to co-parent, and to be friends or allies as the isolation of the family from the outside world becomes more intense. Children, consequently, receive highly inconsistent and unclear messages about who they are and about the meaning of their relationship with the parent. Often they experience themselves not only as the parent's friend, and confidante, but also, by extension and unconsciously, as the parent's lover. Consequently, when their roles shift, the result is an intense sense of abandonment, betrayal, competitiveness, jealousy, and anger that is always perpetuated in future relationships. Similarly, relationships between siblings may shift. Intense ties that may have evolved in the absence of strong parental figures may be broken as the parent becomes more involved with the family, or a child who was previously a spouse surrogate may attempt to assume a parental role with other siblings who will very likely rebel. Competitivenss among siblings for parental or spouse roles may result in either overtly hostile or highly distant relationships among siblings. This intensity or enmeshment may be implicit in the family interaction while overtly, on the surface, relationships may appear to be somewhat detached or disengaged.

Work with children in the adjustment and maintenance phases after sobriety is crucial to the family's process of recovery and restabilization and crucial to prevention or recurrence of symptoms in the alcoholic, the spouse and in the children themselves.

Issues for Children in the Adjustment Phase

The alcoholic parent feels tremendous guilt and defensiveness over his absence of parenting while drinking. He overcompensates by becoming overly involved or intrusive with the children and parenting in a rigid, punitive manner. All family members feel resentment and hostility that the "incompetent" member of the family is now attempting to be competent. The spouse may react by sabotaging any attempt that the alcoholic makes to assume parental responsibility. Equally likely is the possibility that the alcoholic will remain detached from the family so that roles remain unchanged. This tends to be a temporary situation during which anger and resentment build because the family's positive fantasies about having a sober parent do not materialize.

In the first situation, the overfunctioning child frequently becomes depressed, while other children in the family may act out in an attempt to restore the nondrinking spouse's role as the competent one. They may rebel against the rigidity of the alcoholic's behavior. Acting out also functions to permit the expression of anger or to deflect anger that exists between the two spouses. Again, the family at this stage may be feeling, for the first time, the intensity of its anger towards the alcoholic, but anger is one emotion that the family has typically never learned to express constructively.

Alateen and Post-Teen are very helpful for youngsters at this phase. These groups normalize some of their feelings and give them peer support in dealing with the problem, thus addressing some of the isolation that is typical in an alcoholic family. However, Alateen without at least some therapeutic intervention can sometimes compound the child's problems. Alateen teaches children that the alcoholic suffers from a disease, often making it very difficult for the child to express normal anger. It is difficult to justify anger at someone who is sick. The therapist needs to help the family give the child appropriate channels for expressing anger to avert severe depression or acting-out behavior.

Children in this phase feel confused about which parent's authority to accept. They are uncomfortable with the alcoholic's attempts to reestablish a relationship if this occurs. They experience a sense of loss of old patterns of relating and are usually able to verbalize these feelings, particulary if they are adolescent or preadolescent.

Treatment Goals in the Adjustment Phase

1. Help parents to assume appropriate parental responsibility and to set limits in a calm, nonreactive manner. Have them practice or enact this process directly within sessions.
2. Encourage children to acknowledge their anger and sadness and to talk about the ways that things are different with the drinking stopped.
3. Normalize the family's reactions and responses.
4. Help the parents to evolve new ways of responding and relating to the children that will facilitiate a process of "reparative nurturing."
5. Assess the roles each child has played in the presobriety family and work with the parent to establish new expectations, allowing each child a substitute reward to replace the power, specialness, or immunity inherent in the old mode of functioning.

Particularly in regard to the fourth item, above, it is important to remember that children cannot be expected to respond to limit setting that is harsh or rigid, nor can they be expected to feel kindly towards parents who only set limits without attempting to repair any of the damage done by alcoholic behavior and the lack of nurturing that was characteristic prior to sobriety.

For instance, some alcoholic families have never had the experience of enjoying leisure time or recreation together. Outings should be assigned for specific children individually with a parent or for the whole family together. While these may seem like minor interventions, they do represent nurturing experiences to children. It is often necessary literally to teach the family how to play and enjoy themselves. Members of alcoholic families typically suffer from a deprivation of such experience and once a common activity can be decided on, the therapist frequently has to direct the family step by step in terms of how to follow through with the activity.

The following transcript illustrates the major theme of work with children in the adjustment phase: loss of role. Although Tom, the alcoholic, has been sober for two years, his family is considered to be in the adjustment to sobriety phase, because he has not really accepted that he is alcoholic and, consequently, sobriety is still somewhat tenuous. Judy is Tom's second wife, and the family has come into therapy identifying sixteen-year-old Alice's acting-out as the major problem.

In this part of the session, the therapist is attempting to shift the focus of attention from Alice's acting-out to Alice's loss of role now that Tom is sober.

THERAPIST: [to Judy] One of the patterns that I notice very, very commonly is that when one of the parents is drinking, forget the label alcoholic, o.k., but when there's controversy around the drinking, the other parent is usually particularly close to at least one of the kids. And my guess is the last couple of years you and Alice were close.

JUDY: Well, it's hard to withdraw—Alice told me she couldn't stand it once he [Tom] stopped drinking because daddy noticed everything. [Alice experiences Tom's attempt to parent as critical and intrusive. She has difficulty accepting him as a parent and his reinvolvement threatens to disrupt her "friendship" with Judy.]

THERAPIST: That's one of the changes that happens when the person who is drinking, the adult who is drinking, sobers up—he notices everything. But other roles in the family change too, o.k.? Alice had a very important role when you were drinking. [to Alice] You were a very important part of this family. You were very important to her [Judy].

JUDY: Very much so.

THERAPIST: O.K. [to Tom] And all of a sudden what happens is you get sober and you think things are going to be better now. Except that all of a sudden she [Alice] has problems and I don't think it's just because you're noticing her. [to Alice] I think your problems probably have gotten worse.

ALICE: Um hmm.

THERAPIST: You don't get a whole lot out of his stopping drinking. Do you? You lost something. You lost the good relationship with her [Judy], didn't you?

ALICE: Yeah, I guess.

THERAPIST: You really did. You still have a lot of anger about the stuff that happened when he was drinking.

ALICE: Sadness maybe.

THERAPIST: Yeah. Sadness. Talk some about that sadness, Alice, if you can. You're probably not too used to doing it.

ALICE: No, I don't. . .

THERAPIST: No. I know. I know. [Judy starts to interrupt.] Judy, I want you to control yourself, I really do. Come on, I want Alice to have center stage and I want her to have center stage in a different way than she usually has it.

ALICE: Uhmm, when I got really close with Judy, I hardly ever saw my mother [who was alcoholic too], and it's like that's when I started realizing that Judy was like more of a mother than my mother was to me and I don't know when I started to get in trouble and she started, I don't know, she turned on me. Me and Judy were really close, we went shopping and everything. And I guess it's like it's partly my fault, but I just, I get mad at her and everything and I just, I don't care.

THERAPIST: Well, I guess sometimes it's really kind of like Judy knows best how to relate to people when there are problems, because that's what she's been having to do for the past few years. And it's like, almost like you two don't know how to talk to each other except when you're talking about a problem over here. So you get mad—it's like you've lost her.

ALICE: Yeah.

THERAPIST: Judy, send the other kids over to Tom. Let him take care of them for a minute here. [*Therapist removes the two younger children from between Judy and Alice.*]

ALICE: Only when there's some sort of problem with my sister, me and Judy start getting close or something. [*When Alice and Judy didn't have Tom's drinking to discuss, other problems were substituted.*] When she starts feeling bad. When it's my problem, when I get in trouble or something, then they're so quick to just ground me or something, you know. They ask me why, like they're mad [*crying*]. [*Alice experiences it as unfair that she is consulted about other people's problems, but reacted to punitively when she has her own.*]

THERAPIST: So, it's like you don't have any way of getting close to Judy anymore, do you?

ALICE: Only if there's another problem [*crying*].

THERAPIST: When do you and your father talk?

ALICE: We talk.

THERAPIST: Hello, goodbye?

ALICE: No, yeah. We talk, you know, but we don't talk about anything.

THERAPIST: Anything real. So you and Judy only talk when there's problems.

ALICE: We used to talk all the time.

THERAPIST: But, you don't anymore. That's part of one of the things you're saying about it.

JUDY: I stopped that on purpose. There was a day I said I'm sorry—it wasn't like a gradual thing.

THERAPIST: Why did you stop?

JUDY: Okay, I gave up on Alice. I just feared where Alice was concerned. Come this winter. Alice ran away three times in the course of over two months, o.k., and not just for a couple of hours, I mean these were overnights, a couple of days' search and whatnot. And the first time she ran away, you know, I was upset. We talked like—'come on, what's the problem?'—we tried to get at it. The second time, we tried working through it. I tried getting therapy for Alice. I took her to [*therapist*]. I went to the school; I talked to people on the child study team. Alice was the main thing on my mind for months, every day looking on her face how she's doing, how she's feeling. I saw Alice being miserable and I hurt for her cause I loved her so much, o.k., and I was going to try everything I could to help Alice feel better in any way I could. But, I think I deserve a little bit more respect and love from Alice in return. Not the kind of kid that goes to school in the morning saying goodbye to you—everything is fine—and then just doesn't show up for four days, doesn't come home after school. [*Judy makes Alice responsible for her own sense of adequacy—in return for her love and attention Alice is expected to behave appropriately. The fact that she doesn't is viewed as a statement that she doesn't care about Judy. Alice is in the difficult position of being in the child role but expected to meet adult needs.*]

THERAPIST: [*to Alice*] Did they come looking for you when you ran away? Did you want them to? You don't have to admit it out loud to them, you can just tell me.

ALICE: Well, yeah.

THERAPIST: You did want them. You wanted them to come looking for you, didn't you? [*Therapist attempts to help underline that Alice is a child who needed a response from her parents.*]

Tom's sobriety has disrupted Alice's role with Judy. She and Judy were friends, relating around the issue of the problems with Tom, until Tom's reentry into the family as a sober parent eliminated Alice's function and pushed Judy into a more parental role with Alice. Alice experiences herself as "demoted" to a child role. As Alice reacts by running away, Judy becomes more punitive and begins to distance from Alice and react negatively to her much as she did with Tom when he drank and the other children when they had problems. Any problem with another member of the family seriously threatens Judy's sense of her own adequacy, and she becomes angry that her feelings aren't "taken care of." Alice is only vaguely aware that she is asked to be an adult with Judy on the one hand (talking with her about others' problems), but is clear that something is not right when she is suddenly treated again as a child. Her running away could be viewed as a request for clarification of this confused role status as well as a reaction to her loss of adult status.

The goal of therapy is to help realign the family so that both Judy and Tom parent Alice in a developmentally appropriate way while working to bridge the distance in her relationship with each of them individually.

Later in the session, the therapist works with Alice's relationship with Tom and works directly on reparative nurturing, giving each parent assignments to spend individual time with Alice outside of the session.

Issues and Treatment Goals for Children in the Maintenance Phase

When families appear for treatment after two or more years of sobriety have elapsed, the presenting problem is typically child-focused and generally suggests that issues of role loss and change have not been negotiated and resolved. The family may have achieved a functional balance around the continuing distance of the spouses while either one or both become involved with AA or Al-Anon. In other words, problems in the family tend to occur both when roles do change *and* if they don't.

Goals for treatment in this phase are similar to those for the adjustment phase, and, typically, addressing these issues will relieve the presenting symptoms unless the marital relationship is highly dysfunctional. The difference with cases appearing for treatment at this point is that there tends to be less anxiety about a recurrence of drinking and much of the intensity of the initial family responses to sobriety will have lessened. The system tends to be more "settled" into sobriety and less precariously balanced, although the problems continue to simmer quietly under the surface and emerge through the child's symptoms. Rebalancing the family interaction along lines of role complementarity is a primary focus of concern (see Chapter 7).

A Case Study—The Jones Family

In addition to work on role loss and parenting in the maintenance phase it is frutiful, whenever possible, to move beyond the child's symptoms to work on the marital interaction. The following case illustrates work that is characteristic in the maintenance phase with children. Since phase-of-treatment issues are never absolutely distinct, some adjustment issues are resolved in this case also.

The Jones family sought treatment at a point when Joe, the alcoholic, had been sober for two years. The presenting problem was the behavior of the youngest of two daughters, Linda, age fourteen, whose grades in school had been deteriorating at the same time that she was becoming more and more belligerent and withdrawn at home. A specific incident of acting-out behavior involving some concern as to whether or not Linda had been sexually abused by an older adolescent precipitated the family's seeking therapy.

The family typically reacted to Linda's behavior in a predictable, repetitive way: Linda would have a temper tantrum or behave badly and her mother, who usually took responsibility for limit setting and discipline, would scream back and impose some consequence. Linda would storm away and remain distant from the family, preferring always to be with friends. Joe would either avoid any confrontation with Linda altogether or make a halfhearted attempt at a later point to "talk" to Linda, whose response was usually to laugh or be otherwise disrespectful, a sequence which was frequently repeated in sessions. Recently, the father had begun to feel violently angry toward Linda, had imposed some very punitive consequences, and feared he would become physically abusive. In contrast, he expressed utmost respect and approval for his older daughter, an accomplished art student who rarely, if ever, behaved badly.

Some of the issues in the family typical of the maintenance phase were the following: Mrs. Jones, Mary, was the daughter of an alcoholic father. She tended to be highly overresponsible for all the functional and maintenance tasks in the family and rarely asked the girls to take any responsibility for their own living environment. She refused to attend Al-Anon, and felt deeply unsure of her adequacy as a wife and mother. She did make an effort to respond to the emotional needs of the girls, but often parentified them in the sense that she looked to them to enhance her sense of adequacy. She had often asked Linda to "keep her company" when her husband was out drinking and on one or more occasions directly asked Linda to tell her father how badly he had behaved after a night of drinking.

Mr. Jones, Joe, was an only son and oldest child of two nondrinking parents. He had two younger sisters. Joe was given the clear message that he was "special" as the only son in the family and was never asked to assume any responsibility. He was raised to believe that financial success was of paramount importance and had little sense of connectedness with his sisters. He tended to remain distant both in his family of origin and in his nuclear family—his time spent drinking was replaced in sobriety by either working long hours or marathon running. He admitted that he had no sense of how to relate to his daughters and preferred to avoid responsibility for parenting. Ironically, it had been his impulse to call for therapy, as if to find someone else who could "do something" about this daughter. He felt a great deal of guilt and shame about his drinking and was eager to make up for it, but didn't know how. At one point in the session, he broke down and sobbed about his feelings of helplessness and guilt over Linda, then expressed shame at having been so emotional. His wife remained at a loss as to how to respond to this display of emotion and Linda stormed out of the room.

Linda was continually overshadowed by her older sister and appeared to have a speech problem that made her withdrawn and shy. She refused any assignment in school that involved oral presentation or reading out loud. The parents had never thought to have her tested for possible learning problems. She emphatically denied in sessions that her father was an alcoholic.

The older sister, Jane, was an overachiever who seemed comfortable with herself, but rarely expressed feelings or opinions about herself or events in the family. She was emotionally very protective of her younger sister on the one hand, but kept her at a distance by constant squabbling over the room they shared, or clothes Linda borrowed. As Linda improved in treatment, occasionally it was revealed that Jane was not as "together" as she appeared and she began to talk more about some of her own typically adolescent difficulties.

In general, the emotional climate of the family was one of tense distance. While both Joe and his wife were adamant that their marriage was a good one and though Mary was, in fact, much less resentful and bitter about the drinking than was usual, both seemed comfortable with a relative degree of distance in the marriage. The family lacked spontaneity, rarely disrupted its typical routines, and tended to avoid vacationing together. The older sister's art activities provided a diversion in that they frequently required travel to art exhibits and school events.

The therapeutic goals with the family were defined as follows:

1. The typical sequence of behavior surrounding Linda's acting-out was to be reversed. This was accomplished by putting Joe in charge, with the mother's agreement, of all limit setting and discipline with both girls. The parents were to discuss and agree on rules and expectations for the girls and Joe was to enforce them.

2. Parents were coached to work at reparative nurturing—to parent differently in areas where emotional needs of the girls had been neglected. It was suggested that a stronger relationship with the school be developed and that learning evaluations be requested to assess what help could be made available to Linda in the school environment. Both Mr. and Mrs. Jones were asked to begin "training" the girls for independent functioning by asking them to take responsibility for various tasks around the house.

3. Once the immediate symptoms were addressed, the therapist moved to establish a different emotional equilibrium in the family and to shift roles further. This was accomplished by discussing the family's reactions to alcoholism at length. Joe was asked to help Linda accept and understand his alcoholism, and to hear and respond to her anger about it. Her sister, who listened to this process intently, obviously benefited. Linda, meanwhile, was asked to function in the role of co-therapist and to direct a family sculpture of the emotional relationships in the family as they were and as she would like them to be. With much support from the therapist, she became very involved with this task and managed to render quite an accurate portrait of the family's life together. Her perceptiveness impressed even her father and she gained new status in the eyes of all the family members as well as her own.

A comparison was made between the way that Joe's drinking served to rock the boat in the family and the way that Linda's behavior had a similar effect. It was recommended that the two team up to "rock the boat" in a positive way and that they plan a surprise event for the family which others must agree to be involved with. This task quickly elicited Joe's fear of planning something that the others wouldn't "approve of." Similar tasks were proposed for other combinations of family members at various points in time.

The family was asked to bring in scrapbooks and pictures of family events, baby pictures of the girls, and to reminisce together about some of the events the pictures portrayed. The girls in particular became quite involved in this process and were quick to point out which of them had been more or less the focus of attention at which points in time.

4. Finally, Mary was asked to talk about her feelings in response to Joe, his alcoholism, and their relationship. Joe was asked to find ways to be more responsive to Mary and she to him. At this point, Joe became depressed. He began to feel discomfort with his greater involvement with the family—he began to attend fewer AA meetings. The therapist refocused attention on the importance of AA, consolidated the gains that the family had made, and reduced the frequency of therapy.

Outcome and Comments

Linda's school functioning improved and her acting out significantly lessened. She became much more a vital member of the family and she noticeably smiled more frequently and was, in general, more responsive. The parents had shifted their parenting patterns and the family began to experience a loosening of the rigidity that had characterized their interactions. Patterns of over and underresponsibility were shifted and an adjustment to the reality of alcoholism and its effects in the family's life was accomplished.

Joe's depression and discomfort with his new role were viewed as direct evidence of sex role issues. Joe felt very uncomfortable with feeling because it made him question his masculinity. He talked frequently of not understanding women and yet he, like Linda, was one of the more emotional members of the family. His greater involvement with the family clearly made him uncomfortable and even though he felt pride in his ability to take a more active role in family life, greater emotional involvement also aroused a great deal of fear and anxiety. The therapist discussed this fact directly with both him and Mary, and talked about the stereotypes of masculine and feminine behavior that both had learned in their families. Since Joe and Mary both expressed satisfaction with the current marital relationship the therapist finally opted not to push for further change in this relationship and to assume that the two would find a balance comfortable for them. On follow-up two years later, Joe is still sober and the family remains free of symptoms.

It is important to be aware that even adult children who no longer live in the home may have reactions in their own relational contexts to the sobriety of a parent. It is useful to include as many family members as possible in postsobriety sessions to help address unresolved issues and dysfunctional relationships that may still occur between the adult child and his parent(s).

Family Treatment When the Child Is the Alcoholic

When the family enters treatment because of an alcohol problem in a child, or when a child-focused problem reveals itself to be alcohol abuse, three considerations are important: Is the symptom one that is functioning to mask problems in the marital or family structure of a dry or sober family? Is the child's alcoholism deflecting attention from parental alcoholism? Or is the child's alcoholism creating other family problems? In any case, the alcoholism must be the primary focus of intervention, but the issues and technqiues involved will differ.

The Alcoholic Child with an Alcoholic Parent

If a parent in the family of an alcoholic child is actively drinking, it is frequently the case that the child's alcoholism serves the function of deflecting attention from the parental drinking. Alternatively, the family may deny the child's alochol abuse and deny the parent's alcohol abuse equally. Frequently, alcohol abuse in the child suggests concurrent multiple drug abuse as well.

A system in which both parent and child drink resembles a single parent system (Beal, 1980) in that the only member of the family functioning in a parental role is typically the spouse—again, frequently aided by a sibling of the drinking child who becomes the surrogate spouse/parent.

The therapist must intervene to stop the overfunctioning of both the spouse and the overresponsible child. The spouse should be referred to Al-Anon, the child to Alateen, and the overresponsibility of both should be engaged in the positive interests of encouraging the drinking spouse and drinking child into various parts of the program. Initially, the most efficient work that may be done with this type of family is to encourage the drinking child to attend Alateen to address the parent's drinking and the parent to attend Al-Anon to address the child's drinking. Frequently, a client who attends one program in the interest of another family member recognizes and is able to admit his own problem with alcohol. The therapist must use her judgment in terms of deciding what course of action is likely to be palatable to which family member—it is important to motivate whatever family member one can to attend any program for whatever reason in the interests of beginning to shift the family dynamic and change the way family members perceive the problem. Working towards establishing lines of responsibility that are structurally consistent is ideal.

As an example, in one family, both the father and adolescent daughter drank alcoholically. The mother was in effect a single parent because the parents were divorced. The noncustodial father was asked to come in to help with the child's acting-out, but it soon became apparent that his drinking allowed the mother to disqualify him as a parent and, in fact, he did operate very ineffectually with his two children. The therapist was able to motivate the daughter to go to Alateen where she acquired information about alcoholism. She then participated with the rest of the family in an intervention in which she confronted the father about his drinking. He went into treatment, got sober, and began to take a more effective parental role in terms of joining forces with the mother to set limits with the daughter. He eventually developed a relationship with his daughter in which he was able to encourage her to go to AA to address her drinking problem so that AA became a vehicle for facilitating a growing closeness between them. In this case, the mother had adamantly refused Al-Anon attendance, and the change in the family was really precipitated by the alcoholic daughter's taking on a new and more palatable (to herself) role by agreeing to attend Alateen. Once sobriety had been achieved somewhere in the system, more conventional structural work could be done and the adjustment phase of sobriety work was carried out.

Alternatively, the therapist—again, based on his judgment about who can be motivated to do what—may attempt to empower the drinking parent and elicit her support initially in addressing the child's alcoholism by limit setting, attendance at Al-Anon, and cooperative work with the spouse to impose consequences and control the child's drinking. The therapist may suggest that the parent take the child to AA herself. If this fails, the "bending the bow" principle applies and the case can be made that the child's behavior is uncontrollable because of the parent's drinking. This will leave the spouse with the decision as to how he will handle two hopeless alcoholics and will typically motivate him to cooperate more fully in terms of attending Al-Anon, curtailing overresponsible behavior, taking positions, and setting limits. Ultimately, it may result in a decision to leave the alcoholic.

In these situations, the nondrinking parent is frequently more motivated to focus on the child's alcoholism than on the spouse's and may go to great lengths to get the child into treatment programs while essentially ignoring the spouse. The sober child may induce the parent to stop drinking or the child may come out of a treatment program and relapse—in which case the parent may "throw in the towel" out of guilt and get sober. The outcome of this type of situation is frequently that the two alcoholics alternately achieve sobriety and then relapse until the family dynamics can be significantly reversed and restabilized. Sobriety for the parent is the more crucial to achieve in terms of lasting change for the family as a whole, but sobriety wherever it can be achieved is a starting point for further change in the family.

The Alcoholic Child and the Sober Alcoholic Parent

Families frequently seek treatment for alcoholic children at the point that a parent is in the early phases of sobriety. Focus on the child's problem at this particular phase in the family's adjustment to sobriety represents a number of structural dynamics:

1. Shifting of the symptom to another family member.
2. A reaction to loss of role in the child.
3. The child's cooperating in shifting unresolved anger and defusing anxiety in the parental subsystem by redirecting the family's focus towards him.
4. The effects of the child's problems having gone unnoticed during the adult alcoholic's drinking. The parents are now available to shift their attention to the child, and the child's behavior represents a reaction to their attempt to resume a parental role.

As the following case illustrates, a child's alcoholism, when it occurs in the early phases of a parent's sobriety, may serve to restabilize the family around drinking and may eventually return the family to its former balance with the focus on the drinking spouse.

Following Hank's tentative achievement of sobriety, the focus in the family shifted to sixteen-year-old Diane, the second child of Betsey's first marriage. Diane had always been Hank's "understudy," functioning as her mother's emotional partner during his drinking, but in many ways she had a covert coalition with him against her mother. Her loyalty conflicts were severe. As her drinking and drug use escalated, overt battles between her and Betsey emerged, battles which replicated the battles that Hank and Betsey had when Hank was drinking.

The therapist managed to unite the parents in a decision to place Diane in a rehabilitation program. The therapist asked Hank to be the "villain" and to tell Diane that she was to leave for the program right after the therapy session. The intensity of Diane's reaction to Hank's taking charge and telling her he had made arrangements for the rehab that very afternoon was a very clear indication that a real structural shift had taken place, however temporarily, in the family. Diane was enraged. However, she went, and has remained sober since. Hank acted as a very competent co-parent when Diane first came home, but relapsed very shortly afterwards and continues to do so. Eventually, he was admitted for a second time to a rehabilitation program himself.

The periods in which everybody remains in control or "sober" in this family have been fleeting. They are still in a very unstable phase.

In the family where a child's alcoholism emerges during the adjustment phase of sobriety, issues of parenting style are crucial to address. Typically, before sobriety, parents have failed to control the child at all or have controlled on all the wrong issues. After sobriety, tension about drinking behavior is high—even children in the family who do not engage in problem drinking will be interrogated, accused, and generally distrusted. The parental style reverts from nonattention and no (or inappropriate) limit setting, to overinvolvement and very punitive measures to control the child. Parents, particularly the nondrinking spouse, express frustration and a sense of helplessness about "knowing the right thing to do," while the sober alcoholic, out of guilt, alternates expressions of rage with attempts at "understanding" the child.

In general, parents in the adjustment phase of sobriety with an alcoholic child need to apply the general parenting principles outlined on page 211 for families with postsobriety issues. The goals specifically have to do with role loss, limit setting, and reparative nurturing in response to the alcoholism of one or more children in the family.

As Stanton and Todd's (1982) treatment model with substance abusing families indicates, the parents must be united in their decisions on how the child is to be dealt with. The therapist can anticipate that with a newly sober alcoholic and a still resentful, angry spouse, accomplishing this task will be the most difficult since it involves the alcoholic assuming, perhaps for the first time, a cooperative, competent parental role with a spouse who may continue to be invested in her view of herself as the only competent parent. The therapist must work very carefully to frame this situation in a way that makes it both palatable and necessary for both spouses to save face enough to enter into a working relationship around the child's drinking. New role behaviors should be coached in the session and the likelihood of one spouse sabotaging agreements should always be anticipated and predicted.

Once an agreement to work cooperatively has been reached, parents can be coached to take the following steps:

1. Take positions about what will and will not be tolerated regarding drinking behavior in and outside the home. Establish specific consequences when rules are violated.
2. Give up overresponsible behavior—do not take any responsibility for tasks, behaviors, or feelings of the child that are appropriately his to deal with.
3. Don't protect the child from the consequences of her actions—do not bail her out of situations that may arise as the result of drinking. For instance, do not pay for car insurance if she drinks and drives, or for lawyers' fees to defend her against drunk driving charges.

4. Depending on the age of the child, parents may decide to take responsibility for putting the child into a treatment center or for requiring attendance at AA meetings. With younger children— aged thirteen to sixteen—this decision is frequently effective in stopping the drinking, and relapse is less likely to occur if the first three steps are consistently maintained. With older children of seventeen or eighteen, this type of intervention is frequently less effective and the adolescent needs to be allowed to "hit bottom" and "agree" to treatment in much the same way that the adult alcoholic would.

Once the child's sobriety has been achieved, and during the course of attempting to achieve it, many of the marital issues common to postsobriety treatment will be raised. In general, the therapist is always dealing with restructuring of roles for the entire family, and as better parenting and more stable sobriety evolve, the more difficult issues of power, control, pride, intimacy, and sexuality in the marriage can be addressed.

It is important to bear in mind that although the adjustment to sobriety phase has been defined as occurring from six months to two years after drinking has ceased, if a family presents themselves for treatment with an alcoholic child after five years of sobriety, the therapist may usually assume that early adjustment issues have not been resolved and may proceed with treatment accordingly.

The Alcoholic Child with Nonalcoholic Parents

Situations in which children of nonalcoholic parents develop drinking problems usually involve a pattern in which parents are overly responsible for the child, but underresponsible in terms of self-focus and have difficulty with appropriate limit setting. The alcoholic child or others in the family may be triangled into the marital relationship as a spouse surrogate or as a scapegoat for marital conflict. Frequently, there is an intergenerational progression of the alcoholism—one or both parents typically had one or more alcoholic parents, and the dynamics that may maintain or provide a context for alcoholic drinking are usually present so that the symptom occurs again at this new generational level.

Many alcoholic traits may exist in the family in terms of the extreme complementarity of roles and sex role conflicts. The drinking child is often emotionally overresponsible for one parent and tremendously angry at the other and frequently plays the "bad" scapegoat role while another sibling may play the "good" compliant role.

Frequently, nondrinking parents from alcoholic backgrounds communicate intensely high expectations to their children and, consequently, parentify them in the sense that the child's accomplishment and behavior is viewed as a direct commentary on the parents' adequacy. Similarly, the parent may seek from the child approval he never received from his own parent so that limit setting and appropriate parental behavior are absent. Sibling position and sex of the child may figure heavily in terms of which child is focused on and parentified and, consequently, which one drinks.

With this type of family situation, goals for and steps in treatment are similar to those in families with a sober alcoholic parent. Parents must be helped to agree on a plan of action, set limits, and give up overresponsibility for the child. Additionally, they need to be helped to disengage from the child in terms of their expectations that she parent them. Marital and family-of-origin issues that may arise as the child achieves sobriety and as the family roles shift may or may not become a focus of treatment. In general, if patterns of over-and underresponsibility in the family are not shifted permanently, drinking is likely to recur either in the same child or in another, and, in some cases, in one of the parents.

Adult Children of Alcoholics

The legacies of alcoholism express themselves in adult children of alcoholics in many of the ways that have been mentioned in earlier chapters on pride structures and in the role types outlined by Wegscheider and Black. Janet Woititz's book, *Adult Children of Alcoholics* (1983), is a useful text that offers an outline of some of the personality characteristics found to be common to adult children of alcoholics.

When adult children seek treatment either with family-of-origin or nuclear family problems, it is helpful to be aware of the following issues in addition to those already mentioned for younger children in alcoholic systems:

1. Adult children of alcoholics in a high percentage of cases are either married to an alcoholic or will become an alcoholic themselves.
2. The adult child typically operates at one complementary extreme of either overresponsible or underresponsible behavior in either the functional or emotional dimension.
3. He will usually respond with intense pride or defensiveness in areas in which he feels particularly emotionally vulnerable and inadequate.
4. In many cases, the alcoholic environment she has lived in has tended to distort her perceptions of self and others, and she has

difficulty realistically assessing life situations and achieving the gratification of basic needs.

5. Many typically alcoholic defenses such as rationalization, intellectualization, or denial are typical of the adult child.

6. He typically experiences the world as a very unsafe place in which people are either to be avoided, placated, or overpowered, but never trusted.

7. She is either very emotionally constricted, or tends to live at extremes of either intense emotion or lack of feeling and responsiveness. She either tends to be very reserved and self-contained emotionally or to act out, potentially through alcohol or drug abuse. She often experiences intense ambivalence about almost all relationships and life decisions.

8. He typically experiences very low self-esteem, feels valueless, and longs for recognition and emotional contact, but cannot bring himself to do the very things that would result in recognition or emotional responsiveness from others. No realistic success is owned or experienced as "adequate enough" and emotional response or support from others is blocked because it arouses tremendous fears of dependency and helplessness. He often experiences chronic emptiness or sadness related to the lack of a responsive parental figure.

9. Sexual preference and identification may be conflicted as a result of the inappropriate blurring of boundaries often experienced between parents and children in alcoholic systems. Relationships with the opposite sex may be impaired by experiences of real or implied incest, overinvolvement or extreme distance of a same or opposite sex parent, feelings of betrayal, attack, or rejection by a same or opposite sex parent.

Treatment Goals for Adult Children

1. Using the family genogram, coach the adult child to identify and reverse to whatever degree possible the role she assumed in the family.

2. Encourage an awareness of self-experience over time in the family and define how that experience relates to his present relational difficulties.

3. Relabel or reframe obvious misperceptions about self or rigidly fixed perceptions of other family members in the context of an understanding of alcoholic behavior and systemic dynamics typical in an alcoholic family.

4. Encourage an awareness of self in the feeling dimension and explore the ways the client does or does not respond to and express her own needs and feelings in various relational contexts (spouse, work, parental, siblings, etc.).
5. Suggest behavioral changes related to the above emotional patterns that will encourage self-responsibility without a tendency to fall into or perpetuate over or underresponsible behavior.
6. Help the client to become aware of his pride issues—grandiose thinking, self-effacing tendencies—and encourage realistic goal setting.
7. Encourage the client to act on one aspect of her characteristic ambivalence and to explore more fully the sadness connected with an experienced absence of parenting.

Adult children who are not alcoholic benefit from intervention that is supportive, instructional, and involves a great deal of reality-based feedback about themselves, their behavior, and the requirements of adult responsibility. The therapist must walk a fine line between becoming overresponsible and parental with the adult child, and responding appropriately to the real personality and developmental deficits that result from life in an alcholic environment. Directness, self-disclosure, and encouragement of participation in groups and workshops providing interaction with other adult children are productive interactional tools when the adult child is treated in an individual context. The rationale for this approach involves the following points:

Support conveys an acceptance of the client's particular world view and self-experience and defines a context in which the client can reverse his tendency to defend against feelings, be distrustful, and withhold self-expression. Instruction or "teaching" or coaching of appropriate responses to problem situations restores some of the real developmental learning or emotional experience that may never have taken place in the client's family environment. Reality-based feedback provides an interactional framework in which the client gains a sense of what is "normal" interactionally and "true" about her experience of self. Self-disclosure defines the relational context as one of equality, portrays the therapist as an equally limited human being, and avoids a complementary relationship in which dependency is fostered so that the client continues to feel inadequate or incompetent but "liked or helped" by a benevolent therapist. The ultimate goal with adult children is to empower them to accept and take responsibility for needs and feelings in a realistic way.

Finally, family-of-origin work, that is, an exploration of roles, behavior, and emotional patterns of the family and a coaching and rehearsal of specific behavioral changes with family members, is an organizing principle for individual treatment.

For instance, Bill, the second son in his family, functioned as an oldest and was exceedingly successful in his own company. He never knew any way of life except that of overachieving. He entered therapy as his marriage of some thirty years was breaking up, partly due to his wife's anger at feeling that she had lost a sense of herself in relationship to this tremendously competent man.

Bill had never related his overfunctioning to his mother's alcoholism until the therapist commented on some of the common characteristics that adult children of alcoholics share. He readily related. In therapy he is being coached to repair emotional cutoffs of long standing with his sons and his brothers which ultimately repeated themselves in an emotional cutoff in his marriage.

Jane, a younger of two daughters, had always been expected to meet her own needs as a child. The family focus of attention was alternately on her sister, who was epileptic and probably schizophrenic, and on her alcoholic father. Following her sister's death, in the hope of gaining her mother's love, Jane willingly triangled herself into her parents' marital conflict, listening for hours to her mother's complaints about her father's drinking. When her mother refused to go to Al-Anon, however, and quoted Jane to her father, she cut off from both parents. Some five years after the cutoff, as her father was dying, she was coached to reopen her relationship with him, and he, shortly before his death, acknowledged his alcoholism to her. She is now working on strengthening the relationship with her mother.

When clients are not able to work directly with a parent to reverse their typical role behavior, or when a parent is dead, letter writing is another useful tool for helping to unblock unexpressed feeling and open potential new behaviors in a relationship.

Following are two excerpts of letters from daughters to their alcoholic fathers. The first writer, Babs, has been in therapy for bulimia. Her mother is alcoholic and now sober and her father continues to drink. Babs is twenty-one.

Dad:

I wish I could calmly say to you what I can only express here on paper.

I want to confront what in my eyes is a drinking problem you have. Quite frankly, it worries the heck out of me. I find it detrimental not only to yourself, which is bad enough, but as well to the rest of the family. I do not know if the drinking is increasing, or I am just becoming more aware of if. But, whichever is the case, it is overwhelming. It's not only worrisome but it's scary, unhealthy, anger-causing, and isolating. I think it's a large cause of the isolation you say you feel from the family. You say you are never told what's going on, that no one tells you, even though we may have discussed whatever the issue for literally days prior to the event. If we haven't told you it's either an oversight of pure honesty or personally I just gave up, thinking, "Why bother? He won't remember or care if he does remember." It sets a huge barrier which I watch grow higher and higher with every drink that I think you may have taken.

It seems insane. I get so angry, Dad! Here is a man I love and respect more than most anyone I know. Yet, I find myself looking around to see if you've had a drink or not, figuring out if you're sober or drunk, getting angry at you for being what I would consider "under the influence" in a way which you cannot control. (I know it's a disease, though you seem not to accept it as such.) And this man is my father? . . . I used to think I hated you. But now I know it's not you I hate, for you're a good man. You're kind and loving and a lot of fun when I catch you at the right moments . . . mostly the a.m. or when you're just home from work . . . your sober moments. It's the alcohol which I hate for it has robbed me of my father.

I always feel that I shouldn't say anything. Who am I after all? What do I know? Who am I to tell you what I see as a problem? And do I really think you're going to listen to me? You're just going to get angry, perhaps you may even drink more . . . at me. But that's what I'm risking in spite of how important your approval has always been to me.

And now back to my questions. . . . Who am I? I am your daughter . . . I've lived with you 21 years now. I'm one of the 7 other family members of yours who all are terribly concerned. What do I know? Well, perhaps more than anyone would think. I know the world is a big place, a bit complicated at times, it's scary, it's hard (life ain't always easy) . . . especially for a man who's head of a family like ours. It can get lonely . . . overwhelmingly so . . . and it's hard to turn to someone else. God knows none of us wants to appear weak or afraid or troubled. Especially, probably, a man. I myself am lonely a majority of the time . . . even when I'm with people. So I know from my experience. But, you know what? (I've had to learn this) we are only human. God made us that way. We all make mistakes and mess up. We all have emotions, we all have feelings, and we all have to express the feelings and emotions sometime. Somehow, we all need someone. That's why there are more than just one human. Now, who am I to tell you what I see as a problem? As I've said, I'm someone who is deeply affected by this problem which I see as alcoholism. You and I both know I've got my problems too. Anorexia and bulimia. And I'm not proud of them either. But, I'm trying to fight them, I'm trying to save myself. I'm hoping the same for you. I hope you will listen to me and at least consider what I'm saying. For it affects us all, just as my problem affects us all. But no one can help me 'til I'm willing to help myself. Then I can open up and receive and utilize others' support. No one can help you, Dad, but you. I'm here and so is the rest of the family to support and help you in any way we can. But the first step must come from you. I'm trying my steps, and trying to handle my diseases. I may not ask you for help. That is because how can I if I feel you are "not all there"?

Dad, I hope you will consider what I'm saying, for our sakes as well as your own. I cannot force you and nor would I want to. It's your life. I just want to, hopefully, open your eyes and just ask.

Because I love you,

—B—

Babs's father never acknowledged the letter from Babs although he tried for a time to do something about his drinking. She, however, felt considerably freed by having said things openly. It is important to remember that the client is being helped to change herself, not to change the other person.

In the next letter, Sarah is in her fifties. Her father is dead.

Dear Daddy:

All of my life you have been very important to me. You always sent me letters and postcards and I knew that I was always being thought about. And when I was having problems in school you always wrote to me with very good advice. I knew that you cared. And I knew that you loved me. I always felt as though you and I were the closest ones in our family and I felt as though Bill and Betsey were jealous of me because of the attention that you paid to me and because of the gifts that you gave to me. I always felt that I was the special one in the family because of you.

But, the drinking that you did always confused me. I couldn't understand why you would treat yourself so miserably when life was so beautiful and when others needed you so very much. I was embarrassed to be with you when you were drinking and embarrassed that you would show up at the events I was involved in—drunk. And, many times you did. I remember those days at college when you would appear at the reception room of my dormitory drunk. I was so very embarrassed. I wished that you had not come, but I wanted to get out of there as fast as possible so that not too many would see you and embarrass me. I did not like to tell you not to come because I knew that you wanted to see me. I would have rather stayed with my friends sometimes.

I know you did all that you could for me and you also did all that you thought was right at the time. I would have liked to have gone to Boston Country Day for high school, but I always felt that although you wanted me to go you were not strong enough in convincing Mother that that was where I should have been.

I spent a lot of my time thinking about you . . . whether you would be drinking or not, and what things would be like at home. Although you and I were the closest ones in the family and I could talk to you, I wasn't able to tell you everything and sometimes felt a little strained in my conversations with you. I knew that you wanted me to do well and was always trying to achieve, but I never really felt as though I did as well as Bill and Betsey.

I often felt sorry for you because you seemed to be so alone and Mother never really expressed her love to you. She was always making excuses for you. But you were such a kind man and were always put down by Mother. Of course, I do remember you making fun of Mother's family and I guess that was hard for her to take. I hated it when you two drank cocktails at nighttime and got into terrible arguments. This was when I was living at home after college and I don't feel now that I should have been there at that point in my life. I felt as though you and Mother thought it would be disgraceful if I left home before I was married. But those years living at home were very difficult for me.

Daddy, I knew that I was the apple of your eye and I knew that you loved me and always wanted to do things for me. I enjoyed going to the football games that you took me to, but I was always afraid that you would drink and I would be embarrassed. One thing strange that I remember was when I started to develop you put your arms around me and I don't know whether you did it on purpose or not, but you always seemed to touch my breasts from my back. It made me feel funny.

I loved being with you, Daddy, because when you were sober you were always quiet and peaceful. We had fun working in the garden and cutting the grass and fixing up the house. I enjoyed going on trips with you, especially when you took me to all the historic sights in Boston. We had such a good time during that period of my life. I also enjoyed going on business trips with you. You taught me so much about traveling and about the towns that we visited.

Thank you for being my dad and making me feel special.

I loved Christmastime so much . . . it was almost scary to me. The anticipation of the holidays overwhelmed me. When they were over, I was so very depressed. I could not take the tree down because it was so very sad. Most often on Christmas—as on many holidays—you got drunk. I can remember Christmas eves waiting for you to come home, and when you finally did, you were drunk. It was always such a tremendous letdown. Christmas morning you loved, as I did, and we had such a good time. But then later on the drinking started and Christmas dinner was always hard. I know now that you couldn't help the drinking because you did have this disease.

I appreciated the help that you gave me with my school projects, especially in sixth grade history—you helped me get to sit in the number one seat in the class. It was fun doing the projects with you. I also remember the help you gave me in Girl Scouts—with my merit badges.

We had a lot of bad times and a lot of good times. You were always special to me.

I regret that after I was married, I did not see you so very much and my visits to Boston were cut down. I guess I felt an obligation to be with Bob and since he did not want to make the trip, I just did what he wanted me to do. Of course, he was drinking a lot, too, and I was growing in my illness of being addicted to the alcoholic. When you were in the hospital the last time, I never came to see you and did not get a chance to say good-bye to you. I don't know why I never got there because I felt so lost when you died. There aren't any excuses for my not being there toward the end. And when Martha called me collect at 5 a.m., I felt so alone and it made it so impersonal. I'm glad that we had so many good years together—I'm just sorry that our later years weren't closer. I am glad that you knew Susan when she was such a tiny girl. That made me so very happy. I am glad that I have a picture of the two of you. You are the two most special people in my life.

Good-bye, Daddy—I love you.

When the treatment context is the whole family, the therapist's role changes in that changes in role behavior between parents and child may be orchestrated directly within the session. Parents can be coached to assume a more appropriate parental role and, to some degree, to repair the emotional gaps.

Again, it is important to be aware that the adult child frequently does not *know how* to deal effectively with relationships, with adult responsibilities, and with interpersonal problems. His skills for meeting his most basic needs are often inadequate, and his protestations to this effect are real and not usually manipulative bids for caretaking. The therapist must acknowledge an understanding of the client's dilemma and avoid unresponsive or punitive interactions, while at the same time stressing that ultimately it is the client's responsibility to learn how to deal with his problem. As a general rule, the therapist should respond directly to "how" questions and then proceed to comment on the client's failure to use the information he has asked for and been given if this behavior pattern emerges. Frequently, the adult child needs to mourn the lack of adequate parenting in his background before he can free his energies to assume appropriate self-responsibility.

Summary of Primary Treatment Goals with Children in Alcoholic Families

Presobriety

1. Educate children about drinking.
2. Provide a safe environment in which feelings about drinking and the drinking parent can be discussed. Relieve the child's sense of being responsible for the problem.
3. Rule out potential abuse.
4. Attempt to restore appropriate parenting to whatever degree possible.
5. With older children, assess the potential that one or more children in the family can exert influence in getting the parent sober with the therapist's support. Children are not necessarily included in all sessions. Do not attempt to deprive the child of functional survival roles at this point in treatment.

Adjustment and Maintenance Phases

1. Assess presobriety roles and help the child adjust to new role demands that may evolve as sobriety progresses.
2. Normalize and help the child to express feelings of rage, sadness, and fear at the changes in the family.
3. Help parents to assume appropriate parental responsibility stressing the need for reparative nurturing. Children should be

included in all sessions until the focus of treatment shifts to specific marital issues.

The Alcoholic Child

1. Encourage parents to make a commitment to cooperate in parenting and setting limits for the child.
2. Ask them to take positions, set limits, and to give up overresponsible behavior, particularly around the child's drinking.
3. Depending on the specific situation, have parents assume responsibility for admitting the child to a rehabilitation or treatment program.

The Adult Child of the Alcoholic

1. Examine in detail the role the adult played in her family of origin and trace the ways she perpetuates that role in current relationships.
2. Help reframe the client's self-perceptions based on an understanding of what dynamics typically occur in an alcoholic-system—in other words, help the client to "name" his experience in a way that defines it as normal in the context of an alcoholic environment.
3. Support, encourage, and—when necessary—teach appropriate, realistic responsibility for self in both functional and emotional dimensions. Provide reality-based feedback.
4. Coach a shift in role behavior in family and other primary relationships.

CHAPTER 11

The Role of the Therapist
Limitation and Right Relation

THE PREDOMINANT focus of this book has been on thinking and on doing, on relating ways of conceptualizing about alcoholism to concrete actions the therapist may take to work with the family affected by alcoholism. Finally, it seems important to discuss the "being" of the therapist—how his or her attitudes and ways of thinking about self and role in the therapy of alcoholic systems and people is likely to affect the outcome of treatment.

As David Berenson (1979) has pointed out, the therapist's relationship with an alcoholic system or an alcoholic relationship can often replicate the dynamics that occur within the relationship itself. The therapist becomes overly invested in "doing something" about the alcoholism, in changing the alcoholic or the system in much the same way that the nondrinking members of an alcoholic family focus on and try to change the drinker. This need to "do something" replicates the "incorrect complementarity" that exists in the system in two ways. First, and most obviously, it reestablishes the overresponsible, underresponsible dynamic between the therapist and the family. The therapist now overfunctions emotionally, perhaps functionally, in an attempt to "help" the family.

Second, and more subtly, it replicates an "incorrect complementarity" or an incorrect relationship that is endemic to the nature of the therapeutic context itself: It establishes one person (the therapist) as better than, more knowledgeable than, more expert about the problems of being and living than the other (the client). Thus, the therapist seems "in control," the client out of control. The therapist seems independent, the client dependent. The therapist is objective, the client subjective. The one-up/one-down nature of the interaction between alcoholic and nonalcoholic is thus subtly replicated between therapist and client and the pride systems of both become activated in much the same way that they do within the alcoholic interaction. The more one-down, dependent, and helpless the client feels, the more he will resist change, and the more powerless, ineffectual, and out of control the therapist feels, the more she will reassert her dominance, her expertness, her attempts to *do* something about the client's situation. Soon the therapist becomes a victim of the false trap in which the alcoholic is caught. She denies limitation and denies dependence—like the co-alcoholic, she begins to take ultimate pride in her ability to help or do for others, and this is precisely the attitude that will likely provoke the alcoholic to drink more or the family to rigidify its already dysfunctional boundaries and structure. If one refers to the pride wheel (Figure 3–2), the therapist frequently experiences herself squarely at the top of the wheel in the "God" position—that is, dominant and in control, while the client experiences himself squarely at the bottom. This incorrect complementarity may occur to a greater or lesser degree in any therapist-client interaction, but it is particularly dysfunctional when it occurs in the therapy of alcoholic systems.

What steps can a therapist take to foster a "right relationship" when working with alcoholic systems?

First, the issue of attitude is of crucial importance. Many people have very negative attitudes toward alcoholism, and frequently these attitudes have to do with a fundamental intolerance for, or a belief that all dependency is a bad thing. Often, as psychotherapists, we tend to perpetuate the false myth that absolute independence and control over our own lives is both desirable and attainable. Negative attitudes toward Alcoholics Anonymous are frequently extensions of this thinking that dependency is bad. One hears many therapists speak of AA as a crutch, even while paying lip service to its "utility" in "doing the job" of keeping alcoholics sober.

Since an acceptance of mutuality, interdependence, limited control, and limited dependence is crucial to the alcoholic's recovery, these countermessages can be very damaging indeed. They tend to evolve from the same "false epistemology" or false view of self in the therapist that maintained the alcoholic's drinking. And yet, they are more the norm than the exception in terms of the way therapists view their role.

For example, one of the authors was supervising the therapy session of an alcoholic mother who had achieved sobriety through the Pentecostal church. The therapist asked how the woman had stopped drinking. The response was "God." The client then went on to explain that she had been reluctant to mention it because she thought that psychiatrists did not believe in God. The therapist's reponse was, "It's not my role to make judgments, if it works for you."

In the training group discussion that followed, the therapist maintained initially that by saying, "if it works for you" she meant to convey that it was o.k. With urging from the trainer the group began to process their feelings about spirituality. The actual transcript of the discussion follows.

TRAINEE 1: . . . Plus giving God the credit always makes me angry because she's [*the client*] the one who stopped drinking, you know, and I don't believe in giving God the credit.

TRAINEE 2: But, it's like wanting to give the psychiatrist the credit—it's the same thing.

TRAINEE 3: Well, I guess my own spirituality has been an ambivalent process because of my ambivalence about being dependent, about being vulnerable in relationships, and my conflicts when that happens. It's my relationships with people and with God and my struggles with vulnerability and dependency that I think would interfere with my attitudes about the Pentecostal view of spirituality. That's very polarized from my position. In that session I would probably have felt a little nervous inside, a little queasy, a little anxious. That part of what she [*the client*] said I would have wanted to ignore . . . to push away.

THERAPIST: . . . J [*Trainee 3*] was talking about the sessions raising *his* anxiety, but mine was there even though I verbalized being nonjudgmental. I mean my initial reaction was "That's the stupidest thing I ever heard of."

TRAINER: Was it?

THERAPIST: Oh sure. I mean that was my gut feeling . . . uh . . . this woman . . . I'm not one of these fanatics and that was my initial reaction.

TRAINEE 1: That was my initial reaction to AA. I went to a large, open meeting and I just felt this whole thing about trading one dependency for another and when I left I said to myself . . . I know that what works, works . . . but . . . what's the real issue . . . what's the real problem here . . . I just had that feeling.

Clearly, it is important for the therapist to examine his own views about dependency and spirituality. Alcoholics and alcoholic families will not be likely to be treated effectively if the therapist's attitudes about AA and dependency of any kind are negative and reactive. The therapist should be honest enough to acknowledge this attitudinal problem if it exists, and refer the client or family elsewhere.

Some clues that therapist attitudes may be hindering therapy are: (1) too great a willingness to accept the client's resistance to AA, (2) neglect to check on or encourage the client's real involvement with the program, (3) impatience with AA rehetoric, (4) a tendency to encourage greater dependency on the therapeutic situation than on AA, (5) failure thoroughly to understand or learn about the principles of the AA program.

Finally, if the therapist is to establish a "correct complementary" relationship with his alcoholic client or family, she must struggle with the concepts of limited control and limited dependence just as the alcoholic does in achieving sobriety.

The implications of this struggle are subtle, yet profound in terms of the therapist's style of "being" or working with the client. Acceptance of limited control defines the therapist as of less importance or as less central to the client or family than the larger family, group, or community in which the family operates. Limited control does not suggest that the therapist takes no responsibility. Fundamentally, the therapist must realize that while he makes well-thought-out interventions—while he *does* things—his basic position is one of powerlessness. He must do things knowing that he can do nothing. He must realize that ultimately therapy may involve simply sitting with the client (or sending the client away), helping her to stay with a sense of despair and hopelessness long enough that the client can take advantage of the opportunity hopelessness provides for change. In other words, the therapist is required to be in correct relationship with the client, while allowing the client to "hit bottom" and to begin the process of taking responsibility for her own life.

The therapist must then be willing, as Berenson points out, to sit with her own anxiety and hopelessness. She may also need to accept the criticisms of colleagues, the anger of the client, and her own reproach if hitting bottom doesn't occur before a car accident or a suicide.

In short, acceptance of limited control means that the therapist must be courageous enough to take calculated therapeutic risks and to take the consequences of those risks. Sometimes he must be willing *not* to intervene. He must constantly question his judgment as to the appropriate degree of responsibility to take.

Finally, true acceptance of limited control would mean that the therapist could rejoice when the client gave all the credit for his growth to his sponsor in AA, or even to God. This last remark is really a statement about the nature of limited dependency which suggests, for the therapist, a recognition of the degree to which she may seek to have clients, rather than people in her immediate interpersonal environment, meet needs for self-validation or power. The therapist who acknowledges or accepts the concept of limited dependency may recognize that the activity of "doing" therapy helps her to avoid uncomfortable feelings of dependency or vulnerability that might emerge in more mutual, equal interpersonal relationships. True mutuality of relationship would suggest that the therapist could temper her own perfectionistic tendencies with clients, admit error to them, and acknowledge the degree to which she needs her clients. She may also acknowledge the degree to which the activity of "doing therapy" cannot address the experience of personal isolation, hopelessness, or powerlessness.

These comments may seem to suggest that all therapists who work with alcoholic families need to shift their epistemological premises to be more consonant with those of AA. While this is not the case, it is important that a respect for AA be communicated to the client and that the therapist examine his own belief system, particularly, as it relates to the issues of responsibility, control, power, dependency, and spirituality. At the very least, therapists are encouraged to examine roles and issues within their own families of origin in a structured way in order to have some experiential understanding of premises that are corrective for the alcoholic family.

Alcoholism in families is a problem of epidemic and tragic proportions, but it is eminently treatable. More than many other symptomatic problems that plague families and society, it is highly predictable in its patterns and effects and responds, over time, to specific types of interventions. More often than not, however, those interventions will involve two important factors: The first is knowledge of objective facts about the effects of alcohol within a system and knowledge of the subjective experience of the alcoholic. Second, the therapist must *be* in correct relationship with the client or family. The treatment of alcoholism in families is one form of therapy in which it is often important to do nothing in an informed way.

Thus, the "treatment" of alcoholism may be as paradoxical as the symptom itself. Certainly for all that it is tragic in proportion, the growing understanding of alcoholism can teach us a great deal about human needs and can reveal a great deal about the ways in which our prevalent social structures fail to meet those needs. If it is our social context that influences how we think about ourselves, and if the way we think about ourselves pushes us to abuse drugs to correct self-experience, then we need not only to find better corrections, we need to change the context itself. Alcoholism tells us, more than most problems, some very important things about the way our social context needs to change. It remains for us, as a society and as mental health practitioners, to hear that message and to act differently in response to it.

Notes

Chapter 1.   Alcoholism: A Systemic Perspective

1. For a concise overview of the literature relating to the etiology of alcoholism see Royce (1981).
2. We are grateful to David Berenson for his discussion of some of the above concepts and their relevance to this text. They derive directly from his presentation at an international conference on Alcoholism and the Family in Dublin, Ireland, July 1984.
3. Bateson defines relationships as either "symmetrical" or "complementary." The symmetrical relationship is competitive—more of a particular kind of behavior in A stimulates more of the same behavior in B. A complementary relationship is one in which more of a particular behavior in A stimulates less of a different, but related behavior in B. See Chapter 2 for a more detailed discussion.

Chapter 2.   Alcoholism and the Interpersonal Context

1. The concepts of complementarity and symmetry are elaborated by Sluzki and Beavin in their chapter in *The Interactional View* (Watzlawick and Weakland, 1977).
2. The concept of the one-up/one-down nature of the complementary relationship is developed by Watzlawick (1964) and Haley (1963).

3. For a discussion of the concept of "emptiness" see Fogarty's paper "On Emptiness and Closeness" in *The Best of the Family: 1973–1978*.
4. An interesting exploration of this theme in more psychoanalytic terms is presented in Miller (1981).

Chapter 3. Alcoholism and the Self

1. The AA program consists of twelve steps that guide the alcoholic in his recovery. Step Two states, "Came to believe that a Power greater than ourselves could restore us to sanity" (AA World Services, 1952).

Chapter 4. Alcoholism and Gender

1. See Corrigan (1980); Powell, Penick, and Read (1980); Boothroyd (1980); Parker, Parker, Wolz, and Harford (1980); Scida and Vannicelli (1979); and Zucker, Battistich, and Langer (1981).
2. See Hare-Mustin (1978) and Libow, Raskin, and Caust (1982) for discussions of the relationship between feminism and family therapy.
3. See Beckman (1975) for a discussion and partial review of the literature on this issue.

Chapter 5. Assessing Alcohol Problems and Setting Treatment Goals

1. The American Medical Society on Alcoholism defines alcoholism as follows:

   Alcoholism is a chronic, progressive, and potentially fatal disease. It is characterized by: tolerance and physical dependency, pathologic organ changes, or both, all of which are the direct or indirect consequences of the alcohol ingested.

   Primary specific criteria for the diagnosis of alcoholism involve physical, emotional, and social changes that are cumulative, "tolerance" for high concentrations of alcohol, withdrawal symptoms when consumption is decreased, inability consistently to predict the duration of the drinking episode or the quantity to be consumed. For further elaboration of these criteria see Royce (1981: 15–22).
2. As well as defining five distinct types of alcoholism, Alpha, Beta, Delta, Gamma, and Epsilon, E. M. Jellinek characterized the disease as progressing through three stages, a Prodromal Phase, a Middle Stage, and a Late or Chronic Stage. The Prodromal Phase is characterized predominantly by increased tolerance for alcohol, preoccupation with drinking, rationalization, and personality changes resulting from drinking. The Middle Stage is often characterized by blackouts, loss of control, drinking alone, interference with

job performance, marital discord, increased psychological and physical dependence manifested by hiding bottles and physical signs of dependence such as tremors, flushed face, and so on. Late or Chronic Stage is characterized by acute physical illness, job loss, moral and ethical deterioration, obsessive need for alcohol and a marked drop in tolerance. For further elaboration, see either Jellinek (1960) or Royce (1981: 87–102).

3. See John Wallace, "Tactical and Strategic Use of the Preferred Defense Structure of the Recovering Alcoholic," paper presented at the 1974 Annual Meeting on Alcohol and Drug Problems of North America. Pamphlet published by National Council on Alcoholism, Inc., New York.

4. A useful questioning technique used by strategic therapists is described by Selvini-Palazzoli, Boscolo, Cecchin, and Prata (1980).

5. For a description of the development and use of a family genogram, see Guerin and Pendagast (1976).

Chapter 6. Intervening in Alcoholic Systems Before Sobriety

1. In a pamphlet, "I Can't Be an Alcoholic Because . . .," distributed by the National Council on Alcoholism, David Hancock (1969) elaborates on the common misconceptions that prevent people from recognizing alcoholism: "I'm not a skid row bum," "I never drink before five o'clock," "I never drink anything but beer," "I drink only on weekends," "I'm too young," "I can quit anytime."

2. Intervention is a specific, crisis-inducing approach to confronting the alcoholic developed by Vernon Johnson and his colleagues at the Johnson Institute in Minneapolis, Minnesota. For a complete description of the process, see Johnson (1973).

Chapter 7. Intervening in Alcoholic Systems After Sobriety

1. See Carter and Orfanidis (McGoldrick) (1976) for a discussion of the process of coaching work in the individual's family of origin. The original concept of differentiation work within the extended family is Bowen's (1978: 529–547).

2. Bowen (1978: 178). Here Bowen talks about the need for one spouse, by implication the overfunctioning one, to reduce other-directed thinking and acting and focus on self.

Chapter 9. A Model for Group Treatment of Alcoholic Family Members

1. The technique of prescribing reversals is discussed in a chapter by Carter and Orfanidis (McGoldrick) in Guerin, ed., 1976.

Chapter 10. The Role of Children in Family Treatment

1. Treadway discussed this technique at a conference at the University of Medicine and Dentistry of New Jersey, Piscataway, New Jersey, April 13, 1982.

Bibliography

ALCOHOLICS ANONYMOUS WORLD SERVICES, INC. *Twelve Steps and Twelve Traditions.* New York, 1952.

———. *Alcoholics Anonymous.* New York, 1955.

ALTMAN, MARJORIE, RUTH CROCKER, AND DONNA GAINES. "Female Alcoholics: The Men They Marry." *Focus on Women: Journal of Addictions and Health* 1, No. 1 (1980): 33–41.

BAILEY, MARGARET. *Alcoholism and Family Casework.* New York: New York City Affiliate, Inc., National Council on Alcoholism, 1974.

BATESON, GREGORY. *Naven.* Palo Alto, Calif.: Stanford University Press, 1958.

———. *Steps to an Ecology of Mind.* New York: Chandler Publishing Company, 1972.

———. *Mind and Nature.* New York: E. P. Dutton, 1979.

BATESON, G., D. JACKSON, J. HALEY, AND J. WEAKLAND. "Toward a Theory of Schizophrenia." *Behavioral Science* 1 (1956): 251–264.

BEAL, EDWARD W. "Separation, Divorce and Single Parent Families." In *The Family Life Cycle: A Framework for Family Therapy*, edited by E. Carter and M. McGoldrick. New York: Gardner Press, 1980.

BEAN, MARGARET AND NORMAN ZINBERG, EDS. *Dynamic Approaches to the Understanding and Treatment of Alcoholism.* New York: Free Press, 1981.

BECKMAN, LINDA. "Women Alcoholics: A Review of Social and Psychological Studies." *Journal of Studies on Alcohol* 36, No. 7 (1975): 797–825.

———. "Sex Role Conflict in Alcoholic Women: Myth or Reality." *Journal of Abnormal Psychology* 37, No. 4 (1978): 408–417.

Beckman, L. J., T. Day, P. Bardsley, and A. Z. Seeman. "The Personaility Characteristics and Family Backgrounds of Women Alcoholics." *International Journal of Addictions* 15 (1980): 147–154.

Bem, S. L. "Sex-role Adaptibility: One Consequence of Psychological Androgyny." *Journal of Personality and Social Psychology* 31 (1975): 634–643.

———. "The Measurement of Psychological Androgyny." *Journal of Consulting and Clinical Psychology* 42 (1974): 155–162.

Berenson, David. "A Family Approach to Alcoholism." *Psychiatry Opinion* 13 (1976a): 33–38.

———. "Alcohol and the Family System." In *Family Therapy: Theory and Practice*, edited by P. Guerin. New York: Gardner Press, 1976b.

———. "The Therapist's Relationship with Couples with an Alcoholic Member." In *The Family Therapy of Drug and Alcohol Abuse*, edited by E. Kaufman and P. Kaufman. New York: Gardner Press, 1979.

Bissell, LeClair. *Some Persepectives on Alcoholism.* Minneapolis, Minn.: The Johnson Institute, 1982 (pamphlet).

Black, Claudia. *It Will Never Happen to Me.* Denver, Colo.: M.A.C., 1982.

Blane, Howard. *The Personality of the Alcoholic: Guises of Dependency.* New York: Harper and Row, 1968.

Blum, Eva Marie. "Psychoanalytic Views on Alcoholism." *Quarterly Journal of Studies on Alcoholism* 27 (1966): 59–299.

Boothroyd, Wilfred. "Nature and Development of Alcoholism in Women." In *Alcohol and Drug Problems in Women.* Research Advances in Alcohol and Drug Problems, Vol. 5, edited by O. J. Kalant. New York: Plenum Press, 1980, pp. 299–329.

Bourne, P. G. and E. Light. "Alcohol Problems in Blacks and Women." In *The Diagnosis and Treatment of Alcoholism*, edited by J. H. Mendelson and N. K. Mello. New York: McGraw-Hill, 1979, pp. 83–123.

Bowen, Murray. *Family Therapy in Clinical Practice.* New York: Jason Aronson, 1978.

Broverman, I. K., D. M. Broverman, F. E. Clarkson, P. S. Rosenkrantz, and S. R. Vogel. "Sex-role Stereotypes and Clinical Judgments of Mental Health." *Journal of Consulting and Clinical Psychology* 34 (1970): 1–7.

Burtle, Vasanti. "Developmental/Learning Correlates of Alcoholism in Women." In *Women Who Drink: Alcoholic Experience and Psychotherapy*, edited by V. Burtle. Springfield, Ill.: Charles C. Thomas, 1979a, pp. 145–174.

———, ed. *Women Who Drink: Alcoholic Experience and Psychotherapy.* Springfield, Ill.: Charles C. Thomas, 1979b.

Busch, H., E. Kormendy, and W. Feuerlein. "Partners of Female Alcoholics." *British Journal of Addictions* 68 (1973): 179–184.

Carter, E. and M. McGoldrick Orfanidis. "Family Therapy with One Person and the Family Therapist's Own Family." In *Family Therapy: Theory and Practice*, edited by Philip Guerin, Jr. New York: Gardner Press, 1976.

————, EDS. *The Family Life Cycle: A Framework for Family Therapy*. New York: Gardner Press, 1980.

Center for Family Learning and Georgetown University Family Center. *The Best of the Family 1973–1978*. New Rochelle, New York, and Washington, D.C.

CHATHAM, L. R., M. A. ANDERSON, P. PERSON, AND J. KEYES. "Employed Alcoholic Women: The Right to Be the Same or Different." *Labor-Management Alcoholism Journal* 9 (1980): 123–132.

CLARKE, SANDRA. "Self-esteem in Men and Women Alcoholics." *Quarterly Journal of Studies on Alcoholism* 35 (1974): 1380–1381.

CLEMMONS, PENNY. "Issues in Marriage, Family and Child Counseling in Alcoholism." In *Women Who Drink: Alcoholic Experience and Pyschotherapy*, edited by V. Burtle. Springfield, Ill.: Charles C. Thomas, 1979, pp. 217–228.

COHEN, PAULINE AND MERTON KRAUSE. *Casework with Wives of Alcoholics*. New York: Family Service Association of America, 1971.

CONNOR, BERNADETTE AND MARGUERITE BABCOCK. "The Impact of Feminist Psychotherapy on the Treatment of Women Alcoholics." *Journal of Addictions and Health* 1, No. 2 (1980): 77–92.

CORK, R. MARGARET. *The Forgotten Children*. Markham, Ontario, Canada: Alcoholism and Drug Addiction Research Foundation in association with Paper-Jacks, 1969.

CORRIGAN, EILEEN. *Alcoholic Women in Treatment*. New York: Oxford University Press, 1980.

CURLEE, J. "A Comparison of Male and Female Patients at an Alcoholism Treatment Center." *Journal of Psychology* 74 (1970): 239–247.

DAVIS, D. I., D. BERENSON, P. STEINGLASS, AND S. DAVIS. "The Adaptive Consequences of Drinking." *Psychiatry* 37 (1974): 209–215.

DEUTSCH, CHARLES. *Broken Bottles, Broken Dreams*. New York: Teachers College Press, 1982.

DINABURG, D., I. D. GLICK, AND E. FEIGENBAUM. "Marital Therapy of Women Alcoholics." *Journal of Studies on Alcoholism* 38 (1977): 1247–1258.

DINNERSTEIN, DOROTHY. *The Mermaid and the Minotaur*. New York: Harper Colophon Books, 1976.

DOWLING, COLETTE. *The Cinderella Complex*. New York: Summit Books, 1981.

DULFANO, CELIA. *Families, Alcoholism and Recovery: Ten Stories*. Center City, Minn.: Hazeldon Foundation, 1982.

EDDY, C. C. AND J. L. FORD, EDS. *Alcoholism in Women*. Dubuque, Iowa: Kendall/Hunt, 1980.

EWING, D. A. AND R. E. FOX. "Family Therapy of Alcoholism." In *Current Psychiatric Therapies*, Vol.8, edited by J. H. Masserman. New York: Grune and Stratton, 1968, pp. 86–91.

FELDMAN, LARRY B. "Sex-Roles and Family Dynamics." In *Normal Family Processes*, edited by Froma Walsh. New York, Guilford Press, 1982.

FIFELD, L., J. D. LATHAM, AND C. PHILLIPS. *Alcoholism in the Gay Community: The*

Price of Alienation, Isolation, and Oppression. Sacramento: California Division of Substance Abuse, 1978.

FOGARTY, THOMAS. "Systems Concepts and the Dimensions of Self." In *Family Therapy: Theory and Practice,* edited by Philip Guerin, Jr. New York: Gardner Press, 1976.

———. "On Emptiness and Closeness." In *The Best of the Family: 1973–1978.* Compendium of the Center for Family Learning, New Rochelle, New York, and Georgetown University Family Center, Washington, D.C.

Foundation for Alcoholism Communications. *Alcoholism: The National Magazine* (Family Focus Issue) 1, No. 3 (Jan./ Feb. 1981).

FRANKS, VIOLET AND VASANTI BURTLE, EDS. *Women in Therapy.* New York: Brunner/Mazel, 1974.

GITLOW, S. E. AND H. S. PEYSER, EDS. *Alcoholism: A Practical Treatment Guide.* New York: Grune and Stratton, 1980.

GOLDBERG, HERB. *The Hazards of Being Male: Surviving the Myth of Masculine Privilege.* New York: New American Library, 1976.

GOMBERG, EDITH. "The Female Alcoholic." In *Alcoholism: Interdisciplinary Approaches to an Enduring Problem,* edited by R. E. Tarker and A. A. Sugerman. Reading, Mass.: Addison-Wesley, 1976, pp. 603–636.

———. "Drinking Patterns of Women Alcoholics." In *Women Who Drink: Alcoholic Experience and Psycholtherapy,* edited by V. Burtle. Springfield, Ill.: Charles C. Thomas, 1979, pp. 26–48.

———. "Women, Sex Roles, and Alcohol Problems." *Professional Psychology* 12, No. 1 (1981): 146–155.

GREENBLATT, MILTON AND MARC SCHUCKIT, EDS. *Alcoholism Problems in Women and Children.* New York: Grune and Stratton, 1976.

GUERIN, PHILIP, JR., ED. *Family Therapy: Theory and Practice.* New York: Gardner Press, 1976.

GUERIN, P. J. AND E. PENDAGAST. "Evaluation of Family System and Genogram." In *Family Therapy: Theory and Practice,* edited by Philip Guerin, Jr. New York: Gardner Press, 1976.

GURMAN, ALAN AND DAVID KNISKEM, EDS. *Handbook of Family Therapy.* New York: Brunner/Mazel, 1981.

HALEY, J. *Problem Solving Therapy.* San Francisco: Jossey-Bass, 1976.

———. *Strategies of Psychotherapy.* New York: Grune and Stratton, 1963.

———. *Leaving Home.* New York: McGraw-Hill, 1980.

———. *Reflections on Therapy and Other Essays.* Maryland: The Family Therapy Institute of Washington, D.C., 1981.

HANCOCK, DAVID. "I Can't Be An Alcoholic Because . . ." Michigan: Michigan Alcohol and Drug Information Foundation, 1969. (Distributed by the National Council on Alcoholism, Inc., New York.)

HARE-MUSTIN, R. T. "A Feminist Approach to Family Therapy." *Family Process* 17 (1978): 181–193.

HEALTH COMMUNICATIONS. *Focus on Family and Chemical Dependency* 6, No. 5 (Sept./Oct. 1983).

HENNECKE, LYNNE AND VERNELL FOX. "The Woman With Alcoholism." In *Alcoholism: A Practical Treatment Guide*, edited by S. E. Gitlow and H. S. Peyser. New York: Grune and Stratton, 1980, pp. 181–191.

HOFFMAN, LYNN. *Foundations of Family Therapy*. New York: Basic Books, 1981.

HORNEY, KAREN. *The Neurotic Personality of Our Time*. New York: W. W. Norton, 1937.

————. *Our Inner Conflicts*. New York: W. W. Norton, 1945.

————. *Neurosis and Human Growth*. New York: W. W. Norton, 1950.

JACKSON, DON D. "The Question of Family Homeostasis." *Psychiatric Quarterly Supplement* 31 (1957): 79–90.

————. "Family Rules: The Marital Quid Pro Quo." *Archives of General Psychiatry* 12 (1965): 589–1964.

JACKSON, JOAN. "The Adjustment of the Family to the Crisis of Alcoholism." *Quarterly Journal of Studies on Alcohol*. 15, No. 4 (1954): 562–586.

JANEWAY, ELIZABETH. *Powers of the Weak*. New York: Alfred A. Knopf, 1980.

JELLINEK, E. M. *The Disease Concept of Alcoholism*. New Haven, Conn.: College and University Press, 1960.

JOHNSON, P., D. J. ARMOR, S. POLICH, AND H. STAMBUL. "US Adult Drinking Practices: Time Trends, Social Correlates, and Sex Roles." Prepared for the National Institute on Alcohol Abuse and Alcoholism. (Report No. PB 294–044/AS.) Springfield, Va.: U.S. National Technical Information Service, 1977.

JOHNSON, VERNON. *I'll Quit Tomorrow*. New York: Harper and Row, 1973.

KALANT, O. J., ED. *Alcohol and Drug Problems in Women*. Research Advances in Alcohol and Drug Problems, Vol. 5. New York: Plenum Press, 1980.

KAPLAN, HELEN S. *The New Sex Therapy*. New York: Brunner/ Mazel, 1974.

KAUFMAN, EDWARD AND PAULINE KAUFMAN, EDS. *Family Therapy of Drug and Alcohol Abuse*. New York: Gardner Press, 1979.

KELLERMAN, JOSEPH. *Alcoholism: A Merry-Go-Round Named Denial*. Center City, Minnesota: Hazeldon, 1976 (pamphlet).

KINSEY, BARRY. *The Female Alcoholic*. Springfield, Ill.: Charles C. Thomas, 1966.

KISSIN, B. AND H. BEGLEITER, EDS. *The Biology of Alcoholism*. New York: Plenum Press, 1976.

KNIGHT, JAMES. "The Family in the Crisis of Alcoholism." In *Alcoholism: A Practical Treatment Guide*, edited by S. E. Gitlow and H. S. Peyser. New York: Grune and Stratton, 1980, pp. 205–227.

KURTZ, ERNEST. "Why AA Works: The Intellectual Significance of Alcoholics Anonymous." *Journal of Studies on Alcohol* 41, No. 1 (1982): 38–80.

————. *Not-God: A History of Alcoholics Anonymous*. Center City, Minnesota: Hazeldon Educational Materials, 1979.

LANGONE, JOHN AND DOLORES DeNOBREGA LANGONE. *Women Who Drink.* Reading, Mass.: Addison-Wesley, 1980.

LAWSON, GARY, JAMES PETERSON, AND ANN LAWSON. *Alcoholism and the Family.* Rockville, Md.: Aspen Systems, 1983.

LEDERER, WILLIAM AND DON JACKSON. *The Mirages of Marriage.* New York: W. W. Norton, 1968.

LIBOW, J., P. RASKIN, AND B. CAUST. "Feminist and Family Systems Therapy: Are They Reconcilable?" *American Journal of Family Therapy* 10, No. 3 (1982): 3–12.

MADANES, CLOÉ. *Strategic Family Therapy.* San Francisco: Jossey-Bass, 1981.

MANN, MARTY. *Marty Mann's New Primer on Alcoholism* (rev. ed.). New York: Holt, Rinehart and Winston, 1981.

MAXWELL, RUTH. *The Booze Battle.* New York: Ballantine Books, 1976.

McCLELLAND, DAVID C., WILLIAM DAVIS, RUDOLPH KALIN, AND ERIC WANNER. *The Drinking Man.* New York: Free Press, 1972.

McGOLDRICK, MONICA, JOHN PEARCE, AND JOSEPH GIORDANO, EDS. *Ethnicity and Family Therapy.* New York: Guilford Press, 1982.

MEEKS, D. AND C. KELLY. "Family Therapy with the Families of Recovering Alcoholics." *Quarterly Journal of Studies on Alcoholism* 31, No. 2 (1970): 399–413.

MENDELSON, J. H. AND N. K. MELLO, EDS. *The Diagnosis and Treatment of Alcoholism.* New York: McGraw-Hill, 1979.

MILLER, ALICE. *The Drama of the Gifted Child.* New York: Basic Books, 1981.

MILLER, JEAN BAKER. *Toward a New Psychology of Women.* Boston: Beacon Press, 1976.

MINUCHIN, SALVADOR. *Families and Family Therapy.* Cambridge, Mass.: Harvard University Press, 1974.

NICHOLS, MICHAEL. *Family Therapy: Concepts and Methods.* New York: Gardner Press, 1984.

PAOLINO, THOMAS AND BARBARA McCRADY. *The Alcoholic Marriage: Alternative Perspectives.* New York: Grune and Stratton, 1977.

PAPP, PEGGY. "Family Choreography." In *Family Therapy: Theory and Practice*, edited by Philip Guerin, Jr. New York: Gardner Press, 1976.

_____, ED. *Family Therapy: Full Length Case Studies.* New York: Gardner Press, 1977.

_____. *The Process of Change.* New York: Guilford Press, 1983.

PARKER, D. A., E. S. PARKER, M. W. WOLZ, AND T. C. HARFORD. "Sex Roles and Alcohol Consumption: A Research Note." *Journal of Health and Social Behavior* 21 (1980): 43–48.

PARKER, F. B. "A Comparison of the Sex Temperament of Alcoholics and Moderate Drinkers." *American Sociological Review* 24 (1959): 366–374.

_____. "Sex-Role Adjustment in Women Alcoholics." *Quarterly Journal of Studies on Alcoholism* 33 (1972): 647–657.

PATTISON, E. MANSELL AND EDWARD KAUFMAN, EDS. *Encyclopedic Handbook of Alcoholism.* New York: Gardner Press, 1982.

PATTISON, E. MANSELL, MARK SOBELL, AND LINDA SOBELL, EDS. *Emerging Concepts of Alcohol Dependence.* New York: Springer Publishing, 1977.

PAUL, B. B. AND N. PAUL. *A Marital Puzzle.* New York: W. W. Norton, 1975.

PISHKIN, V. AND F. C. THORNE. "A Factorial Structure of the Dimensions of Femininity in Alcoholic, Schizophrenic and Normal Populations." *Journal of Clinical Psychology* 33 (1977): 10–17.

POTTER, JESSIE. "Women and Sex—It's Enough to Drive Them to Drink!" In *Women Who Drink: Alcoholic Experience and Psychotherapy,* edited by V. Burtle. Springfield, Ill.: Charles C. Thomas, 1979, pp. 49–80.

POWELL, B. J., E. C. PENICK, AND M. R. READ. "Psychological Adjustment and Sex Role Affiliation in an Alcoholic Population." *Journal of Clinical Psychology* 36 (1980): 801–805.

ROTHROD, N. H. AND I. G. THOMSON. "Women Alcoholics: A Clinical Study." *Quarterly Journal of Studies on Alcoholism* 32 (1971): 45–52.

ROMER, NANCY. *The Sex-Role Cycle.* New York: The Feminist Press, 1981.

ROONEY, J. F. AND J. N. VOLPE. "The Role of Androgyny in Alcoholism Recovery" (abstract). *Sociologist Abstracts* 28 (Suppl. 103, 1980): 107. Abstract of paper presented at the 1980 Annual Meeting of the Society for the Study of Social Problems.

ROYCE, JAMES. *Alcohol Problems and Alcoholism: A Comprehensive Survey.* New York: The Free Press, 1981.

SANDMAIER, MARIAN. *The Invisible Alcoholics: Women and Alcohol Abuse in America.* New York: McGraw-Hill, 1980.

SATIR, VIRGINIA. *Conjoint Family Therapy* (rev. ed.). Palo Alto, Calif.: Science and Behavior Books, 1967.

SCHWAB-BAKMAN, N., H. APPELF, AND F. RIST. "Sex-Role Identification in Women Alcoholics and Depressives." *Journal of Studies on Alcoholism* 42 (1981): 654–660.

SCIDA, J. AND M. VANICELLI. "Sex-Role Conflict and Drinking." *Journal of Studies on Alcoholism* 40 (1979): 28–44.

SELVINI-PALAZZOLI, MARA, L. BOSCOLO, G. CECCHIN, AND G. PRATA. "Hypothesizing-Circularity-Neutrality." *Family Process* 19 (1980): 3–12.

SELVINI-PALAZZOLI, MARA, GIANFRANCO CECCHIN, GIUIANA PRATA, AND LUIGI BOSCOLO. *Paradox and Counterparadox.* New York: Jason Aronson, 1978.

SLUZKI, C. AND J. BEAVIN. "Symmetry and Complementarity: An Operational Definition and a Typology of Dyads." In *The Interactional View,* edited by Paul Watzlawick and J. Weakland. New York: W. W. Norton, 1977.

SOLOMON, KENNETH. "Counseling the Drug Dependent Woman: Special Issues for Men." In *Treatment Services for Drug Dependent Women,* vol. 2. NIDA/DHHS Publication No. 82-1291. Washington, D.C.: U.S. Government Printing Office, 1982.

STANTON, DUNCAN, THOMAS TODD, AND ASSOCIATES. *The Family Therapy of Drug and Alcohol Abuse.* New York: Guilford Press, 1982.

STEINGLASS, PETER. "Experimenting with Family Treatment Approaches to Alcoholism, 1950–1975: A Review." Family Process 16 (1976): 97–123.

_____. "Family Therapy with Alcoholics: A Review." In *Family Therapy of Drug and Alcohol Abuse,* edited by E. Kaufman, and P. N. Kaufman. New York: Gardner Press, 1979, pp. 147–186.

_____. "A Life History Model of the Alcoholic Family." Family Process 19, No. 3 (1980): 211–226.

STEINGLASS, P., D. I. DAVIS, AND D. BERENSON. "Observations of Conjointly Hospitalized Alcoholic Couples During Sobriety and Intoxication: Implications for Theory and Therapy." Family Process 16 (1977): 1–16.

STEINGLASS, P., S. WEINER, AND J. H. MENDELSON. "A Systems Approach to Alcoholism: A Model and Its Clinical Applications." Archives of General Psychiatry 24 (1971): 401–408.

TIEBOUT, HARRY. "The Act of Surrender in the Therapeutic Process." Quarterly Journal of Studies on Alcohol 10 (1949): 48–58.

_____. "Surrender Versus Compliance in Therapy." Quarterly Journal of Studies on Alcohol 14 (1953): 58–68.

_____. "The Ego Factors in Surrender in Alcoholism." Quarterly Journal of Studies on Alcohol 15 (1954): 610–621.

VAILLANT, GEORGE. *The Natural History of Alcoholism.* Cambridge, Mass.: Harvard University Press, 1983.

WALLACE, JOHN. *Tactical and Strategic Use of the Preferred Defense Structure of the Alcoholic.* New York: National Council on Alcoholism, 1974 (pamphlet).

_____. "Alcoholism from the Inside Out." In *Alcoholism: Development, Consequences, and Interventions,* edited by N. Estes and E. Heinemann. St. Louis: C. V. Mosby, 1977.

WALSH, FROMA, ED. *Normal Family Processes.* New York: Guilford Press, 1982.

WANBERG, K. W. AND J. L. HORN. "Alcoholism Symptom Patterns of Men and Women: A Comparative Study." Quarterly Journal of Studies on Alcoholism 31 (1970): 40–61.

WATZLAWICK, PAUL. *An Anthology of Human Communication.* Palo Alto, Calif.: Science and Behavior Books, 1964.

WATZLAWICK, PAUL, JANET BEVIN, AND DON JACKSON. *The Pragmatics of Human Communication.* New York: W. W. Norton, 1967.

WATZLAWICK, PAUL AND J. WEAKLAND, EDS. *The Interactional View.* New York: W. W. Norton, 1977.

WATZLAWICK, PAUL, JOHN WEAKLAND, AND RICHARD FISCH. *Change.* New York: W. W. Norton, 1974.

WEEKS, GERALD AND LUCIANO L'ABATE. *Paradoxical Psychotherapy: Theory and Practice with Individuals, Couples and Families.* New York: Brunner/Mazel, 1982.

WEGSCHEIDER, SHARON. *Another Chance: Hope and Health for the Alcoholic Family.* Palo Alto, Calif.: Science and Behavior Books, 1981.

WILSNACK, SHARON. "Sex-Role Identity in Female Alcoholism." *Journal of Abnormal Psychology* 82 (1973a): 253–261.

―――. "The Needs of the Female Drinker: Dependency, Power, or What?" Proceedings of the Second Annual Alcoholism Conference, NIAAA, 1973b, 65–83.

―――. "The Impact of Sex Roles and Women's Alcohol Use and Abuse." In *Alcoholism Problems in Women and Children,* edited by M. Greenblatt and M. Schuckit. New York: Grune and Stratton, 1976.

―――. "Alcohol Abuse and Alcoholism in Women." In *Encyclopedic Handbook of Alcoholism,* edited by E. Mansell Pattison and Edward Kaufman. New York: Gardner Press, 1982.

WILSNACK, SHARON AND RICHARD WILSNACK. "Sex Roles and Adolescent Drinking." In *Youth, Alcohol and Social Policy,* edited by H. Blane and M. Chafetz. New York: Plenum Press, 1979, pp. 183–227.

WOITITZ, JANET GERINGER. *Adult Children of Alcoholics.* Florida: Health Communications, 1983.

WOLPER, BENNET AND ZONA SCHEINER. "Family Therapy Approaches and Drug Dependent Women." In *Treatment Services for Drug Dependent Women,* Vol. 2. NIDA/DHHS Publication No. 82-1219. Washington, D.C.: U.S. Government Printing Office, 1982.

ZIMBERG, SHELDON, JOHN WALLACE, AND SHEILA BLUME, EDS. *Practical Approaches to Alcoholism Psychotherapy.* New York: Plenum Press, 1978.

ZUCKER, ROBERT, VICTOR BATTISTICH, AND GINETTE LANGER. "Sexual Behavior, Sex-Role Adaptation and Drinking in Young Women." *Journal of Studies on Alcohol* 42, No. 5 (1981): 457–465.

Index

Made in the USA
Middletown, DE
23 June 2022

67666141R00168